How to Argue

How to Argue

An Introduction to Logical Thinking

David J. Crossley   Peter A. Wilson

University of Saskatchewan

Random House, New York

First Edition
9 8 7 6 5 4 3 2 1
Copyright © 1979 by Random House, Inc.

Library of Congress Cataloging in Publication Data

Crossley, David J   1941–
  How to argue.

  Bibliography: p.
  Includes index.
  1. Reasoning.   I. Wilson, Peter A., 1928–   joint
author.   II.   Title.
BC177.C76   160   78-25799
ISBN 0-394-32131-6

MANUFACTURED IN THE UNITED STATES OF AMERICA

Design by Lorraine Hohman
Cover design by Lawrence Daniels and Friends, Inc.

Preface

Anyone who has ever given or taken an introductory class in logical reasoning or critical thinking will be aware of the particular difficulties and special challenges these topics present. The student requires a treatment of reasoned arguments that is not only adequately sophisticated but also clearly applicable to such activities as writing essays, debating, and evaluating research material. Correspondingly, instructors recognize that the course they plan and the text they adopt must be theoretically sound yet practical as well. Without theoretical structures the student has no basis for understanding the problems involved in the study of argument. Without practical direction the student cannot apply the theory.

How to Argue: An Introduction to Logical Thinking is intended to satisfy both these needs. It explains the basic principles of logical thinking in a clear manner, with the aid of numerous examples, so that the introductory student can easily grasp the essentials of good argument. And it shows the application of these principles to the important practical tasks of evaluating and constructing arguments. One purpose of the book is to point out that arguments surround us daily—in textbooks, speeches, reports, advertisements, magazine articles, and even letters to the editor of a newspaper.

We cover all the topics normally expected in an introductory logic textbook: language and meaning, definitions, fallacies, deduction, induction, explanations, the dilemma, and the *reductio*. In addition the book is innovative in providing concrete tools for finding, evaluating, and presenting arguments. Experience has demonstrated that it is easier to learn the rules of inference than it is to extract an argument from a book or magazine article and then evaluate that argument properly. Throughout we have focused on this latter problem, and the final section of the book presents the unique SCORE and FATE techniques for evaluating, constructing, and presenting arguments.

Exercises at the end of each chapter facilitate review and challenge the reader to employ the ideas and principles just learned. And to permit self-checking of progress as each chapter is completed, answers for all exercises (except the suggested writing topics in the final chapter) are provided at the end of the book. In addition, a glossary of key terms is included for easy reference, as is a bibliography of selected readings for those who wish to study any topic further.

This project began with a class on logical thinking and arguing that we prepared for the Saskatoon Region Community College. We are indebted to the College and to the Extension Division of the University of Saskatchewan for inviting the Department of Philosophy of the University to offer that course.

We thank colleagues and others who offered us encouragement and suggestions about various aspects of the content and presentation of the material. Peter Horban assisted us in the preparation of the text; Isabel Smith, Barbara Curll, and Heather Walker kindly helped with typing and proofreading. We also wish to acknowledge with gratitude the debt we owe to our editor, Jane Cullen, who has wisely advised us on the choice of examples and has helped make many of the arguments clearer and the text in general more readable.

D. J. C.
P. A. W.

Contents

TWO

CLASSIFYING THINGS

THREE

CONNECTING EVENTS

FOUR

EMPLOYING THE TOOLS

How to Argue

1

Introduction

Most of us spend a good deal of our time arguing. Often our arguments are heated, especially when we feel we are being personally attacked for something we did or failed to do, or when we are annoyed by the actions or statements of a local politician or someone we dislike. But an argument doesn't need to involve a torrent of emotion. Sometimes our arguments are calm, like those of the cool movie detective quietly piecing together shreds of evidence to weave a net strong enough to catch and convict a murderer.

An argument is simply putting together, in a reasonable order, facts and bits of evidence so we can reach a rational, logical conclusion. Sometimes you use an argument to try to convince someone of something: "Someone must have been in the house while we were away, because the window was jimmied, there were footprints in the flower garden under the window, and the papers on my desk were messed up." At other times you try to figure out what you should do in a given situation: "Since I am going for a holiday to Italy in six months and will want to know some Italian, I had better enroll right away in that night class in Italian." Sometimes there *is* emotion involved: "You *must* be stupid to have trumped my ace!" Or at other times we make attempts at persuasion: "Smoke *Gaspers*, the cigarette with less nicotine and tar and more flavor."

WHAT ARE THE ESSENTIAL FEATURES OF AN ARGUMENT?

Basically, arguments involve facts or beliefs that are connected in logical ways to arrive at conclusions. Let's take an example. Imagine that you are a cancer researcher, testing a food coloring. You take two groups of rats. To one group, the control group, you give normal cheese. The other group, the test group, eats cheese containing the food coloring. After several months, you discover that nearly all the rats in the test group developed cancerous growths of one sort or another and that there is no evidence of cancerous growth among the rats in the control group. From this you conclude that the food coloring caused the cancers. Also, you would very likely conclude that any human beings who ate the same food coloring in sufficient quantities would develop cancer or run a high risk of doing so.

In this example we have taken some supposed facts and pieces of evidence, shown connections among these facts, and drawn certain conclusions. We connected the *fact* of eating the colored cheese with the *fact* of the cancerous growths. Indeed, we felt that the coloring *caused* the cancer because the rats in the control group did not develop cancer. We then *predicted* that the same would happen to human beings who ate the food coloring *because* we know that rats and people are very similar in terms of their physiological structure and body chemistry. Let us call this whole process an argument—the process whereby we connect evidence in a reasoned, logical way in order to arrive at a conclusion.

WHEN DO WE USE ARGUMENTS?

It's much easier to say when we *don't* use or need good arguments, for we seem to face them all the time. You might write a letter to the editor of a newspaper telling the readers that you are against capital punishment. If you have written a convincing letter, it will undoubtedly state your reasons for opposing capital punishment. These reasons, whatever they are, must provide evidence that can convince someone of your conclusion that the government should abolish capital punishment. Perhaps you are opposed to any taking of human life by other human beings because you are convinced that each person has an inherent, God-given right to life. Your reader will then have to decide whether it is a good reason and might disagree. "Is it not right to kill others during a war?" the reader may ask. Or the reader might agree that *normally* killing is wrong but might claim that it is also wrong for governments to fail to protect citizens from violent people; that we must allow the killing of criminals because the right to, and need for, protection is the more important rule or principle.

Of course, there are many other kinds of situations in which you must be ready to provide good, reasoned, sound arguments: when you have to explain to your neighbors why you won't sign their petition to have stray dogs destroyed, for example; or when you go to small claims court over a dispute with your landlord; or in the frequent disagreements that arise when you are talking in the cafeteria with your fellow students.

WHY DO WE USE ARGUMENTS?

There are four basic purposes you might have for an argument:

1. *Persuasion.* Often we feel we must persuade someone of our point of view or change someone's mind. An example might be to have someone vote for one candidate rather than another in an upcoming election.
2. *Decision.* When it's time to vote, you have to consider the candidates carefully and look at all the reasons for voting for one candidate rather than another. Only if you do this will you be voting responsibly. The evidence you collect and the conclusions it leads you to as you think about it will affect your vote.
3. *Explanation.* Why does a pot of water boil at less than 212° F at the top of a mountain? Because the atmospheric pressure affects the temperature at which liquids boil. Here we connect facts with natural laws. An example of this common type of argument is as follows: all liquids will boil at 212° F at sea level; this water in our pot is a liquid; so this water will be affected in the same way all liquids are—it will boil at 212° F at sea level.
4. *Prediction.* Explanation is connected with prediction in the sense that if you know what is generally true of a group or class of things, you know it will be true of all members of that group or class. For example, if it is a chemical law that burning sodium in chlorine gas produces common salt (sodium chloride), then if you get some sodium tomorrow and burn it in chlorine gas, you will get common salt. We use such arguing to try to predict how people will act, too. For example, the sociologist tells us that people who were tested became irritable, depressed, or even violent when their living quarters were cramped. We expect, then, that any person living in slum housing areas would feel this way. Thus wise city planners replace crowded slums

with spacious low-cost housing, thereby altering the characters of the people living there by reducing the psychological strains they are under. Here we have based a course of action on predictions from our past experience.

TIME TO BEGIN

So much for preamble. The following chapters will outline the basic argument forms that we use every day. The point is to try to help you see how arguments work and to see what constitutes a good argument. If you can recognize good arguments it will help you in two ways:

1. *Defense.* It will help you sort out the barrage of words and arguments you receive daily from TV ads, newspaper editorials, teachers, politicians, and friends. The person who cannot think clearly and logically, who cannot reason and argue soundly, is at a distinct disadvantage.
2. *Offense.* Knowing how to argue and reason well helps in all aspects of life, such as in writing a school or business report, presenting your opinions to others, and understanding the social and physical world in which you live.

REASONING, THINKING, AND ARGUING

You will undoubtedly have noted that thus far we have been talking of arguing as a kind of reasoning or thinking. But what is it to *reason*? What is it to *think* about something?

We normally think about something that puzzles us, some problem we want to find an answer to. Take an example. Suppose your car won't start. Let's say there are a certain number of things that *could* be wrong with your car, any one of which would cause it not to start: it might be out of gas, the battery might be dead, the fuel line might be clogged, and so on. You begin to think your way through this problem. You reason that there is *some* cause of its failure to start, and you make some tests. Here you have engaged in a bit of thinking by first looking for possible causes of your problem and then trying out each possibility. You have reasoned through the problem by *eliminating* possibilities until you arrive at the right one.

In other cases we reason by connecting facts. This is what the good detective does. So does the doctor. The doctor knows that your fever could be a symptom of a number of ailments, so she runs some blood tests. These blood tests turn up a new fact, a high white cell count. These facts—the high white cell count and your feverish temperature—taken together show that you have the disease "daffodil fever," which you caught from a daffodil. The doctor knows that this is the only way one gets "daffodil fever," and her diagnosis was confirmed once she learned that you raised daffodils. Here the doctor connected three facts to decide what your ailment was.

This book is concerned with two connected things: reasoning and rational thinking on the one hand, and the logical argument forms that reflect this thinking on the other. Throughout the book we move back and forth between the two. We will often present an example of someone arguing a point or thinking through a problem and then move on to lay out the structure of that reasoning or arguing.

In other words, arguments, in the wider sense of that term, have two basic aspects: the psychological and the logical. The psychological is the actual real-life engagement of an individual in listening to, analyzing, or presenting an argument. In this the individual connects ideas, draws implications, and considers alternatives. Yet thinking and arguing have patterns, and there are acceptable ways to connect facts and valid argument forms that may be used to structure thinking and arguing. This is the logical aspect.

Consider an example that illuminates this point. John is outraged by his friends' casual attitude about shoplifting and tells them,

> What you are is a bunch of thieves. You just take other people's property without their consent, and thieves are simply people who do exactly that—take other people's property.

The two features this illustrates are:

1. *The psychological*, which is John's actual thinking—the mental process of formulating his beliefs and opinions, of connecting his friends' actions with those of thieves. This is *expressed* in the series of English *sentences* John used to present his thoughts to his friends.
2. *The logical*, which has to do with the *meanings* of John's sentences and how they are *connected* with each other.

In passing, it is worth noting that some people use the technical term "proposition" to indicate what a sentence means. There are two main reasons for distinguishing sentences from propositions. First, many sentences may express the same proposition; that is, two or more sentences may *propose* the same thing. For example, "Bill loves Susan" is a sentence that expresses the same proposition (it has the same *meaning*) as the sentence "Susan is loved by Bill." Also, the

English sentence "It is raining" expresses the same proposition as the French sentence "Il pleut." Second, since the context of a sentence in our language often makes a difference, we can encounter cases in which the same sentence may express different propositions. For example, the sentence "The President of the United States is astute" said by someone in 1978 means (expresses the proposition that) Jimmy Carter is astute; the same sentence said in 1962 meant (expresses the proposition that) John Kennedy was astute. While you will not be at all confused about how these terms are used throughout the book, this distinction is worth noting and remembering. One of the reasons for asking you to note this distinction is that in discussing specific examples, we must be able to talk about and refer to *both* the language someone uses to express thoughts and the meanings that language is intended to convey. The term "sentence" refers to a spoken or written part of a language; "proposition" refers to the meaning expressed by a sentence.

EXERCISES

I. It is important to be able to recognize an argument and to distinguish arguments from simple statements or stories. In the case of each of the following passages, determine whether it contains an argument.

1. All students must study logic in order to be able to write and think effectively. Thus we should make logic a compulsory subject for all first-year students.
2. If we return the books *now*, she may, by the time the due date arrives, forget that we returned them. Hence we had better wait until the last moment rather than return them now, because if she forgets about our returning them she will hold a grudge.
3. If Janice arrives early, I am going to the movie playing at the Odeon.
4. Once we had come to the crossing, Bill looked both ways but did not slow down. Susan saw the train coming and yelled a warning. The rest of us panicked and tried to get out of the car. At the same time Bill stepped on the gas!
5. Either you must study now or you must study later. Since you cannot study now, because of the company coming for dinner, you *must* study later without fail.
6. Some of our friends are politically concerned and active. And given that all politically concerned and active people are in-

telligent, it follows that at least some of our friends must be intelligent.

7. Every time he does a lab test he breaks out in hives. Lab tests must make him nervous, then, because people who break out in hives do so because they are nervous.

8. Bronson is an insufferable snob. In addition, he is conceited, arrogant, and a miserable bore on every trip we take.

9. If Crainsdown leaves that window open again I'll scream. Anyone knows that an open window lets in flies, and flies bring in germs. And no one wants germs in the house, so the windows *must* be kept shut at all times.

10. In view of the fact that the candidates we have to choose from *all* hold unacceptable positions on capital punishment, I am *not* going to vote, because that is the only way I have to express my views on the candidates running in this election. I could vote for one of them only if he or she held an acceptable position on capital punishment.

II. Consider each of the following passages and determine its primary purpose. You will note that virtually all examples present some information and that, therefore, all have something of an explanatory flavor and function. Nevertheless, select the *principal* function in each case; decide whether the passage attempts primarily to: (a) persuade, (b) explain, or (c) predict.

1. Every town with a pool hall has its share of unsavory characters. This is because the pool hall attracts gamblers and all gamblers are unsavory.

2. Everyone invited *must* come to the party. Since we have so much food and have gone to so much trouble and since we did invite you, you *have* to come.

3. Goats that are allowed to eat wet grass often become ill. Since you allow your goats to graze after the dew falls instead of bringing them in for the night early, your goats are bound to become ill.

4. Stars do not really "twinkle." That is, they do not really go off and on. Rather, because of the great distance, a star's light is disturbed by other objects or distorted by the earth's atmosphere so that it appears to go off when the light is blocked by another object or disturbed in some way.

5. Everyone needs Formula X in the home and so you *must* buy some. It will whiten your teeth, calm the dog, and make the grass grow more quickly.

6. If we invest in a new indoor swimming pool for the village,

everyone will benefit. Consider your own children. If we build a pool, *they* will have a place to swim. So you'll surely want to give us a donation toward the cost.

7. Since Great Dane pups tend, unfortunately, to grow into huge dogs and since huge dogs have tremendous appetites, you will soon be eaten out of house and home if you keep that Great Dane pup.

8. In "The Owl and the Pussycat" the pig sells its ring for a shilling. The reason is that at that time a shilling was worth a lot of money in terms of purchasing power, and no one passes up a chance to turn a tidy profit. What else would you expect the pig to do, then?

9. If human beings survive death, it can only be because the human soul is immortal. But for something to survive death, it cannot be physical or it would pass away with the body. Thus you can see that the human soul must be something that is not physical.

10. Liberty is lost if it is not jealously guarded and protected at every turn. In recent times we have let down our guard, and we can expect to suffer the loss of our freedom if we do not soon change our ways.

ONE

WORDS AND LANGUAGE

2

The Trouble with Words

USING LANGUAGE

In spite of the important role that words and language play in our lives, we seldom reflect on the specific words we use in a given context or on the various functions of our language. Yet we can easily think of several distinct ways that we employ language. For example, you use certain words and phrases to describe your Aunt Harriet to a friend and others to explain to someone exactly where you were until 2:00 A.M. last night. You might also call your dog, shout a warning, issue a threat, or order a lunch. You can purposely say something to annoy or embarrass your neighbor. And you can choose words that inform someone that you are annoyed, embarrassed, angry, or in pain. Words are even sometimes an essential part of entering into a contract. "I do" functions this way in a marriage ceremony. Likewise, shouting out "Five hundred!" at the appropriate stage of an auction is the making of an offer.

While we normally think of language in terms of communicating with others, it is not implausible to suggest that human thinking is necessarily done in and with language. However, putting this possibility aside, we can isolate a few general roles that language plays. (Of course, such classification is not fully satisfactory, given the diversity of language and its uses; but these classes do indicate several clearly perceivable and distinct areas.) *First*, we use language to *describe* the world, events, and ourselves. Such descriptions purport to offer information or facts. *Second*, we *explain* the connections between facts and events. Sometimes we explain the meaning of a word. *Third*, we *express* feelings or emotions, either to communicate these to another person or to exhort that person to sympathize with us. *Fourth*, we give orders, issue threats and use language in other, similar ways in order to *influence* the actions of others. *Fifth*, we use language, usually in conjunction with particular actions or in special settings, to *perform* tasks. For example, you say "I do" in a court of law as part of the action of swearing to tell the truth. "I will," accompanied by raising your hand and stepping forward, is a way of volunteering to go on the dangerous mission to knock out the enemy machine gun.

In this chapter we want to point out some important and useful facts about language, how it is used and how it can be abused so as to lead us or others astray. The initial difficulty is that it all seems so simple. Surely, we think, everyone knows about words and their meanings and about communicating. But is this so? Is every communication really that simple?

COMMUNICATING

Have you ever thought about how people communicate? On the surface, the process seems quite simple. We listen to someone talking, or we read a report or look at a work of art, and we try to determine what it is we heard, read, or saw. Very often what we perceive is not what was intended to be communicated.

Try this experiment: the next time you are in a crowd tell one person a joke and ask him or her to pass it on to the next person, and so on. Then when the whole group has heard the joke, ask the last person to tell it out loud. You would do well to write down the joke at the outset, because the final version will hardly be recognizable. This unintentional alteration of language and meaning is a complex human phenomenon that psychologists, linguists, and others have spent years analyzing.

For our purposes, we are confining our interest to words and their meanings. Experts agree that ideas are generated by cues that we call words and their meanings. Yet some words have a different interpretation for you than for someone else, because various factors come into play that influence your understanding of the word or phrase being used.

We tend, for example, not to read, listen, or look at everything that is directed toward us by the author, speaker, or artist. This is because each of us uses what experts call *perceptual selectivity*. This is a built-in screen that lets key words or pieces of information slip through while others are excluded, even ignored. In other words, we are being deliberately selective; we do not read, hear, or see everything that comes our way—even when we are concentrating totally on the subject matter. What we are doing is piecing together the high-lights and feeding messages to our brain. This is done quickly—and sometimes inaccurately—because, as we have said, there are factors influencing our thinking.

The careful author, the astute speaker, the clever artist have one thing in common: the ability to influence our thinking. For our purposes, we are concerned with the writer or speaker who sets out to argue or win a point. A good writer or speaker knows the value of words. When we say of someone, "She really has a way with words," we mean that she knows how to use words effectively. In other words, she knows that some words will get through our selective screen and make an impression.

What you must learn is the skill to choose words effectively and also to be alert so as to notice when others are trying to influence you. *Psycholinguistics* is the name given to the study of words and how they influence thinking. There are numerous examples of this all around us every day. Advertisers are masters at persuading us that their products are "the most economical," "the fastest," "best for our health," and so on. What advertisers and others are trying to do with words is influence our thinking and behavior—exactly what we are talking about in this book. When you have a point of view, how do you communicate this as effectively as possible to your readers or listeners?

MEANING

Since we communicate with words and since arguments involve statements that, in turn, are words in certain arrangements, we should first pay some attention to the meanings of words. However, there is an initial difficulty because it is not easy to determine the meaning, if any, of certain expressions. For example, if someone runs into the room and yells "Fire!", what is the meaning of what has been said? Is it just shorthand for "There is a fire here"? This hardly seems adequate, because the speaker's intention is more likely to warn you and urge you to vacate the room. Yelling "Fire!" does not literally *say* that, although it is informative to the extent that it indicates the type of danger at hand. While it may be tempting at first glance to analyze all shouts of "Fire!" or "Help!" as short, easy expressions standing for "There is a fire here" or "I need help now," these words usually do not bear their full sense on their face. Understanding them requires knowledge of the settings in which they are uttered and the tones in which they are spoken or written. "Fire!" urges one sort of action on the battleline and another when shouted in an office building. Moreover, it might often be wrong to treat such expressions as shorthand for informative statements. Suppose someone yells "Ouch!" or "It hurts!" Surely these are not always intentional communications to others, although they may be. Often they are mere spontaneous expressions of pain, not *purposely* uttered by the speaker at all.

While certain words play complex roles in our lives and can often be understood only in terms of their settings and accompanying actions, other words serve to point out or designate things we are talking about. If the teacher says, "Jane Soundoff will stay after school," the name "Jane Soundoff" refers to a person: it designates the student that the teacher intends to indicate. Demonstrative phrases such as "this student" or "that cupboard" also are used to indicate, often with accompanying pointing or other gestures, something that the speaker wishes to talk about or draw your attention to.

If we consider general terms such as "dog," "house," or "satellite," which apply to numerous particular items around us, we can see that there is a sense in which these general terms also have a designating or referring role. The term "satellite" can be applied to the natural moons of Jupiter, to the Earth's moon, and to manmade satellites orbiting the earth. We can thereby say that the meaning of "satellite," in one sense, is the group of objects indicated by that term. Meaning in this designating or referring sense is usually called the *extensional* meaning or *denotative* meaning of a term.

Of course, it is not a random or chance thing that general terms designate the objects they do, because the objects referred to by a general term usually have some common feature or set of properties. Satellites and dogs have properties that make them satellites or dogs rather than planets or fish. The common attributes of objects designated by a general term make up the *intension*, or *connotation*, of the term. Intension and extension are related in that it is the *intensional meaning* of a general term that establishes the term's *extension*. That is, it is the definition of "dog," setting out certain essential properties that dogs must have, which determines and justifies our applying that term to Fido, Rover, Spot, and other dogs we meet or will meet.

Looking further at connotation, we note that a word could have either an *explicit connotation* or a *subjective connotation*. By explicit connotation we refer to the accepted interpretation or normal definition of the word, for which a good dictionary is the final authority. By contrast, connotations are subjective when the connotation a word has for a particular person depends in part on the emotional impact that word has on him or her.

Let us take an example to explore these points. Examine this entry from *The Random House Dictionary of the English Language* dealing with the adjective "mean":

mean[2] (mēn). *adj.* 1. inferior in grade, quality, or character: *a mean scholar.* 2. low in station, rank, or dignity: *mean servitors.* 3. of little importance or consequence: *mean, daily gossip.* 4. unimposing or shabby: *a mean abode.* 5. small-minded or ignoble: *mean motives.* 6. penurious, stingy, or miserly: *a man who is mean about money.* 7. offensive, selfish, or unaccommodating; nasty; malicious: *When he drinks he is mean and insulting.* 8. *Informal.* small, humiliated, or ashamed: *You should feel mean for being so stingy.* 9. *Informal.* in poor physical condition. 10. *Informal.* troublesome or vicious, as a horse. 11. *Slang.* skillful or impressive: *He blows a mean trumpet.*[1]

If you look closely at each subentry, you can see that there are several common explicit meanings for the word depending on its possible uses. You will also recognize that this word can have varying subjective connotations. To speak of someone as "mean in his dealings" is quite different from describing that person as "playing a mean game of tennis." These expressions have quite distinct emotional tones. Words clearly have positive or negative connotations, depending on how they are used. For example, the usual meaning of "manipulate," the explicit meaning, is "to handle or to treat by hand"; it has to do with manual dexterity. However, this word takes on a *negative* connotation in a sentence such as, "They resent him because he manipulates the employees whenever he needs to boost sales." Here the employer is said to manipulate or "handle" the employees as though they were mere objects to be exploited for his ends.

If we carry this further, we can reason that if we want a desirable reaction from our listeners or readers, we should be alert to the effect that words have on others. This basically is what psycholinguistics focuses on. Thus we should be conscious of our choice of words when formulating any argument, whether it is written or spoken.

Since most people want a positive reaction to their points of view, knowing how to use words effectively is a valuable tool in arguing. Let's reinforce this by looking at some pairs of words that illustrate our point:

enterprising	opportunistic
bold	audacious
slay	massacre
plan	scheme
ambitious	aggressive

---

[1] *The Random House Dictionary of the English Language*, Unabridged Edition (New York: Random House, 1973). Reprinted by permission.

The content for each pair is evident. But if you were to apply each term to yourself, you would have a different reaction. Try using them in a sentence and the illustration becomes clearer.

Thus strong and mild reactions can be obtained as you become more aware of the power of words. A newspaper report might refer to an execution as a "senseless slaughter." A politician might refer to the "jabber" of an opponent. A letter to the editor might speak of someone as "gross" in manner. No doubt you can find many similar examples from a variety of sources. The psychological implications of words can work to your advantage.

The business world has been aware of the psychological power of words for some time. How you describe your business or your goods can shape your image into something acceptable to the public and can persuade people to invest in your stocks or buy your product. As an example, credit card companies know that the word "credit" has unpleasant connotations, carrying the idea of borrowing, of debt, of needing financial help. As a result, some companies have introduced the phrase "courtesy cards" to describe what we more ordinarily call simply "credit cards."

In *The Moneychangers* Arthur Hailey includes several brilliant passages about credit cards that illustrate our point about the power of words and the importance of using the right ones to describe what you are doing. In one place, Alex, one of the main characters, is told that the banks are aggressively pushing credit cards on people who cannot handle them properly and reaping the rewards of high interest rates, a practice that is described as the "Shylocking eighteen percent interest all bank credit cards charge." The coined adjective "Shylocking," with its clearly negative connotations of pitiless greed, is especially effective in making the point. To this Alex replies:

> I've told you that credit cards are a packaged commodity, offering a range of services. . . . If you add those services together, our interest rate is not excessive.[2]

Doesn't it sound better to talk of a "packaged commodity," of something that *offers* you *services*, than to talk of a *credit* card? In the conversation from which the above quotation is taken, Alex goes on to explain that there are no *necessary* interest charges because a person can pay the charges in full every month, thereby avoiding all interest fees. Through another character Hailey points out that the majority of people do not do that, but rather pile up long-term debts at high interest rates by paying just the minimum balance. Hailey's

[2] Arthur Hailey, *The Moneychangers* (New York: Doubleday, 1975), p. 72.

character blames the banks for this, in part, because they push their credit cards by announcing them as ways of enjoying things *now* and paying for them *later*. Even Alex, the banker, dislikes this approach and quashes an ad campaign that was to have slogans such as:

Why Worry About Money?
Use Your Keycharge Card
and
Let *Us* Worry for You!

Or:

Bills Are Painless
When You Say
"Put It on My Keycharge"[3]

Note that Hailey's fictional name for the credit card—"Keycharge"— is cleverly chosen with an eye to its positive psychological impact. Presumably, keys are good things: the key to success, the key to the good life, and so on.

Examples of this sort are around you everywhere. Simply pick up a magazine or paper and look at the advertisements. Look at the words and phrases purposely chosen to have positive psychological appeal, chosen to activate your desires, dreams, and hopes. There are no better examples of the persuasive power of words.

An amusing example illustrating the subtle nuances of words occurs in Plato's *Protagoras* when Prodicus tries to convince Socrates and Protagoras that they ought to forget their differences and resume their discussion.

> I as well as Critias would beg you, Protagoras and Socrates, to grant our request, which is, that you will argue with one another and not wrangle; for friends argue with friends out of good-will, but only adversaries and enemies wrangle. And then our meeting will be delightful; for in this way you, who are the speakers, will be most likely to win esteem and not praise only, among us who are your audience; for esteem is a sincere conviction of the hearers' souls, but praise is often an insincere expression of men uttering falsehoods contrary to their conviction. And thus we who are the hearers will be gratified and not pleased; for gratification is of the mind when receiving wisdom and knowledge, but pleasure is of the body when eating or experiencing some other bodily delight.[4]

[3] *Ibid.*, p. 60. Notice also pp. 61, 72–73, and 117.

[4] *The Dialogues of Plato*, translated by B. Jowett (New York: Random House, 1937), vol. 1, p. 107.

SOME PITFALLS: VAGUENESS AND AMBIGUITY

In addition to watching for subjective connotations of words and being alert to the positive and negative impact or tone of words, we must also beware of using words in a vague or ambiguous way. Vagueness and ambiguity are closely related. But in general, a term is vague if it is indefinite or imprecise, while a term is ambiguous if it has more than one meaning.

If a union leader says that the union's strike has occurred because of "poor morale" without explaining exactly what this phrase means, we will have a breakdown in communication precisely because of the vagueness of the phrase. Not only does the expression fail to communicate specific information, but its vagueness would invite different interpretations by the two sides in the dispute.

Communication and arguments also break down if ambiguous terms are employed. We are all familiar with ambiguous terms. Many words in English have several distinct meanings: "bank" can mean either the place where you put your savings or the land that keeps the river in its place. Some words are ambiguous because their common explicit meaning has altered without old usages being totally removed from current usage: for example, "fantastic" is frequently used to mean that products, movies, or people have exceptional qualities, although the word in its original sense means "fantasy-like." Many words, such as "love" as it is used in our society, have a range of meanings so wide as to be equalled only by the number of people using them.

Ambiguity often occurs because of poor grammatical structure or sloppiness in the use of pronouns or referring phrases. For example, consider this story:

> The boys had taken the kittens over to their parents' apartment. They were then treated to a bath.

Who gave whom or what a bath? While we might think of this as a continuing story about the kittens and so construe "they" as referring to the kittens, one could hardly fault an interpretation that suggested other possibilities. Or consider the statement, "John loves lemon pie more than his wife." You can easily see that this remark could cause eyebrows to rise; there are two different meanings one could derive from it.

THE QUESTION OF TRUTH

Now that we have looked briefly at the role words can play in our language, let us move on to the other building blocks of argument: sentences. Let us take an example of an exchange between some mythical executives in a large company. The president and vice-president of this company, let us call it Consolidated Conglomerate, are discussing whether Jones should be promoted to branch manager of the New York plant. The president opposes Jones's promotion and presents the following argument that gives her reasons: "Well, the most important fact is that Jones takes a long time to reach a decision and does not have the backbone to stick by his decision once he has made it. We cannot have such people in high managerial positions in Consolidated Conglomerate because they will tarnish our image for decisive and hard-nosed action and they could cause delays in production, which would hurt our profits. So I say leave Jones where he is— no promotion."

If we analyze this argument we see that the president has made a number of statements. Jones is indecisive. Jones does not stick by his decision but wavers. Consolidated Conglomerate has an image to protect. Indecision by executives tarnishes that image. Delays decrease profits. These are all put out in plain ordinary sentences. The president has also connected some of the facts. Fear of tarnishing the corporation's image is stated as a *reason* for not having men like Jones as managers. The clue to this connection is the "because." The president says that such people as Jones cannot be branch managers *because* they will tarnish the image.

This example points out two things we must look for in an argument. *First*, are the statements that present the facts and the beliefs of the president true or not? *Second*, are the statements connected correctly by the president so that they justify the conclusion she wants?

How do we decide whether a statement is true or not? Here are some sample statements. Which are true?

1. Harold Wilson was once Prime Minister of Britain.
2. The coffee cup on the president's desk is white.
3. Triangles have three sides.
4. Unicorns are white and have one horn on their foreheads.
5. My dog is neurotic.
6. Gravity is a wave of some sort, like a light wave.
7. All cowboy movies are boring.
8. Oh, you must vote for Martha for school president; she's so cool.

Some of these are easy: statement 1 is true, so is 3. You can't at the moment see the president's coffee cup, but if you could, you could easily decide whether statement 2 is true or false. The last two (7 and 8) seem to be quite different, in that they express opinions. Does statement 7 intend to say merely that the *speaker* is bored by cowboy movies? Or does it mean to say that in some sense cowboy movies *really* are boring? But is that a characteristic of a cowboy movie? Could it be like the characteristic of featuring lots of horses, which definitely *is* a characteristic of cowboy movies? Number 8 clearly shows that the speaker likes Martha, but is she "cool," whatever that might mean? What do we say of statements 4, 5, and 6? It's harder to decide whether my dog is neurotic than it is to tell if it is brown and white. And how tricky is statement 4? Mythological stories talk of unicorns and in such stories unicorns *are* white and *do* have one twisted horn. Of course there are no *real* unicorns in our world, but for the world of mythology, this is a true description of unicorns.

KINDS OF STATEMENTS

We can unravel some of the mystery about truth by noting a few distinctions. By and large, the sentences we encounter in arguments are used to state facts, present definitions, or express emotions. Let us look briefly at each of these.

Statements of Fact

Factual propositions claim to assert something about the world we live in. Here are some examples:

Joan has red hair.

My dog has a white patch on his left paw.

Trigger is a palomino.

Each of these states some fact about the world, or at least purports to state such a fact. The key thing about them is that the *only* way to tell whether they are true or false is by experience. You must observe the objects talked about.

You can also put this the other way around: If a proposition must be checked by experience in order to establish its truth, then it is a factual proposition. And remember, by calling them "factual" we don't mean that they are necessarily true. We mean that this kind of proposition *claims* to be stating a truth about the world. But some will be false. For example, many people once believed that the earth was flat, and so they thought that the proposition "The earth is flat" stated a truth about the world. We now know that this statement is false. But since it is *meant* to state a fact or is trying to state a fact, we have called it a factual proposition. These, whether true or false, are some of the building blocks of arguments.

Definitions

Often people do not know how to use a term simply because they are unfamiliar with it or are uncertain of or confused about its application. Such people can be helped by being given a definition of the word in terms of other words that they do understand. A child may not know what "verbose" means but may know what it is to take a long time to make a relatively simple point. Hence the child can be told that "verbose" means to be "wordy," to use an unnecessarily large number of words to make one's point.

A definition always attempts to provide a meaning or to clarify or limit the meaning of a term, by indicating another term that designates the same things or features. A definition is, generally, in the form:

This term means _____ ,

where some synonymous term is placed in the blank, as in

"Bachelor" means "unmarried male."

Since "bachelor" and "unmarried male" are synonymous, they have the same intensional meaning, which also means that they designate the same objects or class of objects and so have the same extension as well. That is, the explicit connotation of "bachelor" is the same as "unmarried male" and both designate or refer to exactly the same individual people. (One qualification is in order here, though. A *persuasive* definition may *purport* to define a term by means of a defining term or phrase that is intended to be taken as synonymous with the term to be defined but that actually is *not* synonymous. This point will become clear later when we discuss different types of definitions.)

A good definition should not be too broad or too narrow. If we defined "fascist" as "a person who supports strong laws and law enforcement," we would undoubtedly include certain conservative yet democratic people. Hence this suggested definition includes too much: it is too broad and fails to allow for discriminations we would want to make. On the other hand, to define "fascist" as "a person who accepted the government of Hitler" is to fail to include people who accept other governments that are or were fascist, such as Mussolini's. Thus this definition is too narrow because it does not include all that it should.

Besides being neither too broad nor too narrow, a good definition should be stated in precise terms so that it does not fail because of vagueness or ambiguity. When defining, we usually are trying to express the essential features or properties of the things referred to by the term being defined. For example, a biologist might define "whale" as "a large marine mammal that has finlike forelimbs and a long tail with horizontal flukes." Here the biologist has attempted to provide a brief statement of the essential features shared by all the mammals designated by the term "whale."[5]

Sometimes definitions are straightforward and cause no difficulties when they are used in communications. If someone defines a tri-angle as a three-sided two-dimensional figure with interior angles summing to 180 degrees, he is reporting the usual conventional mean-ing assigned to the word "triangle" and is indicating the actual, or real, properties of triangles. This might be called a *real definition*.

You can also explain the meaning of a word by a *classificatory defi-nition*, which informs someone of the meaning by indicating *sub-classes* of the things referred to by a term. For example, if someone did not know what "reptile" meant, it would probably help her to be given a classificatory definition something like: "Snakes are reptiles, and so are lizards, turtles, and crocodiles." Here one learns the mean-ing of a general term by discovering the *kinds* or *classes* of things it includes.

In a similar fashion, we explain some terms by pointing out spe-cific examples. If Mary did not know what color was indicated by "mauve," one could only point to examples and say, "This is mauve." Such definitions are called *ostensive definitions*. Ostensive definitions are really the only means we have of indicating what some words mean. How could you ever *explain* what "chocolate" refers to? You cannot describe the taste satisfactorily. You can only say, "Eat this and see what it tastes like; *this* is chocolate."

Unlike the three kinds of definition just discussed, some definitions are troublesome and require careful attention. For example, people will often use definitions that have strong emotive appeal. Consider two definitions of "democracy":

[5] Anyone interested in further consideration of definitions in terms of essential properties should read Plato's Socratic dialogues, such as *Euthyphro* or the first part of the *Meno*. There Socrates tries to find the essential nature of the virtues and assumes that things referred to by a common "name" or term *must* have a common feature.

Definition 1:   Democracy is the freedom to be self-governed.

Definition 2:   Democracy is the tyrannical oppression of the individual by the unenlightened majority.

Each of these is a *persuasive definition*, in that each uses the *emotive* meanings of words to excite a certain response. The first definition is very positive, because it uses the words "freedom" and "self-governed," to which people can be expected to react favorably. The second definition uses negative words—"tyrannical," "oppression," and "unenlightened"—that make democracy seem repulsive and that would cause reaction *against* it. So it is important to detect whether someone is defining a term in a special way to suit certain purposes or in an attempt to gain agreement through the emotive connotations of words. A persuasive definition is one that is weighted or colored in an attempt to influence someone and to excite a favorable response.

Another hazard to clear communication is the *stipulative definition*. In this case someone, or some group, stipulates (decrees) that a word be used a special way. Usually such users of stipulative definitions do not come out and say they are doing this; rather, the way they proceed indicates it fairly quickly. For example, in *Through the Looking-glass* Alice and Humpty Dumpty have the following conversation:

> . . . there are 364 days when you might get un-birthday presents—"
> "Certainly," said Alice.
> "And only *one* for birthday presents, you know. There's glory for you!"
> "I don't know what you mean by 'glory'," Alice said.
> Humpty Dumpty smiled contemptuously. "Of course you don't—till I tell you. I meant, 'there's a nice knock-down argument for you'!"
> "But 'glory' doesn't mean 'a nice knock-down argument'," Alice objected.
> "When I use a word," Humpty Dumpty said, in rather a scornful tone, "it means just what I choose it to mean—neither more nor less."[6]

Clearly Humpty Dumpty is a rather prodigious user of stipulative definitions. Alice wants to deal with real definitions and rightly appeals to the normal meaning people attribute to "glory," and in the next line in the conversation she states that the real question is whether one can "make words mean so many different things."

The moral is that you must be cautious about how to use a word and watch that someone else does not define a word in an unusual

[6] Lewis Carroll, *Through the Looking-glass* in *The Complete Works of Lewis Carroll* (New York: Random House, 1936), p. 214.

way. Most definitions are easy to check: terms such as "triangle" or "whale" have common and well-known meanings. If you are in doubt about your use of a term—or someone else's use—check an authoritative reference source such as a dictionary, encyclopedia, or glossary. But also be alert to the "special" uses to which definitions may be put.

Before we leave definitions, we might note an interesting use of them that has arisen in commercial advertising. If you heard a laundry detergent commercial on your radio similar to the fictional one below, you would not find it much different from many others:

> Try *Blammo* detergent for a whiter, brighter wash. *Blammo blasts* the dirt away. And remember, only *Blammo* has "Purex," the patented miracle ingredient that gets all your clothes whiter than white.

In our culture, we are impressed by science and what it can do; so advertisers sometimes use names and words that *sound* scientific to evoke a positive response. Here the technical- and scientific-sounding word "Purex" is introduced as the name for a special chemical ingredient. Of course, laundry detergents do contain chemical agents, but this advertiser has given some common ingredient a special name in order to impress the consumer with the scientific properties of the product. "Purex" has been defined so that it refers to a certain ingredient and registered as a trademark. Hence only Blammo *can* have "Purex" because no one else can use that name. The unwary consumer buys a detergent containing what is very likely an ordinary ingredient, but an ingredient that seems unique because it has a unique name.

This is a special use of a word in which the word is purposely *defined* but also in which the word *selected* has a special flavor, or quality. Such specially defined words are partway between persuasive and stipulative definitions, sharing features of both.

Expressions of Emotion

A large number of the things that we say are quite different from statements of fact and definitions. "Foreigners are lazy" may truly express your feelings but could hardly be considered either a statement of fact or a definition. "Rock and roll music is irritating" is a statement with definite emotional overtones. Some people would contend that it is a statement of fact, but basically it is an emotional statement or expression. A sentence that is emotive is usually not said to be true or false.

The thing to note is that much of our language is emotional. As such, it is very difficult to deal with. One can use emotive words in order to prejudice people or influence them. In fact, you will remember that emotive words are the key feature of a persuasive definition. Consider the difference between the following two sentences:

1. Custer's army lost many men at Little Big Horn.
2. Custer's army was butchered at Little Big Horn.

The first is fairly neutral and describes an event. The second conveys an emotional feeling by the use of "butchered." In the second the speaker is creating a bias by suggesting that something inhuman and immoral happened to Custer's army. Many people have claimed that the history of the North American Indian has been purposely misrepresented by the use of such colored terms. It *does* make an enormous difference, of course, if we call all Custer's victories "battles" and all the Indian victories "massacres."

Be careful about how you use terms and cautious about how others use them. Avoid the emotional trap!

Arguments frequently break down because people become angry or emotional. And often emotional reactions are sparked by the use of emotive terms or abusive language. Someone who calls you "insensitive, immoral, and boorish" is likely to do more than catch your attention.

Here are two examples of arguments that deteriorate because tempers and emotions run high. The first reports a conversation between Boswell and Dr. Johnson. By and large this is not an exciting conversation; it is not even an illuminating argument. However, if you read it twice and imagine it as an actual spoken conversation, you can begin to feel the emotions and the anger building in the last few lines:

> We resumed Sir Joshua Reynolds's argument on the preceding Sunday, that a man would be virtuous though he had no other motive than to preserve his character. Johnson. "Sir, it is not true: for as to this world vice does not hurt a man's character." Boswell. "Yes, Sir, debauching a friend's wife will." Johnson. "No, Sir. A man is chosen Knight of the shire, not the less for having debauched ladies." Boswell. "What, Sir, if he debauched the ladies of gentlemen in the country, will not there be a general resentment against him?" Johnson. "No, Sir. He will lose those particular gentlemen; but the rest will not trouble their heads about it." (warmly.) Boswell. "Well, Sir, I cannot think so." Johnson. "Nay, Sir, there is no talking with a man who will dispute what every body knows. (angrily.) Don't you know this?" Boswell. "No, Sir; and I wish to think better of your country than you represent it."[7]

[7] James Boswell, *The Life of Samuel Johnson* (New York: Random House, 1952), p. 415.

The debate fails because Johnson gets angry at having someone dispute his position. This leads Johnson to attack Boswell, in the last of his speeches quoted, by implying that Boswell either is so stupid that he doesn't know things commonly known by all people, or else that he is stubborn enough to debate commonly known truths. Now no one likes to be called stupid, even in subtle language, so Boswell *also* gets angry as he reacts to Johnson's angry remarks. In turn, he suggests that Johnson is next to a scoundrel to think so badly of his country. Emotion builds on other emotions.

The second example occurs in *The Moneychangers*. At a party, Alex and Margot have the following heated exchange:

> At one point Margot had demanded, "Who the hell are you?"
> "An ordinary American who believes that, in the military, discipline is necessary."
> "Even in an immoral war like Vietnam?"
> "A soldier can't decide morality. He operates under orders. The alternative is chaos."
> "Whoever you are, you sound like a Nazi. After World War II, we executed Germans who offered that defense."
> "The situation was entirely different."
> "No different at all. At the Nuremberg trials the Allies insisted Germans should have heeded conscience and refused orders. That's exactly what Vietnam draft defectors and deserters did."
> "The American Army wasn't exterminating Jews."
> "No, just villagers. As in My Lai and elsewhere."
> "No war is clean."[8]

In this debate the emotional atmosphere is dense. Note the use of highly emotive terms and phrases: "Nazi," "heeded conscience," "immoral," "draft defectors," "exterminating." Also note how Margot puts an emotional tone on her position by comparing the Vietnam War to the treatment of Jews by Nazi Germany during World War II. Hardly anyone will fail to be repulsed at what occurred during World War II, and by the comparison she draws Margot is trying to evoke a similar repulsion in her opponent in reaction to the Vietnam War. Of course she starts things with a bang in the first line quoted: anyone would be irritated by a question like "Who the hell are you?"

WINNING AN ARGUMENT

There are two sides to every story. Take capital punishment as an example. Some people are for it, some are against it. Suppose Cindy is opposed to capital punishment and her friend Barbara is for it.

[8] Hailey, *The Moneychangers*, p. 76.

Imagine Cindy and Barbara sitting down over coffee one day and beginning to discuss this topic. Cindy wants to win Barbara over to her point of view on this issue. How can she do this? First, she must try to present her case in a clear, logical way. This means she must:

1. Be sure her statements are true.
2. Connect her statements in a logical way.
3. Draw her conclusions so that they clearly follow from the facts.
4. Avoid any errors or fallacies in her reasoning.

Up to this point in the chapter, we have been talking about point 1—the question of truth. Numbers 2, 3, and 4 take practice, and you will learn from this book several easy steps in acquiring these useful skills. Once you thoroughly understand the preliminary ideas in the first part of the book, you will be able to make use of the techniques for analyzing and evaluating arguments that are presented in Chapters 10, 11, and 12.

Besides presenting her own argument in a clear, logical way, Cindy must try to show up any weaknesses there may be in Barbara's side of the story by applying the principles just mentioned:

Cindy should check Barbara's statements. Are they true? Did Barbara try to gain an advantage by using emotive language or persuasive definitions? If she did—or if she said false things—Cindy can critically attack on those points.

Cindy should consider whether Barbara made any logical mistakes in connecting her facts. (Again, later chapters are meant to help the reader recognize such errors.) Cindy wins if there are any such errors, for Barbara's case is not acceptable.

Cindy should ask herself whether she can lead Barbara to contradict herself or say something that is not consistent with the rest of her argument.

CONTRADICTION AND INCONSISTENCY

While it is sometimes hard to end arguments because, like people, they can be very complex, there is no doubt that an argument is over when one of the positions ends in a contradiction or inconsistency.

Suppose George says he believes that every person has complete freedom to do whatever he or she wishes. Suppose he also believes that the government has the right to collect an income tax from every citizen. You can see that George's positions are not consistent. If a person has complete freedom, no one (or no institution) can take away his freedom to spend his own earnings as he wishes (which an income tax does). Contrariwise, if the government has the right to redistribute everyone's money by collecting income taxes and spending these revenues on highways, social programs, and so forth, then people do not have complete and absolute freedom to do whatever they wish with their property.

The best way to show the errors of this kind of argument is to try to construct a formal contradiction. We can do this with George's beliefs in the following way:

George's First Belief	George's Second Belief
"I am absolutely free to do as I wish."	"Governments have the right to levy income tax."
	↓
	This belief entails that the government can take some of my money (in taxes) and spend it as the government sees fit.
	↓
	Which means that I do not have the freedom to spend the money they take.
	↓
	Which means that there is one area in which I am not free to do as I wish.
	↓
	Which means I am *not* absolutely free.

Here we have spelled out the implications of George's second belief to show that we end with a belief that contradicts belief 1. So we have a formal contradiction if we add these two beliefs. Belief 1 says "I am absolutely free." Belief 2 says (once it is spelled out): "I am *not* absolutely free." So George believes at one and the same time that "I am absolutely free and I am not absolutely free." This is not acceptable and so George's position is to be rejected, just as we would reject the claim of someone who said "Right now, at 2:30 P.M. on

Thursday, March 9, it is both snowing and not snowing." Things just don't work this way.

In passing, it might be worth remarking the difference between *contraries* and *contradictories*. "White" and "black" are *contraries*: no object can be both black and white at the same time and in the same respect, but that object need not be one or the other. For example, your car cannot be all black and all white at the same time, but it could be neither; it could be yellow or blue. However, "white" and "not-white" are *contradictories*: no object can be both at the same time, but every object must be one or the other. Again, your car cannot be both white and not-white but (because "not-white" refers to *all* colors other than white) it *must* be one or the other.

Propositions can be distinguished in a similar fashion. Propositions are contraries if both cannot be true at the same time and if neither needs to be true. For example: "My house is a bungalow" and "My house is a two-story house" cannot both be true at the same time, provided "bungalow" means a *one*-story house. However, both could be false. Propositions are contradictories if both cannot be true at the same time yet one of them *must* be true: "My sibling is a male" and "My sibling is *not* a male" are contradictories: both cannot be true at once, but one *must* be true provided the speaker *has* a sibling. A more obvious example of contradictory propositions is the pair: "It is raining now" and "It is *not* raining now." A *self-contradiction* is merely a statement that contains a contradiction. For example: "I am over 20 and I am not over 20" is a self-contradiction.

The subject of contradictions and the issue of whether their presence settles a dispute once and for all came up in the course of the great Fundamentalist religious debates in the United States in the early part of this century. One of the key historical episodes in the rise of Fundamentalism in the early 1900s was the Niagara Bible Conference of 1895, which put forward a statement of the five essential points of the Christian faith. These became known as the Five Points, the first of which was belief in the infallible, literal truth of the Bible. While the Five Points were subsequently and frequently revised or, at least, issued in varying versions, every statement of these essential Christian doctrines accepted the literal truth of the Bible as one of the crucial beliefs of Christianity. Of course the Fundamentalists had opponents, especially during the early part of this century when Darwinian evolutionary theory provided an explanation of man's origins rivaling the account in Genesis. On the subject of the Fundamentalists' belief in the literal truth of the Bible their opponents argued that, since the Bible had contradictory claims in it, it follows that not every claim in the Bible is literally true.

One example of a contradiction in the Bible occurs in the accounts

in Acts of the Apostles of the experiences of Saul and the men traveling with him on the road to Damascus. Here are the contradictory
claims, with the key passages underlined:

Acts 9:7.   "And the men which journeyed with him stood speech-
less, *hearing a voice*, but seeing no man."

Acts 22:9.   "And they that were with me saw indeed a light and
were afraid; but *they heard not the voice* of him that
spoke to me."

Given the context of the first passage, the voice said to have been
heard by the men must have been the voice that spoke to Saul. However, this makes the two claims contradictory. Regardless of what
actually happened on the road to Damascus, the company either heard
a voice or did *not* hear a voice during the same event. So *one* of the
accounts, either that recorded in Acts 9:7 or that in Acts 22:9, must
be false. Therefore, it was concluded, the Bible cannot be literally
true in every claim it makes.

Since we do not pretend to be theologians, we are not going to suggest how the Fundamentalist case might be saved here. The point we
wish to illustrate is that to be caught in a contradiction destroys your
position. The Fundamentalist belief in the literal truth of the Bible
is not justified if the Bible has contradictory statements in it. If there
is even one contradiction in the Bible, then the Bible necessarily has
at least one false statement; because for every pair of contradictory
statements we have, one *must* be true and the other false. And if the
Bible has one false statement, then the Bible is not infallibly true or
literally true in every respect.

Sometimes a contradictory position or use of words simply con-
fuses people. In the spring of 1977 many newspapers ran a full-page
paid advertisement entitled "God Is Alive—Religion Is Dead." It
turned out that the group responsible for the ad was officially registered as a religious organization calling itself "Christianity Without
Religion," and donations to the group were held in a trust fund
registered in that name. Many people were subsequently upset because the group seemed to them to present non-Christian views in
the garb of Christianity, perhaps even just using the appeal of Christ
and Christianity to gain followers. But more to the point for our
purposes, many people were confused by the group's claim to be a
Christian but nonreligious group, especially the claim that they were
not an "organized religion." Since they were registered under a name
using the term "Christian" and gathering donations, they certainly
apeared to be an organized religion. Moreover, since there can be no
doubt that Christianity is a religion, is it not just a straightforward

contradiction to claim to be a form of Christianity yet *not* a religion? It makes sense to claim to be a *true* religion in the midst of misguided sects, but it makes no sense to claim *not* to be a religion while claiming by your official name to be a branch of the Christian religion. And it makes no sense because the very title of the organization entails a contradiction.

Views and beliefs that involve or entail contradictions must be rejected. Arguments are automatically lost if they involve contradictions, and you can win an argument by discovering a contradiction in your opponent's position.

One must also be *consistent*; a person loses credibility by being inconsistent. A parent who advises a teenage son or daughter against smoking cigarettes on the grounds that smoking is unhealthy, yet who smokes himself, is not going to gain the unquestioned obedience of the teenager. Usually when one is inconsistent there is a contradiction in the background. For example, the smoking parent, by his advice to the teenager, is in effect claiming that "No people should smoke." Yet by his example he is saying, "Some people (namely, I) should smoke." These propositions are contradictories.

Contradictions and inconsistencies create difficulty because people sometimes fail to see them. In fact, people often fail to see the consequences and implications of their words and deeds. A rather humorous illustration is an event that occurred in England in January 1977. The printers' union of the London *Times* went on strike for one day, making it impossible for the *Times* to publish. The underlying problem was that the printers' union refused to set the type for an article that the newspaper's editors wished to carry in that issue. And what was the article in question, which the members of the printers' union refused to set? It was an article claiming that the printing unions practiced censorship! One wonders whether the union members realized what they were doing; could they really have failed to see the implications of their action? Did they not realize that their actions merely confirmed the accusation in the article?

This bears an important lesson for us. Since many arguments are lost because of ensuing contradictions and inconsistencies, it pays to recognize and be alert to the implications of what one says and does. This is especially true because most contradictions are initially hidden and come out only after some probing and debate.

RHETORIC

As we have pointed out, words can be useful tools—but they can also be devastating weapons. We are sometimes intimidated by the haughty clerk who makes us feel awkward by saying to us, "Some people just don't recognize *quality*." Or how often have we heard the flowery rhetoric of the politician who harangues his opponents with the high-sounding observation, "*Our* party cherishes democratic ideals and we will fight *all* those who oppose social justice." It is apparent from these examples that the speakers are implying more than is being stated. By emphasizing the italicized words, one can readily see that there are shades of meaning beyond the stated words. Powerful speakers and effective writers know how to make good use of language. Not only must we be alert to the uses to which we ourselves can effectively put words, but we must also learn to defend against the misleading use of terms by others.

There are several kinds of misleading device that appear innocent enough on the surface but that, when looked at closely, can be seen to have the power to trap one into conceding a point without realizing it. One of these strategies is the *rhetorical question*, in which the answer to the question is hinted at or implied in the very question itself. When someone says, "You don't *really* want to go to *that* movie, do you?" it is obvious that "No!" is the expected response. Watch for this kind of "loaded question," which immediately puts you on the defensive. In this example the burden is now on *you* to state why you would possibly feel otherwise about the movie.

Another rhetorical device is *irony*, in which the speaker or writer suggests the opposite of what is stated. For example, in Shakespeare's play *Julius Caesar*, Mark Antony, addressing a mob, says, "For Brutus is an honorable man." Yet throughout this portion of the scene it is clear that Antony, in part by repeatedly reminding the mob that Brutus is "honorable," is able to rouse them against Brutus.

Somewhat close to irony is the *understatement*. An example of this is: "I can understand why you could forget; you had so much to do today." This in effect makes the listener think twice about his or her behavior. In addition, there is the *overstatement*, which everyone has experienced: "Oh, yes, I know. You are *much* too clever to have ever thought of something as simple as that!" In both cases, there is a hint beyond what is literally said that something is not acceptable to the speaker or writer.

Numerous examples of rhetorical speeches are to be found in George Orwell's *Animal Farm*. Intended as a satire on dictatorship, the story is about a group of farm animals who drive out their master, Mr. Jones, and take over running the farm themselves. All begins well enough—everyone is excited by the new spirit of freedom and of sharing in tasks and the farm's produce. But leadership, which falls to the pigs, has its pitfalls and gradually the original ideal order becomes changed in ways that increasingly make it like the old despotic rule of Farmer Jones. As each fateful change occurs some new rationalization is presented to justify it. It is in such contexts that the spokesman for the pigs waxes eloquent in speeches filled with rhetorical flourishes.

The first occurs when it is discovered that the milk and the apples are not being shared equally but are going to the leaders, the pigs. Squealer, who speaks for the leader, Napoleon, says:

> You do not imagine, I hope, that we pigs are doing this in a spirit of selfishness and privilege? Many of us actually dislike milk and apples. I dislike them myself. Our sole object in taking these things is to preserve our health. Milk and apples . . . contain substances absolutely necessary to the well-being of a pig. . . . The whole management . . . of this farm depend[s] on us. . . . It is for *your* sake that we drink that milk and eat those apples. Do you know what would happen if we pigs failed in our duty? Jones would come back![9]

Notice that Squealer opens with a rhetorical question. He then argues that it is not pleasure—a point backed up by the personal testimony that he dislikes milk and apples—but *duty* to the others that forces them to eat the distasteful food. This automatically puts opponents on the defensive because of the association of the welfare of all with the eating of apples and drinking of milk by the pigs. And at the end, the argument is dramatically closed by threatening the event they fear the most—the return of Jones.

Fine turns of phrase, the use of rhetorical questions, understatement, and overstatement are all part of Squealer's bag of rhetorical tricks. Sometimes he appeals to the hopes and dreams of the animals by vivid accounts of how it will be when the present goal is achieved. Squealer's peak is probably the explanation he gives when it is discovered that one of the rules against manmade and manlike things has been altered, that the pigs are now sleeping in beds. Here is part of Squealer's speech:

> You have heard . . . that we pigs now sleep in the beds of the farmhouse? And why not? You did not suppose, surely, that there was ever a ruling against *beds*? A bed merely means a place to sleep. A pile of straw in a stall is a bed, properly regarded. The rule was against *sheets*, which are a human invention.[10]

Note how this proceeds. The first two sentences admit the "crime" and so take by surprise anyone who expected denial. The second is

[9] George Orwell, *Animal Farm* (Harmondsworth: Penguin Books, 1951), pp. 32–33.
[10] *Ibid.*, p. 60.

another rhetorical question that *challenges* the audience of farm animals so that they are now on the defensive. The third sentence, beginning "You did not suppose," again is a rhetorical master stroke; because to suppose otherwise is to admit stupidity. This is quickly followed by the implication that all the animals sleep in beds, because even straw in a stall is a bed. So who is free to complain? No one wants to be thought stupid or to leave himself open to attack, yet Squealer has maneuvered so that those who wish to complain must risk both. Later in the speech Squealer will again remind the animals that the pigs need good rest in order to do all the brainwork required to run the farm, and so the beds are only a necessary means to the performing of the pigs' duties of leadership. Lastly, the threat of the return of Jones is thrown in for good measure.

Squealer's abilities hardly know any bounds. He even uses gestures well in setting a mood. The horse Boxer has been moved to the hospital, or so the animals are told. However, some suspect that he was sent by the pigs to the glue factory. But who could doubt that Boxer died in the hospital, well cared for, happy at the last and firm in his belief in the revolution and the pigs' leadership, after hearing Squealer's account:

> "It was the most affecting sight I have ever seen!" said Squealer, lifting his trotter and wiping away a tear. "I was at his bedside at the very last. And at the end, almost too weak to speak, he whispered in my ear that his sole sorrow was to have passed on before the windmill was finished. 'Forward, comrades!' he whispered. 'Forward in the name of the Rebellion. Long live Animal Farm. Long live Comrade Napoleon! Napoleon's always right.' Those were his very last words, comrades."[11]

Surely this is the ultimate rhetorical appeal: the message, from the deathbed and in his own words, from the one simple and honest friend and coworker they all had, whom they all trusted and looked up to for his many sacrifices for the good of Animal Farm.

CUTTING YOUR LOSSES

You must also learn what things can and cannot be argued over. We can discuss and argue about how the world might have begun. We can also argue about who has the hardest shot in professional hockey, or about whether a God exists. But you can't argue against the claim that someone likes chocolate ice cream better than any other kind (unless you think the person is joking or lying on this occasion);

11 *Ibid.*, p. 105.

matters of taste are not debatable. Factual statements and definitions can profitably be debated, but emotional exclamations seldom can—an exception being the case where an emotional outburst contains a factual claim ("Damn it, Jones is so nauseatingly polite!").

Politics, morality, religion, and a great many other subjects *are* worth discussing and can be pursued with some success. But just remember that people often reach a point where they will not discuss things further. Or they may think the particular subject is a matter of personal preference or that discussion of it is in poor taste. There is nothing to be gained by pursuing what someone considers a delicate subject or by trying to continue a discussion that the other person wishes to end.

EXERCISES

I. For each of the following, determine whether the basic intention of the passage is to:

(a) provide information or an explanation,
(b) express or evoke emotion,
(c) command, give directions, or give advice,
(d) define a term.

If more than one is involved, indicate the portion of the passage that determines each.

1. We cannot come to the party because we have another engagement that evening.
2. You must vote against the proposal. If it is accepted, the war will continue for at least another year. This means another year of terrible agony for the injured, the homeless, and those who will lose a loved one; consider the tears of pain and anxiety on the faces of the children and widows.
3. Identical twins are the only ones being used in the current study in genetics.
4. The phrase "identical twin" refers to twins that are the result of the division of a single fertilized egg.
5. Although we tend to treat all military leaders as heroes, some of them were of the lowest sort, being cheats, scoundrels, and indecisive, whimpering cowards.
6. University professors are the most boring, egotistical, self-centered people I have ever met. You would do best to avoid them.

7. A tenured teacher is one who holds a position permanently and who cannot be removed from the position, so long as the duties of the position continue to exist and so long as the teacher is not guilty of moral turpitude.

8. In our culture, the moral principles of many of our outstanding, exemplary citizens result from their religious beliefs. Given this, it would be a good idea to have more religious training and study in the schools. This would improve the morality of our total society.

II. Read the following statements and decide whether they are:

(a) vague,
(b) emotional,
(c) factual,
(d) a definition.

1. Gun control is a sort of forced law.
2. Laws are made to be obeyed.
3. Butter pecan ice cream is fattening.
4. All modern art is trash.
5. A sister is a female sibling.
6. The latest space odyssey is terrific and wonderful; it's an *experience!*
7. A snack is a light meal.
8. Every person on welfare is a no-good, lazy bum.
9. Oranges grow in subtropical countries.
10. All criminals are low-down, no-good con artists.
11. One requirement of a citizen is to vote.
12. No centipede really has a hundred legs.
13. Art is the expression of emotion.
14. The intern at the hospital said that Cyril was sick because he had a "bug" of some kind.
15. Milk and cheese are sources of protein.

III. In each of the following determine whether there is an ambiguous term. If there is, explain the different senses in which the term is used or, in the case of an ambiguous pronoun or referring phrase, the different possible referents of the term.

1. Some of the people can be fooled all of the time and all of the people can be fooled some of the time. But they cannot all be fooled all of the time.

2. Many of the people who voted for Nixon were embarrassed by

Watergate. Our neighbor Jones, however, said he would *still* vote for Nixon even today. This caused Smith to remark that it didn't surprise him that Jones would still vote for Nixon. "He has such an innocent face," said Smith, "so it's little wonder."

3. When the arrogant king was told that the peasants were revolting, he said, "I couldn't agree more."

4. Everyone agreed that Stockton *must* be a good teacher because he was such a good soldier in the war and, in addition, was very good in college.

5. The researchers at the regional veterinary college were examining a cow that had just given birth to an abnormal calf. Dr. Johnson claimed she had never seen one like it, although she had studied large animals for most of her life.

6. The judge said that the law could only hold fully sane people responsible for criminal acts and, therefore, Green was not going to be sent to the penitentiary because it had been shown conclusively that Green was mentally disturbed. One of the jurors remarked that if Green was not responsible for the act, he should not have been arrested and tried in the first place.

IV: Criticize the following definitions in terms of their being either:

   (a) too narrow,
   (b) too broad,
   (c) vague.

1. A dinosaur is a prehistorical animal.
2. Violence is forcing someone to do something against her or his will.
3. An identity is the sharing of identical features by two or more things.
4. Morality is the doing of what is morally right.
5. Philosophy is the study of the works of Plato.
6. Photography is the process of developing and printing film.
7. Love is an emotional response.
8. Learning is a form of intellectual stimulation.

V: Consider each of the following pairs of statements. Determine whether the pairs constitute:

   (a) contraries,
   (b) contradictories,
   (c) neither.

1. All my bathing suits are white.
   All my bathing suits are black.
2. All people who swim every day are fit.
   All people who swim every day enjoy the water.
3. No lions are ferocious.
   All lions are ferocious.
4. No wild lions are ferocious.
   Some wild lions are ferocious.
5. It is cold here today.
   It is not cold here today.
6. Violence influences young children.
   Violence can be seen on TV every day.
7. All fruit is nutritious.
   Some fruit is not nutritious.
8. No cowboys live in the city.
   All cowboys live in the city.

3

Don't Let Them Fool You: Some Common Fallacies

Language is a powerful tool, but it can be misused. People will try to persuade you by means of all sorts of appeals—by playing on your sympathies, your likes and dislikes, your fears, or whatever. In the last chapter we emphasized the need to watch for emotive language. In the present chapter we shall point out some devices to watch for and avoid, either by not using them yourself or by not letting others use them on you. The key point about all of them is that they are very frequently successful as persuasive measures. But they do not succeed by logically connecting facts and drawing reasoned conclusions from them; their effect depends on trickery, emotional appeals, or threats of one sort or another. Such tricks and illogical moves are called *fallacies*.

FALLACY OF APPEAL TO THREATS AND INTIMIDATION (APPEAL TO FORCE)

The uses of intimidation can be fairly subtle—it need not only be a threat to hit or punch someone. Imagine a representative of a bargaining group presenting suggested legislation to a member of Congress. She could try to present the group's case rationally and logically to the congressman in order to try to persuade him of its merits. But she might also just appeal to force by telling the congressman that the group in question represents a lot of votes and that he had best agree to the reform or lose these votes come the next election. Here the merits of the case are left out and no discussion or reasoned argument used; the group's representative has simply tried to intimidate the congressman. This is not only an instance of a bad argument, but it will be an unsuccessful tactic if the congressman has integrity and courage.

FALLACY OF APPEAL TO PITY
(PLAYING ON YOUR FEELINGS)

The appeal to pity is a technique for bypassing one's thinking abilities. Examples are common in law courts, where an attorney may try to make jury members feel sorry for an accused person rather than leading them to consider the real issue of innocence or guilt. But the law courts are by no means the only places where we can find examples of appeals to pity. If you read the letters to the editor in your local newspaper or listen to someone—perhaps even a fellow student—arguing a cause, you will see that the writer or speaker is often seeking to reach us emotionally and not necessarily rationally. Read the following speech and pretend that it is being given by a senior citizen to a group of city councilors. Underline the words that you consider emotionally charged.

How could anyone consider the unreasonable increase in the price of senior citizen bus passes from $10 to $20 a year? Are you not aware, my dear friends, that you are deliberately penalizing that small and helpless group of older people who built this city of ours? There are many of us who scrimp and save on our meager incomes just to make ends meet—and you want to impose another heavy burden on us at a time when we can hardly afford to keep ourselves alive. I plead with you to reconsider this proposal. If you won't do it for me, then do it for an older loved one who needs your support.

In such a case, the speaker attempts, in part, to gain acceptance of a conclusion by playing upon the hearer's feelings. The speaker tries to achieve that end by the choice of highly emotive terminology. Be wary of the use of such "loaded" language yourself, and be prepared to sift through the layers of rhetoric used by others. Try to avoid *irrelevant* considerations and *illegitimate* appeals.

FALLACY OF APPEAL TO THE MASSES
(APPEAL TO THE PEOPLE)

The appeal to the masses is an attempt to win support by emotional appeal to the sentiments of people in general, rather than by presenting evidence and reasoned arguments. Someone might claim, for example, that a given plan is "for the good of the country." Again one has to cut through the rhetoric and find the real issues.

A common variant of this is to get someone to agree to something because "everybody else does." We have been told that more people buy General Motors cars than any other kind, but this does not mean that these are the best-built cars on the road. One can see that this would be a faulty inference to draw from this fact. Remember that at one time almost everyone believed the world was flat; but that did not make it so.

FALLACY OF ILLEGITIMATE APPEAL TO AUTHORITY

Often someone tries to win the day by either quoting an "authority" or claiming to be one, and thus entitled to a special hearing. While discussing discipline in schools, someone might say, "Well, I'm a parent, so I should know what is to be done." The trouble is, being a parent doesn't guarantee that your views about children are the best or the correct ones. They may or may not produce happy, healthy, well-adjusted children; and they may or may not be effective with other people's children.

TV commercials in which famous people endorse certain products are often based on the same kind of fallacious reasoning. We should not be gullible enough to believe that just because some football star tells us he eats a certain cereal, it is the best cereal; or that just because a beautiful actress says she uses a certain soap, it is the best soap. If truthful, such ads simply give you one person's opinion; they do not provide a legitimate and authoritative testimonial for a product. Beware of appeals to authority.

Of course, there are legitimate appeals to authority; we frequently must rely on experts. Life would be much more difficult if one did not trust and accept the judgments and advice of one's doctor, legal counsel, or stock broker. Few of us can repair our own car, so we accept the authority of the garage mechanic. In writing this book, we have looked up many words in *The Random House Dictionary of the English Language*, so as to be accurate about spelling and usage. The point is that we often *must* appeal to authorities and depend on them.

In arguing, as well, we often have occasion to make legitimate appeals to authority. Whether it is acceptable to appeal to an authority depends on the authority cited and the topic about which that authority is consulted. If a person possesses demonstrated, special knowledge in a field, or if a book has a deserved reputation for being instructive on a specific topic, such an authority can appropriately be used. In an argument about how a muscle spasm occurs, the facts supplied by a neurosurgeon have an important role and it is certainly legitimate to include them in your debates and deliberations.

It would be silly, though, to consult or quote in an argument someone who has no special knowledge. Nor is there any sense in asking an expert about something outside the person's area of expertise. The famous chef James Beard would be worth consulting about making a good soufflé. But unless you knew that he *also* was a great mechanic, would you take your car to him for repairs?

There are several questions you should ask yourself about an authority cited in an argument:

Is the person cited really an authority?

Is the authority talking about something within his or her special field of competence?

Are there *rival* authorities? It is not uncommon for authorities to differ in their opinions. Consider the controversy among doctors and scientists, all authoritative in their fields, about the effects of vitamin C in preventing and curing the common cold.

FALLACY OF ARGUING AGAINST THE PERSON (ARGUING AD HOMINEM)

Sometimes people get off the track and attack their opponent *personally* rather than focussing on their opponent's position and beliefs. (The Latin term *ad hominem* means "to or against the person.") Archie Bunker, in the television show "All in the Family," dismisses many of the arguments put forward by his son-in-law, Michael, on the grounds that Michael is a "pinko commie" or a "meathead." In doing this, he fails to consider the merits of Michael's arguments and reasons; he attacks Michael rather than the beliefs Michael asserts. Remember that even being a member of the Mafia does not automatically make someone's arguments unsound or unworthy of attention.

Fallacious arguing *ad hominem* is commonly divided into two categories. An *abusive ad hominem* involves personal attacks on an opponent's character, ethnic origins, or other irrelevant features, rather than investigations into and evaluations of the truth and logical coherence of the argument presented by that person. To claim that we must not accept someone's proposal just because that person reads *The New York Review of Books* is to indulge in a fallacious inference. Such a tactic could have the psychological effect of transferring negative feelings an audience might have toward a class of people to the proposal in question. But arguing in this way fails to deal with the logical merits of the *proposal* and concentrates on features about the *proposer* that are irrelevant to evaluating the real merits of the case being presented.

The second traditional category of this fallacy is known as a *circumstantial ad hominem.* Here the opponent's personal or professional standing is cited as a reason for discounting his or her argument. It is clearly fallacious to argue that we ought to reject the union negotiators' proposal for a shortened work week simply on the grounds that this is the type of proposal one might expect from the union's representatives. The proposal may be supported by very sound arguments, and we should attend to these argued reasons rather than dismissing the proposal on irrelevant grounds. Similarly, the position of the members of the local gun club that there should be no restrictions on the sale of firearms should not be rejected simply because this is the very type of proposal one might expect from the members of a gun club.

In passing, it is worth noting that other beliefs held by an opponent are not necessarily to be considered irrelevant. One might quite legitimately remind someone of other beliefs that person has expressed as a way of demanding that the person be consistent. In dealing with any purportedly fallacious argument, it sometimes requires painstaking analysis and sound judgment to determine whether an appeal or a rejection is advanced on grounds that are relevant.

Here are two arguments that illustrate the fallacy of arguing *ad hominem.* They are taken from letters to editors of magazines.

Example 1

Well, here we go again with another round of that alltime favorite American game of "Don't do as I do—do as I say."

In this case we have a woman (Marabel Morgan) telling other women how to be happy with a housewife's career, while she is out making a cool $1.5 million plus on the lecture circuit as a writer of popular literature.[1]

Example 2

Considering the influence television has on young people, as you reported (Feb. 21), I propose kids be directed toward reading high-quality publications like *Newsweek*. Then they can be exposed to plenty

[1] *Time*, April 4, 1977. Copyright 1976 Time Inc. All rights reserved. Quoted by permission.

of flashy cigarette ads and glossy booze ads, which happened to make up 22 percent of all advertising in that issue.[2]

In Example 1 the writer attacks Marabel Morgan on the grounds that someone making a lot of money in a different pursuit cannot appropriately tell other women how to make a satisfying career out of being a housewife. This is an illegitimate attack on the person. It is a circumstantial *ad hominem*.

Example 2 employs irony. Here the writer does not address the arguments or disagree with the evidence advanced by the author of the report in *Newsweek*. Rather, he attacks *Newsweek* itself. But what have the ads run by *Newsweek* to do with the magazine's reports and commentaries? Advertisements are sold to gain revenue, and advertising space is sold to those who want it and can afford it. Apparently, the writer is trying to argue that *Newsweek* could have a bad influence on children because it runs these ads and that, therefore, it is *not in a position* to speak out about television. But this argument is not sound. Your doctor may tell you that you are ruining your health by being overweight while she herself is obese. That does not mean she cannot correctly comment on *your* condition. In passing, we might note that this example is difficult to classify as either an abusive or a circumstantial *ad hominem*. It employs ironical, somewhat abusive terms yet, like a circumstantial *ad hominem*, claims that the magazine is not in a position to make judgments about adverse affects on young people.

Let's conclude this discussion of the *ad hominem* fallacy by citing one final variant of it. It seems popular to hold the view that someone cannot be justified in speaking on a topic without having firsthand experience. "What do you know about Uganda and Amin?" someone might say to you. "You've never been anywhere near Africa." Here a fallacy is clearly committed; again it attacks you (the person) rather than your arguments and stated evidence. A sociologist may well be an expert on the effects of crime on our society yet may never have committed a crime.

FALLACY OF ARGUING IN A CIRCLE (BEGGING THE QUESTION)

Sometimes in an argument a person assumes what he or she should, instead, be setting out to prove, with the result that the argument runs in a circle. In other words, the arguer "begs" (avoids or misses) the question at issue. Consider this example:

[2] *Newsweek*, March 14, 1977. Quoted by permission.

GLENNA.   The Bible is the word of God.
ELDON.   But that is only true if God exists.
GLENNA.   Oh, I know God exists.
ELDON.   How do you know?
GLENNA.   The Bible says so.
ELDON.   But how can you trust the Bible?
GLENNA.   It's the word of God!

Here the original question to be decided was whether the Bible is the word of God. But Glenna *assumes* this both at the outset and later in the argument, thereby begging the question. The argument ends in the place where it began.

VAGUENESS AND AMBIGUITY AGAIN

In discussions of fallacies it is not uncommon to divide them into two main types: *fallacies of relevance* and *fallacies of ambiguity*. The fallacies we have been discussing in this chapter are, by this distinction, all fallacies of relevance. They are all devices that involve irrelevant considerations or illegitimate appeals of one sort or another, and, as such, they are common causes of the failure of arguments.

We chose to treat ambiguity in Chapter 2 because it seemed more natural to treat that topic in the context of the meanings of terms. There is, of course, no reason to repeat all that we said there, but we shall review a few points in order to reinforce them.

Whereas vague or ambiguous terms will make your statements unclear or confusing, as pointed out in Chapter 2, an ambiguous term used with two different meanings in two different statements within an argument can make that argument fallacious. That is, vagueness and ambiguity are sources not only of confusion but also of fallacious inferences. Consider the old joke:

1. Nothing is better than heaven.
2. A bread crust is better than nothing.
3. *Therefore*, a bread crust is better than heaven.

Clearly this disregards the different senses of "nothing" in the contexts of statements 1 and 2. Or consider a teenager on a date who argues that a parting kiss is appropriate because the Bible says to "love your neighbor." One can rightly point out that the conclusion— that a kiss ought to be given—does not follow, because *that* is not the sense of loving intended by the Biblical maxim "Love your neighbor."

Vagueness is also detrimental to the clear and precise formulations of one's theories. A scientist cannot test a hypothesis unless the working hypothesis has been formulated in a clear and rigorously precise way. Similarly, our everyday discussions of social concerns falter if the terms we use are so unclear as to fail to communicate our intended meaning. Discussions of philosophical problems can also suffer because a position in a debate is vaguely worded.

Consider the problem of justifying moral standards. We are aware that we do make moral judgments about people and their actions and about our own actions. Typical examples are:

> I ought not to have lied to Uncle Bob.
>
> It was wrong for Celeste to drink beer at the party after she had promised her parents she would not.
>
> People who commit murder should be executed.

Often one's moral judgments or actions are challenged. When this occurs, people sometimes defend themselves by arguing that their actions were right according to the laws of the land or according to the commands of the Bible. Others, however, will argue that all morality is relative and so each individual must personally decide what is right. And some might adopt other positions.

The view that ethical standards or moral rules are relative is called ethical relativism. The first question that must be addressed to someone who says that morality is relative is, What exactly does "relative" mean? Is the theory claiming that morality is relative to a culture? or that it is relative to what our local motorcycle gang believes? or that it is relative to my own personal views, whims, or moods?

The vagueness here can be quickly seen if we imagine someone claiming that the theory of ethical relativism can be expressed by the statement,

> What is right for you to do is not necessarily right for me.

You can see that this statement is indefinite and could be interpreted in at least two ways. *First*, it could be taken as the claim that

> There are contexts or situations in which what is the right or correct action for me is not the correct action for you.

Unfortunately this interpretation does not make morality relative in any interesting sense. To illustrate this, imagine looking into the window of a small store one day and discovering that the owner is being robbed by someone brandishing a knife. If you are a 98-pound weakling, the right action for you would most likely be to run to the nearest phone and call for help. But if you were a police officer in uniform with your gun by your side, the right action would *not* be to run to the phone, but to enter the store and apprehend the criminal. Of course, almost *any* theory of morality will endorse this type of relativism.

However, a *second* interpretation of the original claim might be:

> Moral standards are not necessarily applicable in all contexts, so a given standard may apply to me but not to you.

This is the claim that *standards* rather than actions are relative. Presumably, this is the position taken by someone who believes that blood feuds are acceptable among certain primitive peoples but not in our society. And it is the position taken by the drinking parent who forbids a teenager to drink alcohol. Clearly there are two standards in such situations.

The important point, though, for purposes of this discussion, is that a vague or indefinite word can confuse or fail to communicate what was intended. A vaguely worded theory is indefinite, unclear, and imprecise, and it can lead to more than one interpretation.

A well-known and probably classic case of an ambiguity resulting in a fallacious or questionable inference, at least according to his critics, occurs in John Stuart Mill's *Utilitarianism*. In that work Mill (1806–1873) endorses the theory that actions are to be judged moral or immoral by reference to the happiness they promote. Mill claims that morality rests on what he calls "utility," or "the greatest happiness principle," defined as the thesis that

> Actions are right in proportion as they tend to promote happiness; wrong as they tend to produce the reverse of happiness.[3]

Mill goes on to say that by "happiness" he means pleasure and the avoidance of pain, and he also makes it clear that this principle is altruistic in that it is the happiness of all people involved that must be considered.

After further explanations of his doctrine, Mill asks whether one could *prove* conclusively that it is true. One problem is that since the principle of utility is the *ultimate* moral standard for Mill, he cannot prove its truth by deducing it from some higher principle. Nevertheless, Mill thinks that there is a proof of sorts available:

> The only proof capable of being given that an object is visible is that people actually see it. The only proof that a sound is audible is that

[3] John Stuart Mill, *Utilitarianism* (New York: Bobbs-Merrill, 1957), p. 10.

people hear it; . . . In like manner, I apprehend, the sole evidence it is possible to produce that anything is desirable is that people do actually desire it.[4]

While this proof may seem convincing on the surface, it employs the term "desirable" ambiguously so that it means both "capable of being desired" and "worthy of being desired." Mill requires the first sense— "capable of being desired"—to make "desirable" parallel to "visible" and "audible." But he is trying to prove the ethical theory that the greatest happiness *ought* to be or is *worthy* of being desired, and he must intend "desirable" in the second sense of "worthy of being desired" in order to have that proof. This shift in the meaning of "desirable" makes Mill's proof unacceptable.

Failure to remove ambiguities brought about by equivocations, poorly formulated statements, or shifts of meanings will cause your arguments to falter. Again, one can only urge special care and attention to one's use of language and to the types of appeals made in presenting one's arguments. This has been the emphasis of much of Chapter 2 and of this chapter.

It is instructive to remember King Croesus, for whom an ambiguity proved disastrous. Croesus consulted the Delphic Oracle about whether he should fight the Persians. The oracle said that if he did, a great empire would fall. Taking heart at this, Croesus entered the battle feeling certain of victory. As things turned out, he lost—it was *his* empire to which the oracle was referring. Words are subtle and complex. Always treat them with respect.

EXERCISES

I. Each of the following involves one of the informal fallacies discussed in this chapter. Name the fallacy in each case.

1. You should buy this peanut butter. Of course it's good peanut butter; John Wayne himself eats this kind.
2. A delegate to the leadership convention was told by a certain group that Stover was the person they all favored and the one the delegate herself should vote for. She was, at the same time, "reminded" that her employer was a member of their group and that the employer would be "disappointed" if he learned that the delegate had not voted for Stover, and that he would take appropriate action.

[4] Mill, p. 44.

3. The Flyers are the best team in hockey. I know they are the best team because they will win the Stanley Cup. And they *will* win the Stanley Cup because they are the best team.

4. Don't listen to what Crofton says about why the dock wonders need a pay raise. He's a dock worker himself, so what else do you expect him to say?

5. Mrs. Cratchet was beside herself. "Oh, Mr. Scrooge," she pleaded, "you must give Bob more money, because we have so much trouble making ends meet, with the payments on the Rolls and Tiny Tim's expenses at Harvard. We are so destitute and miserable. You *must* help us."

6. "You keep giving me advice on this project," said Tollspring, "but what have you done *yourself*? You are just a lazy, conceited sponge, living off my position. So there is no reason even to listen to your advice."

7. REAL ESTATE AGENT.   This is an A-1 house. You couldn't get one better.

   PROSPECTIVE BUYER.   What makes it so good?

   REAL ESTATE AGENT.   It's A-1 because it's built by the Schmidt Brothers Construction Company.

   PROSPECTIVE BUYER.   But what makes *their* houses so good?

   REAL ESTATE AGENT.   Well, if you look at all the other houses built by them in this development, you'll find that they are *all* A-1.

   PROSPECTIVE BUYER.   But what makes all *those* houses A-1?

   REAL ESTATE AGENT.   Well, as I say, they are all built by the Schmidt Brothers Construction Company.

8. I am opposed to admitting women to the bar, not because I simply place a value on tradition, even though lawyers *have* traditionally been men. Rather, I take this fact to be the collective judgment of the ages. Over the centuries people have judged that only men should be lawyers. And thousands of people can't be wrong.

9. The principal is the only one on the committee who opposes buying new furniture for the teachers' lounge, complaining that it would cost too much. He met privately with some of the new teachers on staff. In these private sessions he claimed that since he had yet to make his recommendations about next year's teaching appointments, it would be prudent, for new teachers in particular, not to oppose him on this issue.

10. ABERCROMBIE.   The line for the new telephone system should

follow the river bank for the first seven miles and then turn north.

BERKSHIRE. But Cram, our chief engineer, has argued that the river bed is not stable, so there is reason to believe that the line might be in danger in a few years if the river bed shifts even a little.

ABERCROMBIE. Oh, Cram can go to blazes. He's just an insufferable, officious old conservative with no eye for new ideas. He's not even worth listening to.

II. Some of the following passages present legitimate and acceptable arguments, while others involve fallacious reasoning. Determine which ones involve fallacies and explain the fallacy in each case.

1. "You must get me a bicycle," demanded Susan, "because everyone else in our grade has one and they all think I should have one too."

2. All Smith's cats are white because Smith likes and buys only white cats. So his new cat must be white, provided he bought it rather than its having been a gift or a natural product of the cats he already owns.

3. In court the defense lawyer claimed that her client was a cultured and sensitive person and could not have committed the alleged murder. The prosecuting lawyer then got up and pointed out to the jury that the defendant had long dirty hair and a beard and was obviously a "radical."

4. We only have a proper historical explanation after we have uncovered the *thoughts* of the historical agents involved in a given event. In the case of Caesar's Gallic campaign we are able to get at Caesar's thoughts and planned strategies through the diary kept by one of his officers. Of course, we can only accept that diary as accurate if we have corroborating evidence. Fortunately, we do possess such evidence in the texts of the ancient historians of the period. In fact, those ancient historians based their texts, at least in part, on that officer's diary.

5. POLICE OFFICER. You were speeding just then. May I see your driver's license, please, and the car registration.

MOTORIST. Oh, Officer, I didn't realize I was going over the limit. I've had such a bad week: my

	boss is on my back and my wife is ill. I've just been distracted all day. Surely you can let me go this time, given the circumstances?
POLICE OFFICER.	I'm sorry, but I must give you a ticket. You were driving at an exceedingly dangerous speed, well over the limit for this road.
MOTORIST.	Well, I think it's damned unfair. All you cops are just sadistic brutes who like to use their power and authority on us little guys. You're just a power-mad little dictator. Why don't you do something useful and go out and catch some real criminals, like bank robbers? I don't deserve to get a ticket from the likes of you.

6. Once Mary had gotten clear of the gate, she proceeded down the path to the dock. Because it had rained, Mary had to walk on a fallen log in order to get over a puddle. Then she got into a boat and rowed to the middle of the lake and settled in for her day's fishing.

7. All the fish in the lake have died. A marine biologist at the university who had done extensive studies in the area said that they had been killed by chemicals, put on the surrounding fields by the local farmers, which had worked their way into the lake. So this *must* be the reason for the fish dying.

8. Cynthia, only five years old, had organized the other small children to play "school." This game was apparently based on Cynthia's experience of what going to school meant for her older brothers and sisters. She gave every child a piece of paper, which she said was a "report card" for each of the "pupils" to take home to his or her parents. One child asked why Cynthia was not also given a report card to take to her parents. Cynthia explained that it was because *she* was the teacher and the *others* were the pupils. "But how come *you* are the teacher?" one of them asked. "Because I don't have a report card," answered Cynthia.

9. Reason has no influence over actions. Only our emotions and desire do that. This means that if moral decision making is basically just a type of reasoning, it can never influence our actions. Hence moral reasoning would be useless in helping us decide what actions we should perform.

10. "I see," said Bantingworth, "that Dr. Black is still advocating the use of steam and sauna baths for the cure of mental disorders. I suppose that is what one can expect from someone who did not go to one of the better medical schools. Just knowing where he was 'trained' should cause most of you to discount his opinions entirely."

TWO
CLASSIFYING THINGS

4

How to Classify and How to Draw a Conclusion

SOME INITIAL EXAMPLES OF DEDUCTIVE ARGUMENTS

Who is better at deducing conclusions from the most meager bits of evidence than the famous fictional detective, Sherlock Holmes? The tales of Holmes and his sidekick Doctor Watson are filled with clever pieces of deduction. The remarkable thing about Holmes is not just that he knows so many esoteric and obscure facts, but that he can conclude the most amazing number of facts about a person or an object from the minutest detail or the most obscure clue. The mud on a boot may tell him that a traveler came from a particular remote village because, as only Holmes knows, the mud is of a hue and texture unique to that village. The jewelry case must have lain in a shop window facing south because of the way the velvet lining of the case has faded from constant exposure to sunlight.

At the beginning of "The Adventure of Shoscombe Old Place," Holmes and Watson are together in Holmes's rooms in Baker Street. Holmes has been helping a friend at Scotland Yard who is working on a criminal case in which a policeman was killed. Holmes is examining some material that has been taken from a cap found at the scene of the murder:

> Sherlock Holmes had been bending for a long time over a low-power microscope. Now he straightened himself up and looked round at me in triumph.
> "It is glue, Watson," said he. "Unquestionably it is glue. Have a look at these scattered objects in the field!"

I stooped to the eyepiece and focussed for my vision.

"Those hairs are threads from a tweed coat. The irregular gray masses are dust. There are epithelial scales on the left. Those brown blobs in the centre are undoubtedly glue."

"Well," I said laughing, "I am prepared to take your word for it. Does anything depend upon it?"

"It is a very fine demonstration," he answered. "In the St. Pancras case you may remember that a cap was found beside the dead policeman. The accused man denies that it is his. But he is a picture-frame maker who habitually handles glue."[1]

What has Holmes done here? He has begun with certain evidence: a cap with glue stains on it. From this evidence he has inferred that it very likely belongs to the accused man.

We often make such connections or inferences. Suppose Fred is in a restaurant with his friend George. A woman enters, and Fred says to George, "Boy, I bet she eats a lot." "Who?" George asks. Fred tries to point out the woman but George can't see her, for by now she has sat down. So George asks Fred why he thinks she eats a lot. "Well," Fred explains, "she is terribly overweight." Now in inferring from her size that she eats a lot, Fred has followed a type of reasoning process. And when Fred says, "Boy, I bet she eats a lot," he states or expresses this opinion to George. But so far Fred has not supported his statement in any way or given any evidence for it.

When George asks why Fred thinks the woman eats a lot, he is now demanding this support. He wants to know what the evidence is for this opinion, what Fred's reason is. When Fred then says, "Well, she is terribly overweight," he is offering this evidence and giving his statement some support. If George agrees with Fred's opinion, he will, in effect, be accepting these two statements as an argument in which Fred has reasoned from her obesity to the conclusion that she eats a lot.

But is the argument given in its full form in this imagined conversation? Fred actually presented only the evidence that the woman is overweight, and from this he immediately drew the conclusion that she eats a lot. Is there not, however, a third feature to the argument? Certainly there is: Fred has *assumed* that *all* overweight people eat a lot. So his argument, when fully set out, is

1. All overweight people eat a lot (assumed but not expressed).
2. This woman is overweight (an observed fact).
3. *Therefore* this woman eats a lot.

[1] Sir Arthur Conan Doyle, *The Complete Sherlock Holmes* (New York: Doubleday, 1930), p. 1102.

Failure to express one's reasoning or state an argument fully or to present every bit of relevant evidence occurs frequently in our everyday discussions, and sometimes rightly so. Often some fact is obvious and does not need stating, because all parties accept it as part of the background information. Often, too, we can correctly assume that the persons we are addressing in a report or in a conversation already know certain facts and take them for granted. In such a context it would be a waste of time or even an insult to rehearse the obvious.

The same could be true in our Sherlock Holmes example. As presented above, the argument—the line of reasoning—Holmes is using is not yet fully expressed. But if Watson is familiar with the facts of the murder case Holmes is working on, Watson may immediately see the line of argument Holmes has used to move from his evidence (glue stains on the cap) to his conclusion (that the cap belongs to the accused man). Put out more fully, the line of argument running to the conclusion that the accused man is very likely the owner of the cap involves the following claims:

1. The accused man is a picture framer.
2. Picture framers use and handle glue often.
3. There is glue on the cap.

We could make the argument even more complete by considering and including some of the unexpressed assumptions that are involved. This will give us a *chain of deductive reasoning*. First we could argue:

1. The accused man is a picture framer.
2. Picture framers handle glue often.
2a. *Therefore* the accused man handles glue often.

The sentence labeled 2a gives us a conclusion that we can legitimately *deduce* from statements 1 and 2 and that was assumed but not expressed in the shorter version of the argument. If we make the assumption that people who handle glue often may very well get some on their clothing occasionally, we can add another link to the chain of reasoning:

2a. The accused man handles glue often (from previous link).
2b. People who handle glue sometimes get glue on their caps.
2c. *Therefore* the accused man sometimes gets glue on his cap.

Given this conclusion, we can agree with Holmes that it is reasonable to assume that the cap with glue on it belongs to the accused picture-frame maker—*provided* that he was the only one near the scene of the murder, that there was no other way the cap could have gotten there except by falling off his head, and so on.

To sum up briefly, the examples we have been considering show that an argument involves a group of statements so related that our mind—our reasoning or thinking process—moves from one to another, arriving at a conclusion. The statements that present our evidence are usually the *premisses* of the argument. What follows from these premisses is usually called the *conclusion*. As we noted before (in Chapter 2, the section "The Question of Truth"), the premisses of an argument may fail to support the conclusion we desire if either of two things happens: (a) the premisses are false, or (b) the statements comprising the premisses and the statement of the conclusion of the argument are not properly and logically connected. The question of whether statements are true or false is something we decide in a number of ways, as was discussed in Chapter 2. Some statements, such as "The woman is overweight," we decide by observation. In this chapter we are basically interested in the nature of logical connections.

IDENTIFYING ARGUMENTS

One thing illustrated by the examples discussed so far is that we often do not set out our arguments fully. Frequently, we leave some piece of our evidence unmentioned, either because we think that our listener knows it already or because we assume it to be something that everyone knows.

There can also be times when we don't state our conclusion. For example, imagine that Patrick lights a cigarette. Jean says to him, "You know, many people who smoke end up with serious respiratory problems." In this instance Jean left it for Patrick to draw the conclusion for himself. Clearly Jean is trying to tell Patrick that he ought not to smoke; she is warning him that if he continues to smoke, he may well develop lung disease. Jean's argument here is:

1. People who smoke are likely to have respiratory problems.
2. You smoke.
3. *Therefore* you are likely to have respiratory problems.

Premiss 1 would probably be something Jean learned from a medical study reported in a newspaper or magazine, and she knows premiss 2 because she *sees* Patrick light up a cigarette. The conclusion clearly follows.

One can encounter major difficulty in trying to extract an argument from a piece of writing. Often writers include extraneous details. Often evidence is incompletely presented and logical connections are not made clear.

In Chapter 10, we shall discuss more fully procedures for picking out arguments. But basically, here are the steps to be followed. *First,* find the conclusion. Ask yourself, What is the writer trying to establish? What is the conclusion of the article or report? *Next,* find the reasons being presented. What are the writer's premises? Are they true? Then you must consider the logical form of the argument.

There are three main features that help one to identify an argument:

First, cue words which signal that a conclusion or a premiss is coming.

Second, the nature of the statements used.

Third, the logical form of the presentation.

We can see these features easily in the following argument:

Oranges contain vitamin C *because* oranges are citrus fruits and all citrus fruits contain vitamin C.

The italicized word is a cue word: "because" introduces reasons, thereby introducing premisses. So this argument has the conclusion at the beginning and reasons (premisses) later. Second, the argument contains three statements that are all positive assertions. They are:

Oranges contain vitamin C.

Oranges are citrus fruits.

All citrus fruits contain vitamin C.

Third, we can rearrange these statements, with the premisses first and the conclusion last, to show the logical order of the argument. We end with the argument spelled out in this way:

1. All oranges are citrus fruits.
2. All citrus fruits contain vitamin C.
3. *Therefore* all oranges contain vitamin C.

In ordinary speech or in writing there are certain clues that an argument is either beginning or is in progress or has been underway for some time. For example, we know that someone is about to deliver a conclusion when a statement begins with "therefore," "hence," "thus," "so," or "it follows that." And we know that the person is presenting evidence to us when terms such as "since," "for," "because," "if," or "suppose" are used to introduce a statement. Expressions of these kinds are cue words, and more complete lists of such cue words and phrases are given in the following table.

Cue Words for Conclusions	Cue Words for Premisses (Reasons)
so	since
therefore	for
hence	because
thus	suppose (that)
implies that	given that
shows that	in view of
proves that	in view of the fact that
thereby showing	(one) may infer from
consequently	(one) may deduce from
entails that	as illustrated by
points to	if
(one) may infer	
(one) may deduce	
it follows that	
then	

Much of the trouble you will encounter in finding arguments occurs in cases where no cue words appear or in cases where premisses and conclusions are reversed in their order in a paragraph or sentence. For example, "Mary should get a good night's sleep, given that she wants to do well in her examination tomorrow" is presented with its conclusion first. If we reverse the sentence order, we have, "Given that she wants to do well in the examination, Mary should get a good night's sleep." Or, in other words, "Mary wants to do well in her examination tomorrow; therefore she should get a good night's sleep." The cue phrase "given that" signaled a premiss coming, hence there is no difficulty in ascertaining which is the premiss and which the conclusion.

Without cue phrases, identifying an argument becomes more difficult. In giving a speech, a politician may say, "We support free enterprise. We oppose wage and price controls." These appear to be simply two assertions, and simple assertions do not constitute an argument. Relating a string of facts or telling a story is not arguing to a conclusion. But the context and tone of the politician's speech might make it quite clear that she intends the second sentence to be a conclusion. If so, she is really saying, "*Because* we support free enterprise, we (*therefore*) oppose wage and price controls." This is a genuine argument and intended as such, yet we have no cue words. Fortunately, examples with no cue words are rare.

CLASSIFYING AND CONNECTING THINGS AND EVENTS

As was demonstrated in the previous section, arguments are common, familiar communications that we have no great difficulty in recognizing, even though some complex arguments require analyzing before they can be identified. And we all have frequent occasion to use arguments ourselves. Everyone thinks and reasons. And most people try to present their reasoning in as convincing and logical a fashion as possible so that others will be persuaded to accept their conclusions. Most of us have no wish to be thought silly, illogical, or irrational—incapable of reasoned thought and sound judgment. And most of us wish to understand events, people, and things, because we all have a stake in learning about our general environment. The way to such understanding lies in our ability to reason and to think logically about the world.

When we think about events, people, or things around us, we usually are trying to connect facts or events. In the mundane example of the obese woman, Fred connected overeating with being overweight. The connections established by Sherlock Holmes in solving a murder are not different from the types of connections made by Fred—they are simply presented more dramatically, and they are more complicated because they involve more facts that need connecting. Of course, Holmes is skilled at his trade and is especially adept at connecting pieces of evidence to reach a correct conclusion. But he is simply that—skilled in the art of logical reasoning. He does not really think differently than most people do. If you apply yourself, you too can be as adept as a shrewd detective.

How *do* people think about things? How do they connect events? Putting it rather simply, we think of events in terms of sequence in time or causal relationship. "The dam burst, *causing* the river to flood, which in turn caused Aunt Sue's house to be flooded, which caused the preserves that she had stored in the cellar to be ruined." We forecast future events in terms of past regular sequences we have experienced: "Because there is a low pressure area to the north, we will have rain tomorrow." Or we predict probable events as alternative possibilities: "Because the spring was so dry, either the wheat seeds will not germinate or there will be an infestation of grasshoppers to destroy the crops even if germination occurs."

We also *classify* things, people and events. Voters are Republicans, Democrats, or uncommitted. Cows are Holsteins, Jerseys, or Swiss. Pens come with ball points, felt tipped, or as regular fountain pens. Pens also come with fine, medium, or thick nibs and are available in red, green, blue, black, grey, pink, and orange.

Basically, we view our world as made up of *things* that have *properties*, or *attributes*. Your bed may have a frame made of brass. That *thing*, then—your bed—has the properties of being shiny, golden-yellow in color, and hard and cold to the touch. The mattress may be soft or hard.

Our language reflects this view of the world, because the simplest meaningful sentence we could utter would be one that merely states that some *thing* has a certain property—for example, "My mattress is soft." In saying this, one is classifying the mattress as a soft mattress; it is not hard or medium-firm, but definitely soft. To say, "My mattress is pink," would be to classify the mattress by color—as pink rather than as red, blue, or green. You should be able to see that the obese woman example and the Holmes example from the first section both illustrate this type of classifying.

Classifying is an important part of our coming to understand the world. It is also an important part of thinking and arguing about the world, because if something (thing T) belongs to one class of thing (class A) and that class belongs to yet another (class B), then thing T will also belong to class B. If your tennis racket is strung with gut and if all gut will stretch in the rain, then your tennis racket's stringing will stretch in the rain too.

An illustration of classifying can be found in the following letter to the columnist Ann Landers:

> *Dear Ann Landers:* I am a 21-year-old guy who is perfectly straight. I like to go to a gay bar in our neighborhood because the music is good and the people are very friendly.
>
> My dad sat me down last night and asked me if I was a switch-hitter. I told him absolutely not. He said he was very relieved because he had heard I was a steady at this place. When I explained I liked the ambiance he advised me to find my fun someplace else because everyone assumes that a guy who goes to a gay bar is gay. I think he is wrong. What is your opinion?[2]

Clearly, the father is suggesting that people who hang around known gay bars are going to be classified as homosexuals, so that if his son frequents a gay bar he too will be classified as a homosexual. The father's reasoning took this form:

---

[2] Ann Landers, *The Star-Phoenix*, Saskatoon, March 23, 1973, p. 20. Copyright Field Newspaper Syndicate, 1977. Quoted by permission.

1. Any person frequenting a gay bar is believed to be gay.
2. You are a person who frequents a gay bar.
3. *Therefore* you are a person who is (or will be) believed to be gay.

It is rather surprising that the young man writing the letter thinks this belief would not be prevalent, and Ann Landers quite correctly made that point in her reply. We do classify people in terms of their actions, their friends, and their activities. This is only reasonable: a person cannot be separated from his or her actions, beliefs, and values. Hence, someone who shoplifts, steals from the school lockers, and takes hub-caps from cars at night is a thief. Someone who associates with known criminals is either extremely naive or also a criminal, as any police officer knows. While it may sometimes be unfair to judge a person by the company kept, we are often not in possession of full information about someone and must judge on what information we have.

Classifications and inferences based on classifications are familiar in our experience. Any book about how to improve your grammar or your bridge or about how to win friends is filled with rules that classify certain actions as useful or good ones. Here is an example from a book on tennis that classifies "let" serves:

> The player serving receives two chances; if one of the serves . . . hits the net and lands in the proper service area, the serve is considered a let. The player is . . . permitted the let service over.
> Outside interference, either by another player or ball from a nearby court, results in a let and the point is played over. If the receiver is not ready (in ready position), a let may be called. . . .
> The term "let" in tennis is an abbreviation of the early use of the phrase "let's play it over," used when there was a questionable decision on any point of play.[3]

The last sentence tells us what the term "let" means in tennis, and the earlier part classifies certain types of serves as lets. On the basis of these classifications we could formulate the following inferences about serves, lets, and replayed serves:

1. All serves hitting the net and landing in the proper service area are lets.
2. All lets are serves played over again.
3. *Therefore* all serves hitting the net and landing in the proper service area are serves played over again.

[3] D.A. Armbruster, F.F. Musker and D. Mood, *Basic Skills in Sports for Men and Women*, 6th ed. (Saint Louis: C.V. Mosby, 1975), p. 290.

4. All serves involving outside interference are lets.
5. All lets are serves played over again.
6. *Therefore* all serves involving outside interference are serves played over again.
7. All serves involving an unready receiver are lets.
8. All lets are serves played over again.
9. *Therefore* all serves involving an unready receiver are serves played over again.

While it is rather tedious to draw these out in three separate deductive inferences, it *does* illustrate how classifications allow us to pack much information into a general rule, which we can then apply. When we apply a rule about lets in tennis, we are *implicitly* making one of the inferences just outlined. Rule books and books about skills at a game frequently use classifications and inferences based on classifications. Hence someone who knows what a let is and who knows that it is classified as a serve that can be played over again, will be able to infer that she has the right to another serve when she is interfered with, because such interference is classified as a let.

DRAWING DEDUCTIONS FROM CLASSIFICATIONS

You will recall that in Chapter 1 we distinguished the psychological aspect of arguments, which includes a person's mental processes, from the logical aspect, which refers to the logical structure of the argument. One puts one's thoughts into sentences in some language, and these sentences express propositions. A *proposition* is what a sentence *means* or *proposes*.

Consider again the example of oranges, citrus fruit, and vitamin C that we introduced earlier. The English sentence, "It follows that oranges contain vitamin C because oranges are citrus fruit and all citrus fruit contains vitamin C" actually expresses *three* distinct propositions:

1. All oranges are citrus fruit.
2. All citrus fruit contains vitamin C.
3. All oranges contain vitamin C.

Each of these propositions declares something to be *categorically* true, as opposed to saying that it *might* be true and as opposed to saying that it is conditional upon some other fact, as in "He will return only if we release the hostages." Because of this, we call them *categorical propositions*.

You can also see that each categorical proposition refers to *two* classes of things, and the parts of a categorical proposition that refer to these classes are called the *terms* of the proposition. So the term "orange" in the first proposition, immediately above, is the part of that proposition referring to the class of things called oranges. Likewise, the term "citrus fruit" in lines 1 and 2 refers to the class of fruits called citrus fruit.

It all boils down to this. Our world contains objects that can be classified in various ways—according to their colors, shapes, or whatever. People think about these objects and classifications. Statements of and arguments about classifications are said to express propositions about such classifications. A categorical proposition has two terms and expresses a relationship between the classes referred to by those terms.

Consider the argument about oranges one last time:

1. All citrus fruit contains vitamin C.
2. All oranges are citrus fruit.
3. *Therefore* all oranges contain vitamin C.

Basically, this type of argument states that certain things can be classified in specific ways. It tells us that of all the things in the world containing vitamin C, citrus fruit is among them. Of course there are other things that contain vitamin C, such as broccoli and potatoes. Number 2 tells us that all oranges belong to the class of citrus fruit. It therefore follows that oranges contain vitamin C. You can see the structure of this argument if you consider an arrangement of circles in which each circle represents a class of things mentioned in the argument.

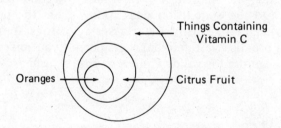

An argument in this form is called a *deductive argument*. That is, we deduce something, a conclusion, from some other fact or facts, namely some evidence. In a sense, then, what this argument says is: since citrus fruit contains vitamin C and since all oranges are citrus fruit, it follows that all oranges contain vitamin C. Someone who accepts both statements in our premisses must logically go on to the conclusion. Anyone who is convinced that citrus fruit contains vitamin C and convinced that oranges are citrus fruit cannot refuse to draw the conclusion that oranges contain vitamin C. If someone did refuse to go on to the conclusion, we would most likely suspect that the person had not understood one of the premisses. The conclusion *necessarily* follows from the premisses in this type of argument.

Deductive inferences of this sort are common, as are the classifications upon which they are based. A handbook on effective writing might say something like this:

> All good writing aims at communicating effectively. Since effective communication requires clarity, good writing is clear writing.

The conclusion is stated at the end of the second sentence. "Since," in the second sentence, cues a premiss, and the first sentence states another premiss. Set out, the passage provides the following deductive argument:

1. All good writing is writing that effectively communicates.
2. All writing that effectively communicates is clear writing.
3. *Therefore* all good writing is clear writing.

Each premiss, 1 and 2, involves a proposition that expresses the relationship of one class of things to another. Premiss 1 classifies good writing as effective communicative writing; premiss 2 classifies effective communicative writing as clear writing. As we mentioned before, rule books and books on how to play games involve many classifications of this sort, especially when such books outline successful strategies.

A simple way of checking to see whether arguments of this form are correct and the conclusion does follow from the premisses is to draw diagrams representing the classes of things indicated by the terms in the premisses. Such diagrams permit you to see immediately whether an argument is valid. Here are some examples.

Example 1

1. All thefts are criminal acts.
2. All shoplifting is theft.
3. *Therefore* all shoplifting is a criminal act.

Now let us show the steps by which classes can be represented by simple drawings.

First Step

Premiss 1 tells us that thefts are classified as criminal acts. So we draw one circle *within* another to illustrate that theft falls within the category of criminal acts.

We know there are *other* criminal acts, such as murder or arson, that are not thefts.

Second Step

Premiss 2 tells us that shoplifting is classified as theft. We then add another circle to illustrate that shoplifting falls *within* the category of theft.

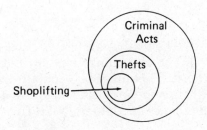

Third Step

We now check to see whether the conclusion stated in 3—"All shoplifting is a criminal act"—does follow from 1 and 2. If it does, the circle representing shoplifting will be *within* the circle designating thefts. An examination of the diagram shows that shoplifting is there. Since the conclusion *does* follow deductively from these premisses, this is referred to as a *valid argument*. If it did *not* follow logically from the premisses, it would be called an *invalid argument*.

Example 2

Here is an example of an invalid argument:
1. All puppies are cute.
2. All kittens are cute.
3. *Therefore* all puppies are kittens.

First Step

The first premiss states that all puppies belong to the class of cute things. As we have already shown, this can be represented by two circles.

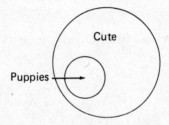

Second Step

The second premiss tells us that kittens *also* are classified as cute. Within the large circle for cute things we now put a separate circle to represent the kittens. This must be separate from the circle for puppies because neither of the premisses has stated that there is any relationship between puppies and kittens, apart from the fact that they are both cute.

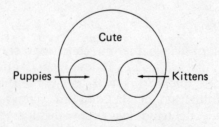

Third Step

You can clearly see from the diagram that the conclusion, "All puppies are kittens," does not follow. Hence this argument is logically invalid.

You can also see that since one represents "All cats are animals" by a diagram having a circle for cats *totally inside* another circle for animals, you can represent "No cats are dogs" by two separate circles —one representing the class of cats, the other representing the class of dogs.

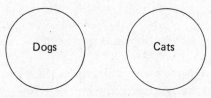

To show that *part* of a class is included in another class, we let the circles overlap. For example, the statement "Some birds are yellow" would be diagrammed as follows:

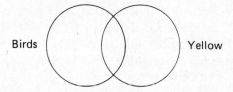

The area of overlap represents the region of the yellow birds.

First, you must be able to *find* an argument when one is presented to you; second, you must be able to *evaluate* an argument; and third, you must be able to *construct* arguments and counterarguments. However, you can only recognize, evaluate, and construct arguments if you are aware of the different kinds of logical thinking that go into presenting a good argument and if you are able to distinguish valid from invalid arguments. The exercises for this chapter will help you develop these skills.

EXERCISES

I. Consider each of the following passages and pick out the cue words it contains. Then say whether the cue word indicates a premiss or a conclusion.

1. Some liberals are unrealistic, so some idealists are unrealistic, since all liberals are idealists.
2. All working horses are large. Therefore, all horses on our farm are large, since all horses on our farm are working horses.
3. Every *real* baseball fan buys a season ticket, for every baseball fan is a fanatic about the game and no fanatic about the game fails to buy a season ticket.
4. Because no one in our family lives in a glass house, anyone in our family, therefore, can throw stones if he or she wishes, since only people who live in glass houses shouldn't throw stones.
5. In view of the fact that Jane is taking the introductory class in abnormal psychology this semester, it is not surprising that Jane believes she has a neurosis, because every student taking the introductory class in abnormal psychology ends up believing that he or she has a neurosis.
6. The last photograph sent by those on the class trip has a kangaroo in it, and kangaroos only live in Australia. Hence, those on the class trip are in Australia.
7. No messy people are particular about the clothes they wear. Yet some children are messy; hence, some children are not particular about the clothes they wear.
8. In view of the fact that people who voted for Sandstone expected him to introduce a bill that would lower personal income taxes, and given that everyone living in Greystone Heights voted for Sandstone, we can conclude that everyone living in Greystone Heights expected Sandstone to introduce a bill that would lower personal income taxes.

II. Write out the premisses and conclusion of each passage in excrcise I.

III. List the classes referred to in each of the following. Do not be concerned with the relationships between classes; simply identify *all* classes mentioned in each.

Here is an example:

Vegetables are nutritious. The carrots in my garden, the carrots in the supermarket, and Mrs. Alright's turnips are all nutritious.

These sentences are about the following classes of things:

Vegetables
Nutritious things
Carrots in my garden
Carrots in the supermarket
Mrs. Alright's turnips

Now try these yourself:

1. While all the serious students did well and most of the lazy students did not do well on the test, there were some lazy students who *did* do well. The latter must be naturally clever students.
2. Charlie's horses all speak a language. Most of them speak German but a few speak Chinese.
3. Of course, all battles are bloody. In the history of naval battles, the Battle of Trafalgar was perhaps the most bloody.
4. The bread from the local bakery is usually very good; however, the bread we get from the supermarket is often tasteless.
5. She always buys penny candy. She buys a few licorice braids, a few jujubes, some toffees, and a jawbreaker or two.

IV. Consider each of the following arguments and, with the aid of a diagram, decide whether it is valid or invalid.
Here is an example:

1. All my cats are Persians.
2. All my pets are cats.
3. *Therefore* all my pets are Persians.

This is valid, as the diagram illustrates.

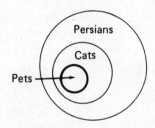

Now complete the following:

1.
    1. All coffee is expensive.
    2. All cocoa is expensive.
    3. *Therefore* all coffee is cocoa.
2.
    1. All rock music has a good beat.
    2. All music we dance to is rock music.
    3. *Therefore* all music we dance to has a good beat.

3.
1. All beer is refreshing.
2. All lemonade is refreshing.
3. *Therefore* all beer is lemonade.

4.
1. None of the voters is married.
2. None of my brothers is married.
3. *Therefore* none of my brothers is a voter.

5.
1. All stars are bright.
2. No planets are stars.
3. *Therefore* no planets are bright.

6.
1. All my good records are 45s.
2. Some of my bluegrass records are good records.
3. *Therefore* some of my bluegrass records are 45s.

7.
1. No crimes are justified.
2. All murders are crimes.
3. *Therefore* no murders are justified.

5

Tools For Testing Arguments: Venn Diagrams

THE BASIC KINDS OF CATEGORICAL PROPOSITION

To understand arguments more fully, we must analyze them to discover what their basic parts are and how these parts are connected.[1] Propositions expressed in written or spoken sentences are the parts of an argument—its premisses and conclusion. And propositions are, in turn, composed of terms, words that refer to classes of things or ideas.

For example, if one argues that all the ancient Roman generals were great military leaders because they won many battles, the argument contains first, the assumed yet unstated premiss that all people who win many battles are great military leaders; second, the premiss that the Roman generals won many battles; and last, the conclusion that the Roman generals were great military leaders. Put out fully, the argument looks like this:

1. All those who win many battles are great military leaders.
2. All the Roman generals were people who won many battles.
3. *Therefore* all the Roman generals were great military leaders.

This argument, then, contains three distinct propositions. And if we look at the individual propositions, we discover that they are similar in that each contains a specific number of terms.

We can see this more clearly if we consider the simple proposition,

[1] In what follows we are discussing the traditional formal logic developed by Aristotle and sometimes called Aristotelian logic.

All horses are fast.

This is about the connection between the class of horses and the class of fast things. The proposition has two terms: "horses" and "fast," and each of these terms has a specific role to play in the proposition. The term "horses" tells us what the proposition is about. It identifies the *subject* of the proposition. Because it identifies the subject under discussion, it is called the *subject term.* The other term, "fast," goes on to tell us something specific about the things referred to by the subject term. Terms of this second sort are called *predicate terms*, because in ancient law courts one could speak of what was *predicated of* (said about or said against) a person appearing before the court. This sense of something "said against" or "charged against" slipped over from practical use in law to the technical sense, in logic, of a predicate as "that which can be said about a subject term."

You can see that propositions of this subject-predicate sort are about classifications. "All horses are fast" places horses in the class of fast things. As such, "fast" is a predicate that can truly be attributed to the things (horses) referred to by the subject term. Or, more accurately, the predicate "fast" indicates a property possessed by the things referred to by the subject term.

Given that all categorical propositions involve a subject term connected to a predicate term and state a fact, we can represent *any* categorical proposition as

S is P,

where "S" represents *any* subject term and "P" represents *any* predicate term.[2] The meaning of a proposition depends on and varies with the terms substituted for "S" and "P." "Dogs are active" means something different from "Dogs are mammals" and from "Ducks are active."

Also, the meaning and the truth of a proposition depend on whether you say "*All* S is P" or "*Some* S is P." For example, it is clearly false to say

All Americans are blond,

but clearly true to say

Some Americans are blond.

A categorical proposition that begins with the word "all" asserts the total inclusion of one class within another and is, therefore, called a

2 Technically, one does not have a proper categorical proposition unless it includes what is called a *quantifier*. In order to present the important points *separately* we have allowed this slight, but harmless, inaccuracy for a brief moment while "S" and "P" are introduced.

universal proposition. A proposition using "some" is *not* about all members of a class; it asserts or denies the partial inclusion of one class within another and is called a *particular proposition.* The words "all" and "some" are called *quantifiers*—from "quantity," because they indicate *how much* of a class is being said to be included or excluded from another class.

We can also distinguish sentences and propositions according to whether they are affirmative or negative. The proposition "All human beings are mortal" *affirms* that the class of human beings falls within the class of mortal things. On the other hand, the proposition "No dogs can fly" is *negative* and denies that the class of dogs falls within the class of flying creatures.

These two ways of classifying categorical propositions are exhaustive; any statement one makes must be either universal or particular and it must be either affirmative or negative. And if we list all possible combinations of these features, we have an exhaustive list of the *types* of categorical propositions:

Universal and Affirmative:	"All S is P."
Universal and Negative:	"No S is P."
Particular and Affirmative:	"Some S is P."
Particular and Negative:	"Some S is not P."

These four types of categorical propositions, which are called the *standard forms*, are referred to by the letters A, E, I, and O. These letters are taken from the Latin word for "I affirm," which is *AFFIRMO*, and the Latin word for "I deny," which is *NEGO*. Hence the affirmative propositions are labelled A and I while the negative propositions are labelled E and O. This can be put in a table:

Name of Proposition	Standard-Form Categorical Proposition
A	"All S is P."
E	"No S is P."
I	"Some S is P."
O	"Some S is not P."

Sentences in ordinary English are extremely varied, and it is often difficult when you first hear or read a sentence to recognize exactly what proposition it is expressing. This is why you should practice analyzing sentences according to the four basic types of categorical propositions. To illustrate how this is done, consider these statements about Western films with which Will Wright begins his Preface to *Six Guns and Society.*

Everyone's seen a Western. Most people like them, some do not, but no American and few in the world can escape their influence.[3]

Here Wright has expressed a number of propositions about people and Western films. If we identify Wright's statements as to type we discover that we can arrange them in parallel lists:

Wright's Sentences	Categorical Propositions
1. "Everyone's seen a Western."	1. All people are people who have seen a Western (an A proposition).
2. ". . . some do not [like Westerns] . . ."	2. Some people are people who do not like Westerns (an O proposition).
3. ". . . no American . . . can escape their influence."	3. No American is a person who can escape the influence of Westerns (an E proposition).

It is worth noting that there are many ways to say something. Hence one can sometimes express one type of categorical proposition in terms of another type. For example, "All senators are intelligent" (an A proposition) means the same as "No senators are unintelligent" (an E proposition). Similarly "Some lakes are polluted" (an I proposition) means the same as "Some lakes are not unpolluted" (an O proposition). "No cars are inexpensive" (an E proposition) means the same as "All cars are expensive" (an A proposition).

We might also note an ambiguity in "All S is P." If we say, "All diamonds are expensive," we mean that diamonds belong to—are included within—the class of expensive things; but we are *not* also claiming that all expensive things are diamonds. But if we say, "All people over 80 and under 90 are octogenarians," it is also true that all octogenarians are over 80 and under 90. Here we have two classes that are strictly *identical*: anything that is in one is in the other, and vice versa. However, since we must never assume anything we are not expressly given, A propositions, expressed as "All S is P," are always interpreted as indicating only class inclusion, not class identity.

THE SYLLOGISM

In one section of the last chapter we introduced a type of argument that had categorical propositions for its premises and conclusion. An argument of this type, having exactly two premises and a con-

3 Will Wright, *Six Guns and Society* (Berkeley: University of California Press, 1975), p. 1.

clusion—all of which are categorical propositions—is called a *categorical syllogism*. The term "syllogism" comes from Greek and means "to say together," hence giving us the sense of putting two thoughts— or two propositions—together in order to draw a logical conclusion from them. Most frequently this argument form is simply referred to as the *syllogism*.

Here is a valid syllogism:

1. All imported cars are small.
2. All sports cars are imported cars.
3. *Therefore* all sports cars are small.

The next, however, is an invalid syllogism:

1. All artists are sensitive people.
2. All artists are poor.
3. *Therefore* all sensitive people are poor.

If this last example causes a little head scratching to sort out, consider the following argument, which can easily be seen to be invalid:

1. All collies are large dogs.
2. All ducks lay eggs.
3. *Therefore* all cats like mice.

In the last chapter you were shown how you can quickly decide whether arguments of this type are valid or not. From the examples of syllogisms just introduced you can further see that every valid syllogism has a key term that appears in both premises and links these together. This connecting term is normally called the *middle term* of the syllogism. This term indicates a common class that links all the mentioned classes together in our thought.

The last example above has no middle term in the premises, so it does not even *tempt* us to think that it is a logical argument. In the first example of a valid syllogism the middle term, "imported cars," provides a connecting link between "sports cars" and "small." The second example has a middle term—"artists"—which occurs in each premiss; however, the argument fails to be valid because the premisses, while indicating classes artists fall into (sensitive people and poor people), do not inform us of any relationship between these classes.

The *rule* of the syllogism is that whatever is true of a class of things must be true of any subdivision of that class. For example, anything true of all dogs must be true of collies. If something is true of all

Europeans, it must be true of Germans and of Italians. Likewise, if we can deny something of a class, we must also deny it of any of its constituent subdivisions. If we can correctly deny that there are any Europeans who trade with Cuba, we can correctly deny that any Britons trade with Cuba.

Consider the following comment by J. Edgar Hoover and try expressing Hoover's argument in the form of a syllogism.

> It is an incontestable fact that our country . . . is the ultimate, priceless goal of international communism. The leaders of international communism have vowed to achieve world domination. This cannot be until the Red Flag is flown over the United States.[4]

If you ignore some of the emotive language, such as "priceless," and translate the last sentence into a proposition about domination of the United States, you have:

1. All leaders of international communism are people seeking world domination.
2. All people seeking world domination are people seeking domination of the United States.
3. *Therefore* all leaders of international communism are people seeking domination of the United States.

The argument is clearly about three classes of people: international communists, those who want to dominate the world, and those who want to dominate the United States. The premises of the syllogism express the relationships between these classes, according to Hoover, and show that the conclusion given in his first sentence does follow validly from those premises. That is, given the relationships between the classes referred to by "international communists"—"those wanting to dominate the world" and "those wanting to dominate the United States"—relationships which are expressed by the premises—the further relationship, expressed by the conclusion, can be validly deduced.

Here is a more complicated example from a letter to the editor of *The New York Times*:

"THE F.B.I. AGENTS COMMITTED NO CRIME"

To the Editor:

Morris B. Abram, in a letter recently published by you, characterized F.B.I. agents as "felons." He apparently referred to those agents who

---

[4] *J. Edgar Hoover on Communism* (New York: Warner Paperback Library, 1970), p. 69.

engaged in warrantless searches in national security cases, as he cites the "Church Committee of the United States Senate" as his source.

A felon is someone guilty of a serious crime. The F.B.I. agents committed no crime as they acted on the authority of the Attorney General. The subject was canvassed at length by the United States Court of Appeals for the District of Columbia on the appeals brought by the Cubans from their convictions in the Watergate cases. Indeed, that court a year ago reversed the convictions of Messrs. Barker and Martinez for the break-in at Dr. Fielding's office because of the refusal of the trial judge to instruct the jury that good faith and reasonable reliance upon the apparent authority of another constituted a valid defense.

It was long the theory of a series of Attorneys General that such searches were lawful. That theory was publicly stated by Attorney General (later Supreme Court Justice) Jackson as regards wiretapping. Reasoning that there was no valid distinction between wiretapping and physical entries, Attorney General Levi publicly refused to prosecute Richard Helms, former Director of the C.I.A., for having authorized the break-in of a photographic studio.

The theory was overruled by the Supreme Court as regards domestic security cases, but the Court expressly left open the question of the propriety of such searches in matters of foreign espionage and intelligence.

Messrs. Barker and Martinez acted on only the authority of Mr. Hunt. F.B.I. agents acted on the authority of the Attorney General, the highest law officer in the land. Certainly their defense is a valid one.

C. Dickerman Williams
New York, May 23, 1977.[5]

Clearly, the writer wishes to refute the claim of the earlier letter-writer—M. B. Abram—that F.B.I. agents were felons. At the beginning of the second paragraph, the writer classifies felons as people guilty of crimes and classifies people who are acting on the authority of the attorney general as people who are not committing crimes in those acts (as the very last sentence of the letter indicates). This provides the following syllogism:

1. All felons are people guilty of crimes.
2. No F.B.I. agents acting on the authority of the attorney general are people guilty of crimes.
3. *Therefore* no F.B.I. agents acting on the authority of the attorney general are felons.

This is a valid syllogism. The reference to the reversal of the convictions of Barker and Martinez provides a further valid syllogistic argument:

[5] *The New York Times*, June 3, 1977. © 1977 by The New York Times Company. Reprinted by permission.

4. All cases of good faith and reasonable reliance on the authority of another are cases of valid defenses.
5. All the cases involving Barker and Martinez *are* cases of good faith and reasonable reliance on the authority of another (namely, reliance on the authority of the attorney general).
6. *Therefore* all the cases involving Barker and Martinez are cases of a valid defense.

Before leaving this topic, we should mention propositions that indicate numbers or use phrases such as "a few," "most of," or "many." Since all classifications either assert or deny the total or partial inclusion of one class within another, we might be tempted to interpret any proposition using "a few" or "many" as particular propositions— that is, as either standard-form I or O propositions. However, this temptation must be resisted, because propositions mentioning "a few" or "many" are more specific than standard-form propositions and require a more thorough and deeper analysis. Usually, arguments that hinge on numerical or quasi-numerical quantifiers such as "many" are treated as not being syllogistic. One of the dangers of interpreting them as standard-form propositions becomes obvious by considering the following argument:

1. All cats are furry.
2. A few cats are bad-tempered.
3. *Therefore* most furry things are bad-tempered.

You can see that such an inference would not be valid. Yet if we were to interpret the second premiss and the conclusion as standard-form I propositions (as "Some S is P"), we *would*, according to that interpretation, have a valid argument.

Sometimes, though, it does not cause trouble to interpret sentences containing phrases like "a few" as standard-form propositions quantified by "some." For example, consider the following argument:

1. All cats are furry.
2. A few cats are bad-tempered.
3. *Therefore* a few bad-tempered things are furry.

With the *same* phrase, "a few," occurring in the second premiss and the conclusion, this looks like a much better argument than the previous one. And if we interpret "a few" to mean "at least one"—which is the minimal interpretation we would give to "some"—we can accept it as valid. But note that to do this we have *stipulated* an interpretation of "a few." You might rightly object that we ordinarily use "a few" when we mean "more than one" but, say, "fewer than some significant portion of the class." So, again, this is a contentious case and requires caution.

Categorical propositions are often hard to detect in ordinary use; seldom does anyone speak or write in standard-form propositions. Thus we cannot *count* on finding cue words such as "all," "some," or "none" to tip us off to the presence of a syllogism. The discussion of classes and their relations is probably the best clue that someone is thinking and arguing syllogistically. Moreover, some phrases can be misleading. For example, propositions such as those which mention "almost everybody" or "all but a few" frequently contain two distinct statements. The proposition,

All but the voters were pleased,

says not only that

All non-voters were pleased,

but also that

No voters were pleased.

Similarly,

Only some of our friends are married

affirms that

Some of our friends are married

and denies the proposition

All of our friends are married.

Because they contain two statements, such compound propositions cannot be interpreted as standard-form categorical propositions. Therefore, these compound propositions cannot be put directly into syllogisms, although we could on some occasions work the contained categorical propositions into syllogistic deductions.

VENN DIAGRAMS

While it is often easy to tell whether a syllogism is valid, there are many tricky cases. Therefore, it is useful to have a method of testing for validity. A pictorial technique for testing syllogisms was developed late in the nineteenth century by the mathematician John Venn (1834–1923). It uses diagrams that are now commonly called Venn diagrams.

Although we want you to learn how to use Venn diagrams because they are tools for *evaluating* syllogisms, you should also treat this section as an opportunity to review, practice, and reinforce the lessons of this and the preceding chapter. You should analyze the given examples by looking for cue words that tip you off to premisses and conclusions. You should pick out the propositions expressed in the examples and write them out in standard form. For example, "Every dog has its day" expresses the universal-affirmative proposition "All dogs *are* creatures that have their day." In doing this you must think about the classes being discussed and think about whether a sentence means to include all, none, or some members of one class in another class. Once you have decided what a sentence *means*, you can express that meaning by a standard categorical proposition.

In Chapter 4 we showed how simple diagrams can be used to test arguments. By putting circles within circles to represent the inclusion of one class within another, and by using overlapping circles to represent the fact that two classes have some members in common, we were able to discover whether an argument was valid.

The Venn diagram technique also uses circles. But the Venn scheme is distinctive in that the circles are placed in the same pattern every time. This has the advantage of making the test standard and simple, thereby eliminating errors that might occur when the relationships between classes mentioned in a syllogism are complex and we would have to think for a while about how they should be represented in a diagram. Basically, Venn begins with an arrangement of circles that allows us to represent all possible relations between classes.

We can see this more clearly if we first consider a categorical proposition. If we ignore quantifiers ("all," "some") for the moment, the basic form of a categorical proposition is "S is P." "S" and "P" stand for any subject term and any predicate term. Since each of the two terms refers to a class of things, a categorical proposition relates two classes. Venn represented these by interlocking (overlapping) circles:

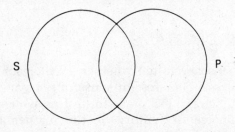

We put the "S" and "P" outside the circles they designate so that we can later mark inside the circles without obscuring the "S" and "P." A proposition in which S and P represented cats and dogs would be drawn as follows:

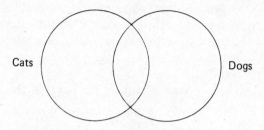

This arrangement gives us four main areas:

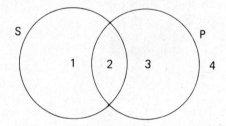

Area 1 would contain anything in the world that belonged to the class designated by "S" but that belonged *only* to that class. Something that belonged to *both* S and P would be in area 2; something that belonged only to P would be in area 3; and something belonging to neither S nor P would be in area 4. Since the propositions employed in the syllogism are concerned to indicate the relationship between members of one class and members of another class, we do not need to deal with the last case. It will never arise. It has been mentioned only to remind the reader that many things will be beyond the scope of the propositions in an argument. Categorical propositions are concerned with the relationship of one class to another and are not trying to deal with the many other things in the universe that may or may not be related to either of the two classes designated by the terms of the proposition.

We next have to decide how to diagram the information provided by the standard types of categorical proposition. Venn diagrams do this in the following ways:

First: if we know that an area in a diagram is empty—that there are no things that belong there—we *shade out* that area. That is, we *black it out* to show that *nothing* can be put in there. Shading means that the shaded out area is empty. Hence A and E propositions require shading because they declare certain regions to be empty.

Second: I and O propositions will not declare regions empty. They are diagrammed by putting a lower case "x" in the appropriate region.

Third: Venn diagrams *always* expect you to assume that if an area is *blank* (containing no shading and no x's), then you have *no specific information* about that region.

Let us now look at the Venn diagram for each of the standard categorical propositions.

I. "All S is P."

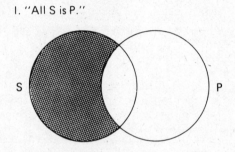

The universal-affirmative proposition, "All S is P," says that each and every S is also a P; in effect, it says that there are no Ss which are only Ss. If something falls into the class S, it *must* also fall into the class P. Hence we *shade out* the part of the circle representing S that does *not* overlap with P; anything now put into the S circle must be put in that part common to S and to P. So "All good dancers are graceful" indicates that any and every person who is classified as a good dancer is also to be classified as graceful. No good dancer will fail to be graceful. Therefore a Venn diagram for this proposition would shade out the parts of the circle for good dancers *outside* the circle for graceful people:

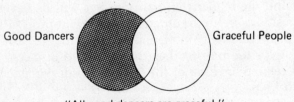

"All good dancers are graceful."

II. "No S is P."

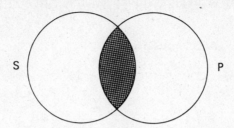

"No S is P" is a universal-negative proposition; an E proposition. The shading in the areas of the overlap indicates emptiness and shows that there is nothing that will be *both* an S and a P. Hence the proposition "No dogs are reptiles" is shaded:

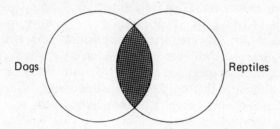

There are no individuals or subclasses that are both dogs and reptiles. Collies go in one and lizards in the other, but neither the subclass collie nor the subclass lizard can be put in the overlapping region because neither is a subclass of both the class dog and the class reptile.

III. "Some S is P."

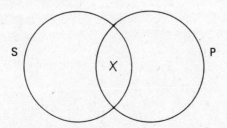

"Some S is P" is a particular-affirmative proposition, an I proposition. We introduce an "x" to diagram a particular proposition.

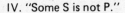
IV. "Some S is not P."

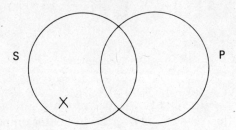

"Some S is not P" is a particular-negative proposition, an O proposition, and is diagrammed as shown.

So far we have seen how Venn represented each of the standard categorical propositions. The important point about the diagrams is that Venn devised them as a method for testing syllogistic arguments for validity. A categorical proposition has two terms representing two classes of objects, and so each diagram for a proposition requires two circles—one for each term. But while a syllogism has three propositions, it has only three distinct and different terms, because each term occurs twice. (A look back at the examples of valid syllogisms presented earlier will confirm this point.) Thus Venn realized that he needed only three interlocking circles to represent the terms of a syllogism. He arranged them as shown in the following diagram, with "M" representing the middle term of the syllogism.

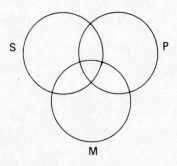

There is a simple and common way to label the various regions of a Venn diagram, thereby providing an easy means of referring to any specific region. Let us begin with a simple case. If we draw a circle to represent, say, the class of all people, we understand the area *within* the circle to represent the class of all people, with all other objects or things that are *not* people falling outside the circle:

All Things That
Are *Not* People

Thus President Carter would fall within the class of people, but his slippers or his pet dog would fall *outside* the class of people. For any class we select there is a complementary class of things that do not belong to the original class. For example, if we take the class horse, designated by "H," then all things not belonging to that class, such as rabbits, belong to the class not-H—represented in the diagram as H. If we take any class S, we can say that the class S has as its complement the class not-S—or $\overline{S}$—which can be diagrammed as follows:

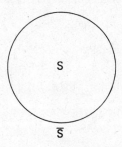

You can see that the classes S and $\overline{S}$ mutually exclude one another and that they also cover everything under discussion. Hence, in talking about living animals, we could let "S" represent the class of all snakes, whereupon "S̄" would represent the class of all things that are *not* snakes: any animal must be in one class or the other, but cannot be in both. And there is no other possibility: something either is or is *not* a snake.[6] Therefore, cobras and pythons fall *within* the class S, while dogs, cats, and elephants fall within S̄.

We can now see that the diagram for standard-form categorical propositions has the following regions:

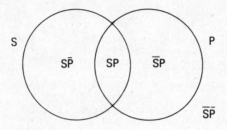

So the region SP̄, for example, diagrams the class of items which are members of S but excluded from P.

Finally, a diagram with three overlapping circles has eight regions and diagrams eight classes:

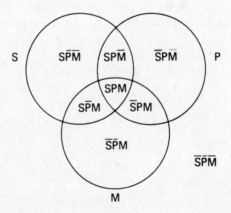

<hr>

[6] The usual way to express these points is to say that for S and S̄ to be complements means that they are mutually exclusive yet jointly exhaustive of their universe of discourse.

Let us take the following syllogism as an example:

1. All sunny days are pleasant.
2. Some Mondays are sunny.
3. *Therefore* some Mondays are pleasant.

This involves three classes within the general category of days, namely days that are sunny, those that are pleasant, and those that are Mondays. We can represent these by overlapping circles.

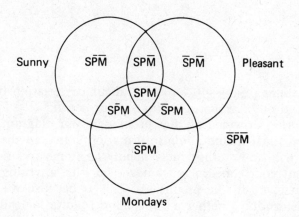

This arrangement allows us to have distinct and separate regions for days that are only sunny, only pleasant, only Mondays, or some combination of the three. We have, at the top left, the region labelled SP̄M̄, which indicates the class of all days that are sunny but not pleasant and not Mondays. The central region, SPM, diagrams the class of sunny, pleasant Mondays. The area outside the circles, S̄P̄M̄, represents everything other than a sunny, pleasant Monday.

Now let us test an argument for validity by using Venn diagrams. Consider:

1. All monsters are pugnacious.
2. All sea serpents are monsters.
3. *Therefore* all sea serpents are pugnacious.

We begin our test by drawing three interlocking circles, one for each term of the argument. Once the circles are labeled, we have the following:

Step 1

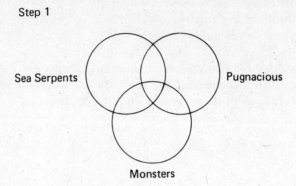

Next we look at premiss 1, which is about the relationship between monsters and pugnacious individuals. Our second step is to include the information provided by that premiss in our diagram. (Remember that you must include *only* information stated in the premisses. Often you will know other facts about the items mentioned in an example, but your concern must never be with anything except the information given in the premisses. This is because we are always trying to determine whether a conclusion follows logically from the premisses stated; we are not entitled to accept a conclusion for reasons *not* stated in the premisses.) In this case we are told, by premiss 1, that all monsters are pugnacious, which means that there are no monsters that are *not* pugnacious. Hence this premiss instructs us to *shade out* the area of M not overlapped by P:

Step 2

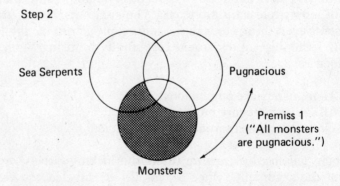

Next we turn to the second premiss and add the information from that to our diagram. Premiss 2, that all sea serpents are monsters, means that there are no sea serpents that are not also members of the class of monsters. So we *shade out* the area of the class sea serpents that does not overlap with the area representing the class monster, thereby showing that (according to premiss 2) there are no individual in that shaded area:

Step 3

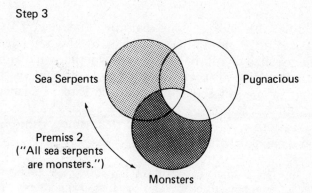

Up to this point—in steps 1 through 3—we have simply added to our diagram the information provided by the premisses. And by now all the information given in the premisses has been included.

We next turn to the conclusion. All we do, at this stage, is look at the two circles that represent the proposition expressing the conclusion of the argument. In our example it is the conclusion "All sea serpents are pugnacious." The rule for our test by Venn diagram is this: if the shading or the x mark required to represent the conclusion pictorially is already in the diagram after the premisses have been shaded or marked, then the argument is valid.

The reasoning behind this rule is that the conclusion of a syllogism simply *draws out* the information contained in the premisses. If the argument is valid, the conclusion should preserve the truth of the premisses. Our test involves putting the information given in the premisses into the diagram; if the conclusion *follows from* those premisses, the information in the conclusion should already be in the diagram after the premisses have been incorporated into it. So we then decide the appropriate shading for the conclusion and compare it to the shading in the diagram.

To return to our example, the conclusion, "All sea serpents are pugnacious," is represented by the following Venn diagram.

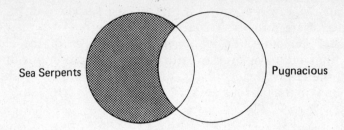

Compare this with the previous diagram, and you will see that the required shading is present. You must, by the way, ignore "extra" areas that get shaded; all that matters is whether what is required has been pictured. Here all that is needed to show that the argument is valid is for the area of S that falls outside P to be shaded—which it is.

Here is another valid argument, this time with one universal premiss and one particular premiss:

> Only human beings are thinking creatures. This means we must consider some robots to be human because some robots are capable of genuine thought processes.

Before reading on, you might try to analyze this argument yourself by writing down the premisses followed by the conclusion. In doing so, you should put the statements of both premisses and conclusion into standard form.

Remember to start your analysis by establishing what the conclusion is and then finding the premisses that are used to arrive at that conclusion. The cue word "because" tips you off that the claim following, that "some robots are capable of genuine thought processes," is a premiss. The phrase "this means" is similar to "it follows that" and indicates that a conclusion is coming—namely the conclusion "we must consider some robots human." The first sentence must therefore be another premiss. If we now put the premisses first and the conclusion last and put them into standard form, the argument is:

1. All thinking creatures are human beings.
2. Some robots are thinking creatures.
3. *Therefore* some robots are human beings.

Note that in putting the sentences into standard form we have "translated out" synonymous terms. This avoids duplicating classes and saves confusion. To be a "thinking creature" and to be a thing

"capable of genuine thought processes" are, for all intents and purposes, the same; so in stating premiss 2, the phrase "thinking creatures" was substituted for the original, "capable of genuine thought
processes."

Note also that this example involves the tricky "only" in the first sentence. To be told that *only* human beings are thinking creatures is
to be told that any and all thinking creatures you encounter will be
human. It does *not* say that all humans are thinking creatures. Sentences of this type, using "only," are tricky because the term that is
technically the subject of the proposition expressed by the sentence
comes *last* in the sentence or, at least, after the predicate term. One
is therefore tempted to place the terms in the wrong order when trans-
lating into standard form. In our example, "Only human beings are
thinking creatures" means "All thinking creatures are human beings."

Let us test this argument for validity by using Venn diagrams.

Step 1

Draw three overlapping circles to represent the classes referred to
by the terms in this argument.

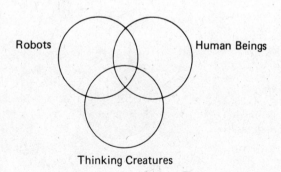

Robots   Human Beings

Thinking Creatures

Step 2

Premiss 1, "All thinking creatures are human beings," instructs us
to shade out all of the area of the circle representing thinking creatures
that does *not* overlap with that for human beings:

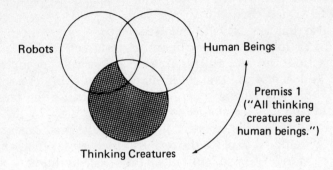

Robots

Human Beings

Thinking Creatures

Premiss 1
("All thinking
creatures are
human beings.")

Step 3

Premiss 2, "Some robots are thinking creatures," is a particular affirmative proposition, and we use a lower case "x" to diagram that proposition:

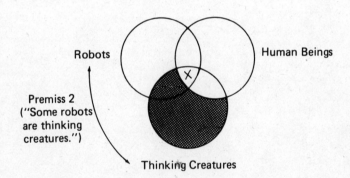

Robots

Human Beings

Premiss 2
("Some robots
are thinking
creatures.")

Thinking Creatures

Note that part of the area of overlap between the circle for robots and that for thinking creatures has already been shaded out because of the information contained in the first premiss. This means that we have to place the "x" required by the second premiss in the remaining unshaded area common to the classes of robots and thinking creatures. In other words, letting "S," "P," and "M" stand for "robots," "human beings," and "thinking creatures," respectively, we can see that the shading for the first premiss included shading the area $\overline{S}\overline{P}M$, which indicates that the area $\overline{S}\overline{P}M$ is *empty*; therefore, since the "x" must be somewhere in the overlap between S and M— that is, in either $S\overline{P}M$ or SPM—we *have* to place the x in the area SPM.

Step 4

We now look at the diagram to see whether the shadings and x-ings achieved by steps 2 and 3 are the same as—or at least include— the area you would have shaded or marked had you diagrammed the conclusion. Since the conclusion demands an "x" *somewhere* in the overlap between the circles for robots and for human beings, and since one is indeed there by the time steps 2 and 3 have been completed, we can conclude that the argument is valid.

The Venn diagram test demonstrates that the conclusion of the argument does follow logically from the premisses given. However, we know that the conclusion is actually false. While this is perhaps disappointing, we have not been guilty of an error. We were in effect asked to *accept* the premisses without question and to discover whether the stated conclusion followed *logically* from those premisses. Remember that a valid deductive argument form only guarantees that the conclusion follows from the premisses given. Whether those premisses are true or not is another matter, which requires a separate investigation. You will recall that the question of truth was dealt with in Chapter 2. Valid arguments with false premisses are not uncommon.

One lesson you should learn from this is that you must question someone's premisses right at the start. To let someone by with false premisses is to allow the person to present an argument that *seems* to lead to a certain conclusion but that may not really lead there at all. Imagine that someone presents the following argument to you:

1. All divorced people are unhappy.
2. All your uncles are divorced.
3. *Therefore* all your uncles are unhappy.

This is a valid argument, because one can correctly draw the conclusion from the premisses. But this is another example in which you must examine the premisses closely. In this case you can see that premiss 1 need not be true, and your uncles may be happily divorced.

Here is another example to test by means of a Venn diagram.

All the wealthy people in the world are Americans. But since some people are not Americans, then some people are not wealthy.

You will have noted that "since," at the beginning of the second sentence, signals a premiss and that "then," after the comma in the second sentence, signals a conclusion. The argument, in standard form, is:

1. All wealthy people are American.
2. Some people are not American.
3. *Therefore* some people are not wealthy.

This gives us the following diagram:

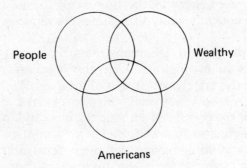

Here is the diagram showing the shading for the first premiss.

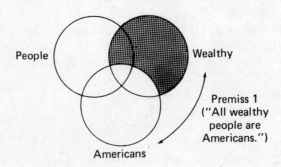

The second premiss is a particular proposition. So we must use an x to diagram that proposition, and the x must be placed in the part of the region designating the class people that does not overlap with the region for Americans:

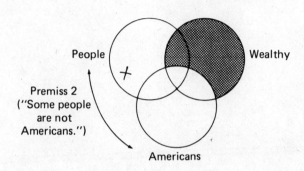

The conclusion, that there are some people who are not wealthy, is a particular-negative, or an O, proposition—like "Some S is not P." Therefore, when you look at the circles for "people" and "wealthy," you should find an x in the region of "people" but *outside* the region for "wealthy." Since such a mark was included among our shadings and markings for the two premisses, the argument is valid. The conclusion does follow from the premisses.

Here is a final example to test by a Venn diagram—this time an argument with negative premisses.

Since no dogs are fond of cats and since no reptiles are dogs, it must be that no reptiles are fond of cats.

The cue word "since" signals the premisses, and "it must be" signals the conclusion. In standard form the argument is:

1. No dogs are fond of cats.
2. No reptiles are dogs.
3. *Therefore* no reptiles are fond of cats.

This gives us the initial diagram:

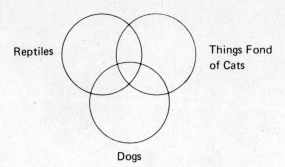

The shading for premiss 1 must show that there is *no overlap* between the class dog and the class of things fond of cats:

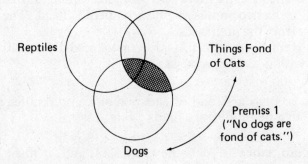

The shading for premiss 2 must show that there is no overlap between the classes reptiles and dogs:

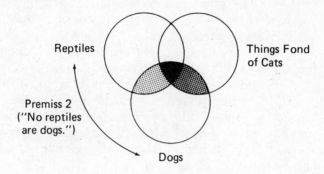

If we look at the conclusion, we can see that it demands the following shading:

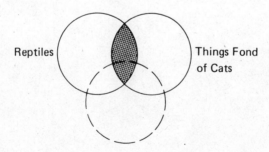

But comparing this to the shadings we obtained by diagramming the premisses, we see that they do not match. The previous diagram, achieved after shading for both premisses, leaves a portion of the area of overlap between the circles for reptiles and for things fond of cats (the area SP$\overline{\text{M}}$) unshaded. This means there *could* be something in that area. Since the shading in the diagram for the premisses does not contain the shading required by the conclusion, the argument is not valid. The conclusion is *not* contained in, does not follow from, those premisses.

One can see why this would be the case: the first premiss tells us just that there are no individuals that are dogs *and* fond of cats. The second premiss tells us that there are no individuals that are both reptiles and dogs. The premisses do not tell us whether some reptiles might be fond of cats—nor do the premisses deny that possibility (as our Venn diagram showed).

By now, you have very likely caught on to the Venn diagram technique for testing the validity of syllogisms. The exercises at the end of this chapter include additional arguments that you can diagram to test your skill. When you set to work on the exercises, you will find it helpful to keep in mind a few points about the procedure.

Shade for universal premisses first. By doing this you *shade out* areas that *cannot* have members. Therefore you will not be tempted later to put an x in such an area.

It is traditional to draw the circles in the order we have shown in the examples. This places the circles representing the terms of the conclusion across the top and makes it slightly easier to locate the conclusion after the information in the premisses has been included in the diagram.

If you are to put an x into a region that is divided, place it on the line forming the division. For example, suppose you had to represent the premiss "Some S is M" in the following diagram.

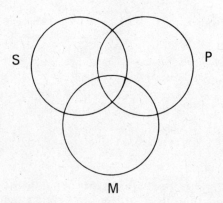

Which area are you to put the x into? It *must* go in the overlap of S and M, but should it go into the area $S\bar{P}M$ or the area SPM? The problem is that the information given by "Some S is M" is not specific enough to tell us. We are being given enough information to know that we must put the x into the area common to S and to M, but not enough to say that it is specifically the region $S\bar{P}M$ or SPM. So the x should be placed on the line:

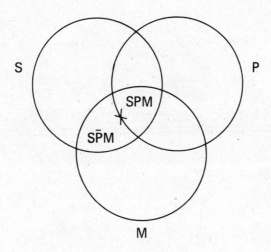

An x on the line in this fashion means that the x is in one of the regions or the other but that we do not have sufficient information to justify placing it clearly in one or the other.

In interpreting this kind of mark when comparing the shading and markings of premises and conclusion in a Venn diagram test for validity, *never* consider an x on a line to be inside an area just because it is on the line. For example, consider the argument:

1. Some cats are mean.
2. Some dogs are mean.
3. *Therefore,* some dogs are cats.

If we use a Venn diagram and mark in these premisses, we have the following:

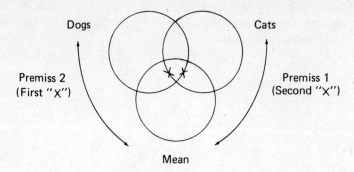

This leaves the circles representing dogs and cats with two x's on the borders of regions:

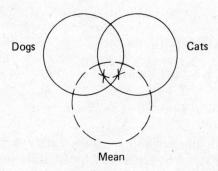

Since these x's *could*, for all we know from the premisses, be outside the region of the overlap between dogs and cats, we are not justified in claiming there is an x *in* the region of the overlap. The argument does not justify the conclusion, which requires an x *clearly* in the overlap between dogs and cats. Hence the argument is not valid.

Finally, it is worth noting that you may encounter singular propositions such as "Trigger is a horse" or "This pen is dry." Rather than asserting or denying the inclusion of one class within another class, such singular propositions claim that a particular person or object belongs to a certain class. The specific horse designated by the name "Trigger" has the essential properties of a horse and so is correctly classified as a horse.

There is some question about how to handle these. Traditionally, singular statements were made to fit the requirements of the syllogism by treating the singular-affirmative statements as A propositions. Thus one treats "Trigger" as designating a unit class (a class with only one member) whose sole member is Trigger. The singular proposition "Trigger is a horse" is thereby taken to mean "All members of the class designated by "Trigger" are members of the class "horse." Similarly, a singular-negative proposition such as "Socrates is not young" is paraphrased as the universal negative proposition "No members of the class designated by 'Socrates' are members of the class designated by 'young'."

There are special problems with singular terms and singular propositions, especially when we have to deal with a fictitious name, which should make us cautious about such paraphrases. Nevertheless, if you are *forced* to deal with singular propositions, you can usually, for the purposes of Venn diagram tests, paraphrase them as either A or E propositions without getting into difficulty.

CONCLUSION

To sum up, if you are interested in good arguing, you must pay attention both to truth and to logic. In assessing someone else's argument, you must ask whether the claims are true. Do the statements really present accurate information that is relevant to the issue being debated? Or are they merely conjectures, unfounded assumptions, or guesses? Do they reflect personal prejudices or biases?

You must also decide whether the statements providing the evidence or reasons actually lead to the conclusion they are said to lead to. How are the statements connected? What is the actual chain of reasoning being used? Is the reasoning complete as it is expressed, or are there hidden assumptions that must be brought to light before the argument can be properly understood? Perhaps there are underlying, unexpressed beliefs that even the person engaged in the argument is not aware of, yet which are crucial to the reasoning being followed.

The same rules apply to your own arguments, of course. You must make certain that your own statements are beyond reproach. Are they absolutely and certainly true? Or are they merely probable or even just likely? The less certain your evidence is, the more cautious and qualified your conclusion must be. To a great extent, the nature of your premises affects and limits the strength of your conclusion.

EXERCISES

To be good at arguing, you must develop your ability to analyze any argument—written or spoken—to determine what propositions it contains and to complete it if it has an unexpressed assumption. The following exercises are designed to help you develop your analytical skills.

I. The first step in recognizing and analyzing an argument is to pick out the various propositions presented. This set of exercises asks you to put the following ordinary sentences into standard form; that is, you must, if possible, translate them into one of the basic kinds of categorical proposition. "Buses are always late" clearly says that *all*, not some, buses are late, and so it is a universal-affirmative proposition equivalent to "All buses are always late." In analyzing each of the following sentences, first think about what the sentence means; ask yourself what type of proposition it is intended to express. Then write the sentence in standard form.

1. Roses are red.
2. Violets are not red.
3. Anything made by Fred's Bakery is good.
4. Nothing that's interesting to eat is free of calories.
5. A few people have snatched victory out of the jaws of defeat.
6. Many poor people are not happy.
7. Every horse is beautiful.
8. Never is an American unpatriotic.
9. People who live in glass houses should never throw stones.
10. If it's a Blamaro, it goes like a bomb.
11. Not everyone who gets an A is super-clever.
12. Only the lonely know the way I feel tonight.
13. He who tells lies lives a lie.
14. The arrogant never see their faults.
15. By and large, tourists are usually obnoxious.

II. When you are trying to understand and to analyze an argument, it is often useful to recognize another way in which you might express a proposition. Consider the following example:

1. No silly people are trustworthy people.
2. All untrustworthy people are to be avoided.
3. *Therefore* all silly people are to be avoided.

In a syllogism such as this we must have a term that appears in each premiss and connects the two premisses together, so that the conclusion follows. However, in this example we have, in premiss 1, the terms "silly people" and "trustworthy people"; in premiss 2 we have "untrustworthy people" and "(people who) are to be avoided." This gives us four terms and four distinct classes; and a syllogism with more than three terms is not valid. However, we can see at once that "trustworthy" people are *not untrustworthy* people. (This is just *double negation*: a person who is *not unkind* is a kind person; it is like algebra, where two minus signs give a positive so that "— —2" is equivalent to "2.") In the example above we can alter premiss 1 to read "All silly people are untrustworthy." This reduces the number of terms in the two premisses to three and allows us to check the argument for validity at once.

Here are a few more examples of the same sort: "All senators are citizens" means the same as "No senators are not citizens." Likewise "No referees are biased" means the same as "All referees are unbiased." And "Some people are just" means the same as "Some people are not unjust."

In each of the following examples, you are to express the proposition in another way. Try to find as many possible alternative expressions, with the *same* meaning, as you can.

1. No cows like children.
2. All pigs squeal.
3. The dunces never failed to stand in a corner.
4. Dogs chew bones.
5. Some boxers are courageous.
6. My neighbors are always annoyed when I sing.
7. Some cultured people are not polite.
8. All insensitive people are intolerant.
9. Some friends are not helpful.
10. No industrious workers are poor.

III. The following drill will develop your ability to find an argument and put it into standard form. In each case, pick out the statements that express the premises and the conclusion. Then put all the sentences into standard form and arrange them in lines, with the conclusion last. It might help you to find the premises and the conclusion if you underline cue words in the text, as in the following example:

Because all the lodge members voted for Nixon and *since* people who voted for Nixon are Republicans, all the lodge members are Republicans.

Here we have italicized "because" and "since," which are cue words for premises. Putting the argument into standard-form categorical propositions, with the conclusion last, we have:

1. All the lodge members are (people) who voted for Nixon.
2. All people who voted for Nixon are Republicans.
3. *Therefore* all the lodge members are Republicans.

Remember that sometimes arguments are not valid and that sometimes premises are false. In this exercise you are not to worry about either. You are only to be concerned about expressing each argument in standard form.

1. Since only rare metals are expensive and since welders do not use costly metals, they do not use rare metals.
2. The delegates went to the reception so they must be supporting Smith, because it was a reception for Smith's supporters.
3. Since the neighborhood dogs don't growl, then they won't bite, because all dogs that growl bite.
4. Some astronauts have seen all the planet Earth at once because they were on the moon's surface and you can see all the Earth from there.
5. Since some politicians love to hear themselves talk and all the people at the party will be politicians, the party will be *totally* a party of people who love to hear themselves talk.
6. No lawyers are labor leaders because no lawyers are socialists and no labor leaders are socialists.
7. It is not legal to possess pornographic films because the vice squad seizes pornographic films and they do not seize items that it is legal to own.
8. As all the completed exam papers are to be given to a supervisor, you are to give your papers to one of the people wearing a name tag. All the supervisors are wearing name tags and no one else is.
9. Some of his ancestors must not have been freed because some slaves were never freed and some of his ancestors were slaves.

IV. Sometimes arguments are not fully expressed. People frequently assume a fact or don't think to mention it, and sometimes people suppress or gloss over one or more of their assumptions. We are then faced with a truncated or abbreviated argument—an argument with either a missing premise or an unstated conclusion.[7] When

---

[7] An argument that is incomplete in one of these ways is called an "enthymeme."

this happens, we must try to find a hidden or suppressed premiss (an implicit premiss), or a missing conclusion, so as to complete the argument.

Here is an example:

The students voted for the communists, so they *must* be crazy.

The cue word "so" means the same as "therefore"; it signals a conclusion. The first part must be a premiss. This leaves us with:

1. The students voted for the communists.
2. *Therefore* the students are crazy.

Obviously, we need another link in this reasoning. What connects voting for the communists with being crazy? It must be that the person making this claim believes that *all* people who vote for the communists are crazy. (And one would expect the person to have evidence and reasons to back his belief.) So here is the hidden assumption that is necessary to make the argument:

1. The students voted for the communists.
2. All people who vote for the communists are crazy (hidden premiss).
3. *Therefore* the students are crazy.

Here are some further examples to try. In each case find the hidden premiss or conclusion and then write down the whole argument in standard form. If the argument appears to be invalid, you should still provide the missing premiss or express the conclusion that seems *encouraged* by the argument.

1. The students in the Grade 9 class cannot be very ambitious or else they would have worked on the school project.
2. This garden is so well kept there *must* be a gardener.
3. The use of hormone injections by athletes has increased to such an extent that it is hard to think of athletic competitions as fair.
4. The conclusion is obvious: the members of the golf club have plenty of money, and some rich people can count on *not* getting what they want from city council.
5. One cannot get downtown on a yellow bus because all school buses are yellow.
6. Everything tasty is fattening, and cheesecake sure is tasty!

7. Since some Armenians are Catholic, all your relatives must be Catholic.
8. People who see violent movies are corrupted, yet the public censors view many such films in the course of their job.
9. One cannot get downtown on a yellow bus because only school buses are yellow.
10. Some American citizens are drafted into the United States Army, and so some women are drafted into the Army too.

V. Take each argument in exercises III and IV and test it for validity by means of a Venn diagram.

VI. Frequently, our deductive reasoning is not simple but involves a longer chain of deduction. Consider this argument:

Because the Giants have excellent pitching, they will win the World Series; for teams with good pitching win most of their games, and winning most of your games means you will win the World Series.

This argument has three premisses and a conclusion. The cue words "because" and "for" signal premisses. The argument can, however, be broken down into two syllogisms, provided we add an unexpressed intermediate conclusion along the way. Put in standard form we initially have:

First Syllogism

1. The Giants are a team with good pitching.
2. Teams with good pitching are teams that win most of the games.
3. *Therefore* the Giants are a team that will win most of their games (unexpressed intermediate conclusion).

We can then use the conclusion, 3, with the other premiss contained in the original argument to give us:

Second Syllogism

3. The Giants are a team that will win most of their games.
4. All teams that win most of their games are teams that will win the World Series.
5. *Therefore* the Giants will win the World Series.

If you are uncertain of the validity of these syllogisms, you can test each by a Venn diagram.

Lewis Carroll, the author of *Alice in Wonderland* and *Through the Looking-glass*, also wrote a book entitled *Symbolic Logic*,[8] which contains examples of arguments involving more than one categorical syllogism. (Such chains of syllogisms are called "sorites," which is both singular and plural; hence, one may speak of both a sorites and many sorites.) Since Lewis Carroll's examples are so delightful and nonsensical, we thought you would enjoy trying some of them. The object is to supply a conclusion in each instance. You must do this by putting them into a chain of syllogisms, supplying missing intermediate conclusions as needed (as we did in the above example about the Giants). Try this one first:

(1) My saucepans are the only things I have that are made of tin;
(2) I find all your presents very useful;
(3) None of my saucepans are of the slightest use.[9]

Here we are dealing with three statements about "things that are mine"; and these are divided into the classes: made of tin; saucepans, useful; your presents. Since we are looking for a connection between these classes, we first look for two premisses that mention the same class. Obviously 1 and 3 do. Putting these in standard form we have the following:

1. All my saucepans are made of tin.
3. No saucepans of mine are useful.
4. *Therefore* no useful things of mine are made of tin (unexpressed intermediate conclusion).

We now take sentence 4 with the remaining premiss 2 and have:

4. No useful things of mine are made of tin.
2. All your presents are useful.
5. *Therefore* no presents of yours are made of tin.

So the conclusion we were looking for is proposition 5.

Now try the following examples from Lewis Carroll's *Symbolic Logic* yourself. In each case you must find the *conclusion* that follows from *all* the premisses supplied. You may have to alter some of the given sentences; altering them to make the argument simpler is acceptable *so long as* you do not change the *meaning* of any. Some-

[8] Lewis Carroll, *Symbolic Logic: Part 1, Elementary* (London: Macmillan 1897).
[9] *Ibid.*, p. 112.

times you will need to put the sentences into standard form, although often they are clear and can be dealt with without doing so.

1. (1) No ducks waltz;
   (2) No officers ever decline to waltz;
   (3) All my poultry are ducks.[10]

2. (1) Every one who is sane can do logic;
   (2) No lunatics are fit to serve on a jury;
   (3) None of *your* sons can do logic.[11]
   (*Hint:* you do not need two classes for the sane and for lunatics. Change around premiss 2.)

3. (1) No one takes in the *Times*, unless he is well-educated;
   (2) No hedge-hogs can read;
   (3) Those who cannot read are not well-educated.[12]

4. (1) All unripe fruit is unwholesome;
   (2) All these apples are wholesome;
   (3) No fruit, grown in the shade, is ripe.[13]

5. (1) Colored flowers are always scented;
   (2) I dislike flowers that are not grown in the open air;
   (3) No flowers grown in the open air are colorless.[14]

[10] *Ibid.*, p. 112.
[11] *Ibid.*
[12] *Ibid.*, p. 113.
[13] *Ibid.*, p. 114.
[14] *Ibid.*, p. 116.

6

Finding Explanations and Making Predictions

EXPLANATIONS AND HYPOTHESES IN SCIENCE AND EVERYDAY LIFE

One advantage of learning to reason and argue effectively is that these skills help you to arrive at explanations. A politician puts forward a line of argument in an attempt to explain the party's views and, thereby, to win over voters. A salesperson explains how a machine works, its running costs, and its advantages over competing models in a persuasive argument intended to convince a prospective client to buy the machine. The detective explains a murder by producing a chain of logical reasoning that demonstrates how the conclusion was reached that "the butler did it." And scientists explain how bone cells regenerate and how knowing that fact led to a conclusion about a possible novel technique for replacing destroyed bone with a specially constructed plastic insert.

A key feature of human thought employed in explanations is the ability to generalize. If someone treats us in a kindly way the first few times we meet him or her, we come to expect similar treatment in the future. We conclude, from our experience, that the person is kindly. In other words, we generalize from our experience. Similarly, a hospital does not have to test every canister of oxygen it buys. Rather, the generalization is made that the oxygen in every canister purchased will have identical properties. We do the same thing in the supermarket. Few of us look at *every* strawberry in a large basket. Instead, we inspect a few and then generalize that the rest will be of approximately the same quality. (Of course, we sometimes get tricked, thereby learning to watch for baskets of fruit that have good fruit placed on the top and fruit of poorer quality on the bottom.)

111

We are generally interested in trying to understand people and things and how they interact. Sometimes we try out theories and possible explanations. In most situations there are so many facts to deal with, one must try to organize them. One must theorize—construct an hypothesis about the way things might be organized—and then test out that hypothesis or theory by experiments and observations to arrive at a satisfactory explanation. Facts by themselves prove nothing. A dead body, a ticket stub, and a cigarette with lipstick on it are only bare facts until the police detective has a plausible theory explaining how these items might be connected.

We all try to find general theories or hypotheses that will help explain things we are puzzled about. Suppose a classmate is acting in a peculiar way. You search for an explanation. Perhaps she is worried that she is losing her boyfriend and is so unhappy because of this that she is not eating properly, therefore losing weight; is becoming inattentive; and so forth. You would feel that you could explain her unusual behavior once you had a theory, or hypothesis, that fitted all the facts. In this example we have a situation that can be analyzed into the following pieces of information:

1. She is worried (our theory; our hypothesis).
2. She is unhappy, does not eat properly, is losing weight, and is inattentive (observed facts).

If we believe that there is a link between worry and unhappiness, failure to eat, losing weight, and inattention, we can add that to the above information. So we now have:

1. She is worried (our theory, or hypothesis).
2. She is unhappy, does not eat properly, is losing weight, and is inattentive (observed facts).
3. People who are worried are usually people who are unhappy, do not eat properly, lose weight, and are inattentive.

We can then connect these into an argument. Stated in normal prose it is:

> *Because* she is worried and *because* people who are worried are unhappy, do not eat properly, lose weight, and are inattentive, she is unhappy, does not eat properly, is losing weight, and is inattentive.

Put in terms of premisses and a conclusion in standard form we have the argument:

1. All worried people are people who are unhappy, do not eat properly, lose weight, and are inattentive.

2. She is a worried person.
3. *Therefore* she is someone who is unhappy, does not eat properly, is losing weight, and is inattentive.

One can see that this is a valid syllogism; it could be tested by a Venn diagram.

What you should note in this example is that we have *first* started with a problem (why does she act in an unusual way?); *second*, we have thought of an hypothesis that might explain the problematic behavior; *third*, we have *connected* the hypothesis and the facts by making them into a valid deductive (syllogistic) argument. By doing this, we have shown that our hypothesis does connect with the facts to be explained, thereby making it plausible that we have advanced a reasonable explanation. Of course, we should next ask whether there are *other* hypotheses that might explain her behavior; if so, one must look again at the facts, see if all the facts fit, and so on, in order to decide which is the *correct* hypothesis.

You can see from this example that this way of searching for an explanation is not uncommon and is, in fact, familiar to everyone. You use it all the time: you cast about for a plausible hypothesis; you connect the facts; you feel that an explanation has been achieved when you can deduce the problematic behavior from your theory and the facts (because this assures you that there *is* a connection between your theory and the facts). And this way of reasoning employs the type of deductive arguments we discussed in the last chapter.

Consider another sort of example: the Canadian ban on the artificial sweetener saccharin. After several studies had shown that rats receiving large doses of saccharin in their diets developed cancer, the government of Canada decided there was evidence that prolonged use of saccharin could cause cancer in human beings. Many groups opposed the ban, and arguments were developed on both sides. One explanation of, and justification for, the ban went along the following lines:

> The test studies have shown that large doses of saccharin over long periods of time will cause cancer in laboratory animals. This means that people who eat and drink foods containing saccharin are most likely going to get cancer eventually. Because of this clear and demonstrated health risk, we are banning the inclusion of saccharin in any food or drink sold.

Put in the form of a deductive argument, the first two sentences provide the following explanation:

1. All food and drugs that are dangerous to people's health should be banned.

2. Saccharin is dangerous to people's health.
3. *Therefore* saccharin should be banned.

The second premiss is presumably supported by the studies—the experiments done on rats. The first premiss states a general principle that most people would accept.

Such an argument received the expected response. Some groups attacked premiss 2 by arguing that not all people use great quantities of saccharin and that in some studies the rats were given proportionally gigantic amounts. Others argued that even if its argument is sound, the government ought not to take away people's choice in the matter. "Why not," they asked, "treat saccharin in the same way as cigarettes, by putting a warning on the packages?" Others pointed out that our society allows things that are much more dangerous than saccharin, such as guns, and that it is too bad we can't prove that guns cause cancer in rats! But despite the counterattacks, the point to note is that a deductive argument in the form of a syllogism was implicit in the original example to help explain and justify a government action.

PREDICTIONS IN SCIENCE AND EVERYDAY LIFE

Suppose you are doing chemical experiments in a lab. You have something in a test tube which you are heating. Suddenly the whole thing blows up. Glass all over the place! "What happened?" someone asks you, and you respond by saying, "The chemicals I was heating produced gas that expanded too quickly as I heated it and the test tube gave way and shattered." Part of your explanation, put in terms of a deductive argument, is:

1. All gases expand when heated (a known law of nature).
2. The chemicals in the test tube turned into gas.
3. *Therefore* the gases produced by the chemicals in the test tube expanded when I heated them.

Your reasoning then moves on to another connected argument built on the combination of this conclusion and the further fact that the glass test tube can only stand so much pressure before it gives way. However, someone who knew that premisses 1 and 2 were true could predict that the chemicals in the test tube would expand when heated. If you know 1 and 2, you can predict conclusion 3. That is, if you know some law of nature and the specific conditions that are going to come into play, you can predict the result. Likewise, you can predict that if a child playing with matches throws a lighted match into the open tin of gasoline an explosion will result and the child will very likely be injured. Here you know a general rule (law) about gasoline and how it reacts to open flames, and you use that as a premiss in predicting a conclusion.

In prediction, if we know the law and the facts, we can draw a predictable conclusion. As we have said, in determining an explanation we have the conclusion and some facts, and we need to find the law (or rule, or hypothesis) from which the result, the conclusion, follows. As you can see, both finding explanations and making predictions are modeled on the type of sound deductive thinking discussed in the last two chapters.

Being able to predict events is important in our lives. We could not plan to have chocolate pudding for supper if we could not predict how the milk, cocoa, starch, and sugar will act when heated. A business executive cannot organize the operations of her branch of the company unless she can count on her employees to carry out the tasks she assigns them and unless she can predict, on the basis of past experience, that they will be able to handle new challenges in their work. Nor could a group of scientists plan a moon landing unless they were able to predict accurately certain facts about gravitational pull, flight trajectories, and the power produced by burning a certain quantity of fuel. All such predictions depend on certain key requirements:

1. We must be able to establish constant regularities—constant relations—between classes of things. (For example, the scientist knows that there is a constant relationship between the distance an object falls and the speed with which it travels.)
2. We must know what conditions will come into play. Sometimes we control these, as in a lab; sometimes we must deduce what these are likely to be, so another logical reasoning process might be linked to the main one.
3. We must be able to make logical deductions—reasoned inferences—about what will happen given the facts established in steps 1 and 2.

You can now see why the deductive logic we discussed in Chapter 5 is so important. That logic dealt with categorical propositions— with simple statements that either expressed relationships between classes or declared the inclusion of one individual or class within another class. The scientist, in searching for laws of nature, uses logic in a similar way. The scientist wants to find connections between classes of things in the world and to determine which connections are constant and, therefore, will necessarily hold under all conditions and at all times. The scientist can use a deductive reasoning form such as the syllogism, because it guarantees that deductions made according to that form result in valid conclusions. Of course, the scientist's main job is to establish a hypothesis. That is, to provide the premiss that can later be fitted into the deductive reasoning process by which explanations can be provided and from which future events can be predicted.

In passing, you might note that hypotheses vary. Some are *universal generalizations*, which are invariably true. Claims about the forces of gravity are of this order. Others are *statistical generalizations*, based on sampling or limited experiment, and are, therefore, only highly probable. The claim that saccharin causes cancer is an example of a statistical generalization.

Throughout this book we are emphasizing effective ways of winning an argument. Your ability to win an argument often depends on the task you set yourself. You cannot argue against claims that are as strongly supported as the laws of nature; you *can* argue against or raise doubts about beliefs that are based only on statistical evidence, such as claims about the effects of saccharin.

Prediction is a common way to *test* an hypothesis. For example, some people in the ancient and medieval worlds wondered whether the *speed* of a falling object was affected by the weight of the object. Would a ten-pound cannon ball fall ten times as fast as a one-pound cannon ball? Our initial guess might be that the heavier object would fall faster than the lighter one. In fact, the ancient Greek philosopher Aristotle believed that the speed of descent of falling objects *did* vary with their size. Nevertheless, some people believed they would fall at the same rate if dropped from the same height.

It is said that Galileo tested this theory in the seventeenth century, by dropping objects from the Leaning Tower of Pisa. He took two objects of different weights and dropped them from a height onto a board. The prediction was that, if the objects fell at the same rate, only one sound would be produced by their hitting the board. The objects were dropped, and there was only one sound. An additional, supporting fact was that they *appeared* to land at the same instant. The prediction was right, providing a confirming instance of the hypothesis. In this example an argument was settled in favor of one theory (hypothesis) over another because the winning theory made possible a prediction about events that turned out to be true and because it was supported by a number of additional experiments done by Galileo's contemporaries.

Scientific prediction also made possible the discovery of the planet Neptune. We are inclined to think that most stars and planets were discovered simply by being observed, and many of them were. But Neptune was hypothesized to exist before anyone had ever seen it. By the first part of the nineteenth century astronomers knew about the orbits of the known planets and about the gravitational force that planets exerted on one another. The orbit of a planet is affected by another planet passing close by it. Astronomers were puzzled, however, by the behavior of the planet Uranus. Its orbital motion was irregular. These scientists tried to explain the irregularities in terms of the attractions of other known planets, but failed. Since there had to be some force causing Uranus to be pulled out of its regular orbit, they came to the conclusion that an *unknown* planet must be responsible for disturbing the orbit of Uranus. Urbain J. J. Leverrier (1811–1877), using the known mathematical formulas about planetary orbits and the facts of the irregular positions of Uranus at various times, finally determined exactly where the new planet should be. He sent this information to the scientists at the Berlin Observatory, and with their large refracting telescope and some newly drawn maps of the relevant part of the sky, they were able to find the new planet, Neptune. Thus a man at a desk, with a theory and some mathematical calculations, deduced a *fact* about the physical world! The prediction of the discovery of a new planet was an hypothesis, based partly on known formulas and facts; and the discovery of the planet established the truth of the hypothesis.

A similar example of scientific deduction occurred more recently. In March 1977 *Newsweek* published the following report in its science section:

THE URANUS MYSTIQUE

The planet Uranus—far out in the void between Saturn and Neptune—was discovered in 1781, but hardly anything is known about it. The largest telescopes gazing through 1.8 billion miles of space have shown only a featureless, bluegreen disk orbited by five moons. Now, two astronomers have added to the mystique by spotting what seems to be either a band of tiny satellites or a system of rings around the planet.

The sighting was recorded when Uranus passed in front of a bright star known as SAO 158687. Separate observations by James Elliot of Cornell University and Robert Millis of Arizona's Lowell Observatory indicated that the starlight started to dim sooner than expected—and then quickly brightened again. The light pattern was repeated four times. The astronomers concluded that the changes could only have been caused by objects orbiting much closer to Uranus than its five known moons. Space scientists will have the opportunity to confirm the discoveries visually in 1985, when an unmanned U. S. spacecraft is scheduled to cruise past the planet.[1]

The astronomers had encountered a remarkable occurrence: unexpectedly, the light coming from the star SAO 158687 had suddenly dimmed and then brightened again. Although not stated outright in this article, it is easy to see that the astronomers were assuming that phenomena of this sort—the light from a star becoming dim—must be caused by an object passing between the star and the observer. This is reasonable, for we know that if an object is large enough and in the right position, it can block out light completely, which is what happens in an eclipse of the sun. Part of the thinking of the astronomers involved this simple but important deduction (expressed briefly):

1. All cases of sudden dimming of light from distant stars are dimmings caused by objects passing in front of the star.
2. All the present observed phenomena are sudden dimmings of light from a star.
3. *Therefore* all the present observed phenomena are dimmings caused by objects passing in front of the star.

Here the astronomers have employed a general rule about such phenomena (expressed by premiss 1) and from this plus the facts (expressed by premiss 2) have concluded that the sudden dimmings of light from star SAO 158687 were caused by some object passing relatively quickly in front of the star—that is, between the star and the observer.

The next question is, "What could the object or objects be?" Since the five known moons of Uranus could not be responsible, they concluded that some other, previously unknown, objects exist near the surface of Uranus. This conclusion is presumably deduced from known astronomical facts (such as the known positions of the five moons) and from observations. The last part of the reasoning of the astronomers involves the deduction:

4. The sudden dimmings observed are caused either by the moons of Uranus or by *other* objects.
5. The dimmings cannot be caused by the moons of Uranus.
6. *Therefore* they are caused by *other* objects.

[1] *Newsweek*, March 28, 1977, p. 87. Quoted by permission.

In steps 4 through 6 the astronomers have considered *possible* explanations and then eliminated one alternative on the basis of established knowledge about the orbits of the moons of Uranus. They have worked *deductively* to a conclusion, in this case to a theory adequate to explain the puzzling sudden dimming of the starlight.

In this last example the deduction employed in the theorized explanation was not in the form of a categorical syllogism. This is not unusual: there are other valid deductive argument forms that may be used in scientific deduction, and some are more helpful than the syllogism when the event involves causal relationships between natural objects. These other deductive argument forms will be discussed later, in Chapter 9.

EXPLANATION AND PREDICTION IN PSYCHOLOGY AND IN MORAL ARGUMENTS

The use of deductive reasoning is not relevant only to scientific explanations and discoveries. We often predict the behavior of people and events around us. Our society employs experts to predict the weather, the state of the economy, future unemployment rates, future sales of certain consumer products, and the number of bushels of corn and wheat that will be produced by farmers this year. Sociologists and psychologists predict the effects of urban life on human beings, what the crime rate will be next year, and how television will influence our behavior.

In the last part of the nineteenth century, when psychology and sociology were just in their beginnings, serious doubts were raised about whether such studies could ever become scientific. These doubts were based on the assumption that to be a *science* and to be fully capable of providing scientific explanations, an area of study must be in command of laws that express absolutely certain relationships between items within the field of study. In other words, it was assumed that scientific explanations must entail deductions from established laws. The reservation about whether psychology and sociology could be considered sciences was based on doubt about the ability of such disciplines to provide *laws* about their subject matter. Is there enough regularity in human character, motives, and so on, it was asked, to allow one to formulate laws about human behavior similar to the laws of astronomy?

We use the same deductive model of thinking in our everyday encounters with ethical problems. The father tells the child that he was bad, that he ought not to have told Uncle Charlie that he had washed his hands before supper when he had not done so. If the child asked why he should not have said this to Uncle Charlie, the father might typically reply by saying, "You should never tell a lie." Here a rule— a moral law—has been evoked to explain why the child was acting inappropriately. Put simply, the implicit argument used was:

1. All people who tell lies are bad (a moral rule or law).
2. You told a lie to Uncle Charlie (a fact).
3. *Therefore* you were bad (the conclusion).

This argument is similar to a scientific deduction, except that we have a moral rule (a moral law) instead of a natural law.

Of course there is much debate about what moral rules one is to follow. But there is no doubt about the *use* of moral rules. They are to help guide our actions and to help us to plan our future actions. If one has a set of moral rules, one can often deduce from these rules, along with the specific facts of a given situation, how one ought to act. The deductive model of thinking discussed in Chapter 5 provides a logical way to connect our moral rules with the actual facts of our situation.

"THINKING UP" AN HYPOTHESIS

You have probably had no difficulty discerning how the type of logical reasoning discussed in the last chapters has an important role to play in scientific thinking and in our everyday thinking about the actions and morality of others and ourselves. However, it might not be clear to you exactly how one goes about *establishing* or "thinking up" an hypothesis in the first place. How does a scientist decide what is a possible and plausible theory? How does the psychiatrist decide which hypothesis to investigate in attempting to explain a child's withdrawn behavior and rejection of his or her parents?

We cannot promise a sure-fire method or technique for all occasions. Unfortunately, thinking up a theory or hitting on an hypothesis in trying to find an explanation does present a challenge. It will often demand that you think creatively. Solving a scientific problem is similar to solving a puzzle, in that both require a search from unexpected connections and the ability to look at a problem in a novel way.

It is important to remember that someone who is trying to explain something is usually trying to connect certain facts together to show that a specific conclusion follows logically from these facts *as connected.* The detective is asking how the cigar butt, the paper knife with the initial "K" on it, the footprint in the flower garden, and the dead man's Siamese cat might be connected in such a way as to allow him to deduce who the murderer was. The kind of deductive reasoning involved in the syllogism involves the connecting of things in terms of class membership and class inclusion. And the notion of connections between and among things and classes of things is the key to finding hypotheses.

Here are five steps you can use in seeking a plausible and possible hypothesis whenever you are trying to understand or explain something.

1. Determine exactly what the problem is.   What specifically needs to be explained or understood? This sounds simple and obvious, but it is amazing how often someone writes a misguided essay or report simply because of having failed to set out the problem clearly and succinctly. Such failure frequently fools the writer and gets the report off on the wrong foot.

2. Determine the relevant facts.   Here you must count on your knowledge and experience about what connections are likely. For example, the thermometer most likely did *not* fall off the wall because it was white rather than red; more likely, it was not nailed up properly, there was a strong draft, or someone bumped against it. The color of the thermometer is not a likely explanation because we know from experience that there is seldom a connection between the color of an object and its falling to the floor. Also, we do not count the pull of gravity as a relevant factor here. Of course gravity is an important background fact, but in this case we want the *specific* factor that came into play and caused the thermometer to fall.

3. Determine the connections you know.   What links between events and things do you already know from your own observations or other data, from theories you have read about, and so forth? Ask whether any of these will account for the event you want to explain. For example, a household guide to plumbing always takes this approach in suggesting how you can "trouble-shoot" your plumbing problems. If the tap drips, we are told, this could be because of a worn washer *or* a worn faucet seat. We are then told to test each possibility, starting with the most frequent kind of problem. You check the washer first, because it is more likely that the washer has worn out than that the faucet itself has worn out and needs replacing.

4. What unknown connections are possible?   If observation and your theoretical knowledge have not turned up an answer, you must search for a *novel* connection between or among things or events. This is where imaginative and creative thinking are needed. You should formulate all possible connections. For example, if your car's starter fails sometimes and you have checked out all the usual possible causes, then you might consider whether there is a design problem. Maybe all starters on this model of car are poorly designed. There are situations that require thinking beyond the norm.

5. *Test each hypothesis.* For each hypothesis you think up you must ask, Do all the facts fit in with my hypothesis? Are there any facts omitted by my hypothesis? Can I think of any counterexamples?

The technique of constructing counterexamples is a particularly useful critical tool for testing an hypothesis. The hypothesis in the example in step 4 above, that all starters in this model of car are poorly designed, cannot be true if you know of several other people who have cars of that make and model and who have never, over a long period of time, had starter problems.

Step 5 is very important because you will frequently encounter competing explanations and competing hypotheses. Sometimes it is difficult to determine which is correct. In the following example no fewer than *three* rival explanations are offered for a problem encountered by residents of the city of Waterloo, Ontario.

POLLUTION, TREE ILLS LINKED

WATERLOO, Ont. (CP) A Waterloo woman says she is convinced that air pollution and not salt has damaged trees and shrubs along her street.

Alma Campbell, one of 31 persons who petitioned the city and Waterloo Region to determine the cause of damage and take appropriate action, told the council this week that exhaust fumes from trucks have caused the damage.

She added that the same black film covering residents' homes and patio furniture also covers trees along the street.

Officials from Kitchener and Waterloo say trees are suffering from an excess of salt spread on the street during the winter.

But road officials say the amount of salt dumped in the area has not changed much from other years and they blame frost for the problem.

An employee of the provincial community services department who had looked at the trees recommended severe pruning, deep watering, and injection of nutrients into them.

Douglas Pollard, Kitchener forestry foreman, said it would cost thousands of dollars to prune, thin, and fertilize the decaying trees. City aldermen agreed the engineering and community services staff should bring back a report on steps that might be taken to cure the problem.[2]

The three causes hypothesized to explain the tree damage are pollution from truck exhaust fumes, frost, and road salt.

Another noteworthy feature of this dispute is that some if not all the parties involved are probably *interested* parties, in that they have something at stake. For example, the road officials do not want to take the blame, so they claim it is not their road salt but frost that is responsible. Perhaps the city officials are worried about being blamed for allowing truck traffic in the area and, because of this, blame it on the salt. They would certainly *like* to be able to prove it is the salt, because they will have to spend a great deal of money to restore and maintain the trees if it is not—as the last part of the report indicates. Perhaps even Alma Campbell has an interest: could she want a ban on truck traffic in her area and so be predisposed to blame the tree damage on the exhaust emissions from the trucks? The last is only speculation; one would need more information in order to decide whether it were so. But you can see how a dispute of this sort might well involve parties with axes to grind or interests to protect. However, Alma Campbell does *back up* her claim by pointing out that the black film, supposedly from exhaust fumes, also covers patio furniture and houses in the area. This makes her hypothesis more reasonable than the others.

No matter how this dispute is resolved, it appears to be a case where more facts must be gathered before one could arrive at the truth.

CHOOSING BETWEEN HYPOTHESES

We expect any hypothesis to be relevant to whatever we wish to explain, to be testable by observations or experiments (even if the testing must be indirect because the things dealt with are not themselves observable), and to be *compatible* with other theories and hypotheses that are considered to be established beyond reasonable doubt. We will reject, or at the very least be highly suspicious of, any hypothesis that fails to meet one of these conditions.

But what do we do if we have two hypotheses that satisfy these minimal conditions? How do we choose between them? There are two further evaluations we can make: we can adjudicate between hypotheses in terms of their explanatory power and in terms of their simplicity.

[2] *The Canadian Press*, May 18, 1977. Quoted by permission.

Explanatory Power

While we expect an hypothesis to be testable in the sense that we should be able to deduce some facts from it that we can observe, we can also determine the range and number of observable facts an hypothesis allows us to deduce. If one hypothesis allows a greater number of facts to be deduced from it than another hypothesis allows, the former hypothesis is said to have greater *explanatory* power or *predictive* power. So, two scientific hypotheses, SH_1 and SH_2, might *both* explain a given number of facts and allow a range of predictions. But if, in addition, SH_1 (but not SH_2) is able to explain or allow predictions over a further range of cases, then we should select SH_1 for this reason. SH_1 has greater explanatory power, a greater ability to predict observable facts.

In passing, we might note that this point about the explanatory or predictive power of rival hypotheses suggests a possible way to refute one hypothesis in certain cases. Since we know that explanatory power has to do with the deduction or prediction of observable facts, we can reject any hypothesis that has as a consequence a result contrary to the established facts of our experience. Thus it may be possible to devise an experiment or a crucial test in order to determine whether the hypothesis SH_1 or SH_2 entails consequences that are not compatible with observed events. Suppose that hypothesis SH_1 entails that a cylinder of chlorine gas under a set of conditions C would expand and then explode. Also suppose that SH_2 entails that the same cylinder of chlorine gas under the same set of conditions C would condense, causing the sides of the cylinder to cave in slightly. Obviously, these results are incompatible; that is, *both* consequences cannot come about. Therefore we can set up the experiment and observe which of the two events occurs. While a cautious scientist might not feel that this decided the issue conclusively, the scientist would undoubtedly agree that failure to expand and explode is evidence *against* SH_1 and evidence *for* SH_2.

Simplicity

If two hypotheses are relevant, testable, in line with established facts and other hypotheses, and have equal explanatory power, we can only choose between them in terms of simplicity. Newtonian science was an advance over ancient theories because it explained everything the ancient theories did with *fewer* hypotheses. Such a test is not unfamiliar. Any parent knows that against almost any explanatory theory the child might advance, the parent's hypothesis that the muddy clothes were the result of playing in a puddle is going to be more acceptable because simpler.

Unfortunately, it is difficult to decide how to define "simplicity." When dealing with explanations of equal power, the one with fewer basic hypotheses seems clearly the simpler. Sometimes, however, writers use "simpler" to mean "more natural." In *The Problems of Philosophy*,[3] Bertrand Russell, faced with the alternative that the world of our conscious experience is only a world of ideas produced by a World Spirit or God and the alternative that the world of experience is the product of our encounter with independent material objects, decided that the latter was to be accepted as simpler because it fits our ordinary view—that is, it was more "natural."

We must, then, warn that while the test of simplicity might be clear in some instances, the notion of simplicity is relatively vague. This, in turn, makes it unclear how to use the test in many cases.

In conclusion, it should be noted that searches for explanations frequently are searches for causes and for universal laws expressing causal relationships. We will discuss causes and methods of finding causes in Chapter 9.

EXERCISES

Each of the following exercises presents an argument that is meant to be an explanation or a prediction. Set out the argument in the standard way introduced in Chapter 5 and test it for validity. Also note any questionable premiss—that is, one that may not be true or that requires further examination. Here is an example. Try it first; then read the answer below to make sure you have understood the instructions.

Charlotte turns her head away from people when talking to them because she has an inferiority complex. We all know that Dr. Knowitall has observed that people with an inferiority complex turn their heads away when conversing with other people.

The cue word "because" signals a premiss. Look next for the conclusion, which we find in the first part of the first sentence. The argument basically is offering an *explanation* of Charlotte's behavior. The explanation involves deducing her behavior from a regularity discovered by Dr. Knowitall plus the knowledge that Charlotte has an inferiority complex. By showing us that we can deduce the prob-

[3] Bertrand Russell, *The Problems of Philosophy* (London: Oxford University Press, 1967), p. 10.

lematic behavior of Charlotte in this way, we are shown the connections that make the explanation logical. In standard argument form this reads:

1. All people with an inferiority complex are people who usually turn their heads away during conversations.
2. Charlotte is someone who has an inferiority complex.
3. *Therefore* Charlotte is someone who usually turns her head away during conversations.

We can test the argument by a Venn diagram, which shows it is valid:

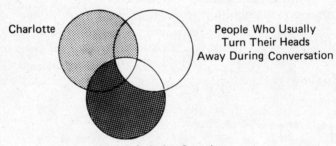

Charlotte

People Who Usually
Turn Their Heads
Away During Conversation

People with an Inferiority Complex

Now try the following:

   I. Because the dinosaurs suddenly became extinct, they can only have died as a result of a great flood. The only great flood known to have occurred at that time is the flood from which Noah and the animals escaped in the Ark.

  II. In *The Big Country*, the hero is an eastern dude who hasn't shot a gun in ten years and doesn't in the film; in addition, all the westerners in this film are mean or crude. *There Was a Crooked Man* is essentially the story of a prison break, which happens to be set in the West, and the hero is a cold-blooded killer. These plots fail to reinforce the mythical structure of the Western, and thus their financial failure lends support to the notion that successful Westerns are determined not solely by stars and advertising but, to a large degree, by the presence of the expected social symbolism.[4]

[4] Will Wright, *Six Guns and Society* (Berkeley: University of California Press, 1975), p. 14.

III. Descartes himself recognized serious difficulties in his position. If mind and matter were totally different things, how could there be a working relation between the two? How could the body act upon the soul, and vice versa? This question caused much trouble; he had to look about for the point of interaction, the "seat of the soul." Some of the ancients had placed the soul in one place, some in another. But medical studies had begun to point clearly to the importance of the brain. The trouble with the brain for Descartes's purposes was that it is "paired," right and left, and divided more finely into smaller structures which are arranged symmetrically on either side. But the pineal gland, the functions of which were unknown, is deeply embedded in the center of the brain. There is only one pineal gland; and it necessarily follows, thought Descartes, that it is the seat of the soul. This gland acted to transmit physical stimuli to the soul, and to transmit impulses from the soul to the body.[5]

IV. Although a patient may complain loud and long about a toothache, it frequently happens that the pain disappears while the patient is sitting in the dentist's waiting room. My guess is that *anxiety* can affect how one reacts to pain situations. Hence the anxiety of sitting in the dentist's waiting room, contemplating the dentist's needles and drills, actually results in the patient's feeling no pain at that time.

V. Pioneer 11, the United States space probe, has provided evidence that Jupiter is a star, not a planet. It found that Jupiter gave off more than twice the amount of heat it gets from the sun. This heat must come from nuclear reactions on Jupiter similar to the nuclear reactions that account for the sun's heat and light.

[5] Gardner Murphy, *Historical Introduction to Modern Psychology* (New York: Harcourt, Brace & World, 1949), pp. 18–19.

THREE

CONNECTING EVENTS

7

Experience Proves the Rule: Inductive Reasoning

INDUCTIVE REASONING

Suppose that a friend of yours—let us call her Arabella—takes a space trip to the planet Mars. After some wandering around, she encounters a Martian. Among other things, she observes that the Martian is green in color and has three eyes. Sometime later she encounters a second Martian who is also green and has three eyes. For the rest of the day Arabella wanders around the surface of the planet Mars and encounters fifty Martians, all of whom are green and have three eyes. After this, she returns to Earth and comes to your house to tell you about the Martians She tells you that all Martians are green and have three eyes. We can express her reasoning in the following way:

Premiss 1: The first Martian I saw was green and had three eyes.

Premiss 2: The second Martian I saw was green and had three eyes.

.

.

.

Premiss 50: The fiftieth Martian I saw was green and had three eyes.

Conclusion: *Therefore* all Martians are green and have three eyes.

An argument of this form is called an *inductive argument*. The thing to note about this argument form is that it moves from specific individual facts to a general conclusion. As you can see, this is different from the deductive argument form, which we looked at in Chapters 4 and 5. In the deductive forms we always had a general claim, such as "All whales are mammals." We then arrived at certain facts based on that general claim in conjunction with some other facts.

In the inductive argument given in the Arabella example, Arabella has taken individual facts, based on her own observations, and worked to a general conclusion. The individual facts, in Arabella's experience, were things such as that the first Martian she met was green and had three eyes, the fiftieth Martian she met was green and had three eyes, and all the Martians in between had these same characteristics. From this she concluded that all Martians have three eyes and are green. We have no reason to believe that she saw every Martian. Note that what Arabella has done in this argument is not just conclude that all the Martians she *has seen* are green and have three eyes, but rather that *all* Martians are green and have three eyes. That is, Arabella now believes that the next Martian that she meets, even though she has never seen it before, and all the Martians living on the planet Mars, have three eyes and are green. And the conclusion of the argument above, which expresses her belief, asserts this to be the case.

An inductive argument attempts to establish a conclusion on the basis of evidence or reasons, just as any argument does. But inductive arguments differ from deductive arguments in that their conclusions go beyond what is strictly stated in their premisses. In Arabella's case she generalized on the basis of a number of particular examples encountered in her experience; hence her conclusion encompassed Martians not mentioned by the premisses. For this reason, inductive arguments cannot guarantee that their conclusions are absolutely true when their premisses are true, in the way valid deductive arguments can. For example, it is always possible that the next Martian Arabella meets will *not* be green. Normally this limitation is expressed by saying that the truth of the premisses of an inductive argument provides support for and good reason to believe the conclusion while not actually entailing the truth of the conclusion.[1]

[1] The terms "induction" and "inductive" unfortunately are ambiguous. The classical sense of induction, to be found in Aristotle or John Stuart Mill, refers to generalization from particular instances. Since this meaning of "inductive" does not cover all types of arguments outside the class of valid deductive arguments, some writers prefer to distinguish deductive from *nondeductive* inferences. The latter are defined as arguments in which the truth of the premisses does not *entail* the truth of the conclusion. There are numerous philosophical problems related to nondeductive inferences that we cannot introduce here. Interested readers might consult the Bibliography for suggested readings on this topic.

The distinction between deductive and inductive arguments can be made simpler by considering two examples. First, consider the valid deductive argument,

1. All flowers are colored.
2. All roses are flowers.
3. *Therefore* all roses are colored.

Here the truth of the premisses *entails* the conclusion. Given the truth of the premisses, it *must* be true that all roses are colored. Next consider this inductive argument:

1. The carrots in sample A were Grade II.
2. The carrots in sample B were Grade II.
3. The carrots in sample C were Grade II.
4. *Therefore* all the carrots in the shipment we sampled are Grade II.

While the testing done on the samples does provide support for the stated conclusion, the premisses of this argument do not entail that the conclusion *must* be true under all circumstances. We might very well find some carrots someplace in the shipment that were *not* Grade II.

Induction in the classical sense of generalization from particular, specific examples is extremely useful, provided we recognize its limitations. We often use inductive reasoning of this type to formulate hypotheses when searching for an explanation. The majority of the general propositions expressing scientific laws and general truths about the world are inductive generalizations based on experience.

This point deserves special attention. In Chapter 2 we distinguished three basic types of statements: definitions, factual statements, and statements that are merely emotive. Factual statements are very important in expressing our knowledge, because they attempt to state something—a fact—about the world. Some of these will be very specific, such as, "My best friend is Frieda Ginger, who lives at 123 Main Street." Some are more general, such as, "All my friends are in college." How do you arrive at general statements? You can only arrive at them by building on specific pieces of information. Billy is in college, Betty is in college, and so on; therefore, *all* your friends are in college. We arrive at general truths and general knowledge by piecing together individual facts. This is how Arabella proceeded in the Martian example. Arabella put together the information she gathered on her visit to Mars and formed the general conclusion that all Martians are green and have three eyes. Because it provides us with important general facts, inductive reasoning is crucial to our ability to think correctly about things and to argue logically.

You can also see from this that inductive and deductive reasoning often go together and that sometimes deductive reasoning depends on inductive reasoning. You cannot draw deductive conclusions about whales and their properties if you have no information about whales. Even if *you* obtain facts from a book, *someone* must have gotten those facts about whales by studying individual whales, gathering information about each one, and piecing that information together. Forming generalizations about whales that are based on specific facts but that go beyond those facts—in that the generalizations are claimed to be true of *all* whales—is an instance of inductive reasoning. And an argument that employs such reasoning is an inductive argument.

You met *chains* of reasoning earlier, in Chapters 5 and 6. In such chains of arguments, premisses of one argument are supported by separate independent arguments. For example, consider the deductive argument,

1. All dolphins are playful.
2. Flipper is a dolphin.
3. *Therefore* Flipper is playful.

This is a valid deductive argument. However, for the conclusion to be acceptable, *not only* must the argument be valid, but *also* the premisses must be true. Thus premiss 1 must be true. But how do we know that premiss 1 is true? Someone must have discovered this general truth by experience—perhaps by conducting experiments in which dolphins were taught games. In other words, this premiss must have been arrived at by inductive reasoning. Therefore the deductive argument about Flipper has a prior link lending support to its first premiss. This link is an inductive argument that concludes, from specific statements of fact, that all dolphins are playful.

DANGERS IN INDUCTIVE REASONING

As suggested at the end of the last section, one must be aware of the pitfalls of induction, just as one must always be aware of and alert to possible misuses of any argument form. There are some general things to watch for in using and in analyzing inductive arguments.

The first rule is: *Never jump to a conclusion.* Although an inductive argument involves going beyond the premisses in that an inductive argument offers a conclusion that exceeds the evidence offered in its premisses, one cannot reach a reasonable and acceptable inductive conclusion from just any set of premisses. While the example of Arabella and the Martians is certainly reasonable, the following is surely silly.

> The vegetables are all terribly overcooked at Bill's Restaurant because the vegetable I had the first time I went to Bill's a couple of weeks ago was overcooked. And I have never gone back.

Obviously, this is hardly a good argument. On the basis of *one* and *only one* experience, the speaker has claimed that *all* the vegetables at Bill's are *always* overcooked. Clearly, one sampling is not enough. But had the speaker gone several times with the same result, and had friends reported similar experiences at Bill's, she *could* legitimately conclude that the vegetables at Bill's are always overcooked. This conclusion has at least a degree of probability high enough to make the speaker certain that if one wants a good dinner one had better avoid Bill's Restaurant. The moral to be drawn is that one must have enough evidence to feel justified in drawing the conclusion. With inductive arguments it is often a matter of judgment to decide when one *has* enough evidence. The error of jumping to a conclusion is sometimes called the "fallacy of hasty generalization."

Another rule is: *Evidence must be relevant.* Consider another example about Bill's Restaurant:

> When we went to Bill's last night my vegetable was overcooked, and Sally was given a soiled napkin, and the lighting was harsh. Obviously they just don't know how to cook food at Bill's.

While this argument *appears* to provide several pieces of evidence—three to be exact—for the conclusion that "they just don't know how to cook food at Bill's," it *really* is just the same argument as the previous one, based on the one overcooked vegetable. This is because the other issues—the soiled napkin and the lighting—are not related to the cooking and, therefore, do not lead to the general conclusion that the food is poorly prepared. However, if this argument presented the conclusion that Bill's is not a good place at which to eat, it would be a much better and stronger argument. Overcooked vegetables, soiled napkins, and harsh lighting can all be related to each other as factors relevant to one's enjoyment of a meal, even though they are *not* all relevant to a judgment about the ability of the cooking staff at Bill's to prepare food properly. The key idea is that when either formulating or analyzing an argument, you must stick to the point.

STATISTICAL ARGUMENTS

Everyone is familiar with statistical arguments, and it is not difficult to see that they fit our definition of an inductive argument by virtue of having conclusions that go beyond the evidence stated in the premisses. As such, the conclusions of statistical arguments are only probable. But the advantage of such arguments is that they allow us to formulate a useful conclusion that has application *beyond* the range of items mentioned in the premisses. Suppose, for example, that we were grading the apples in a bushel basket of apples. Our procedure would be to take a few samples from here and there in the basket. Imagine that 90 percent were found to be Grade A. We would then conclude that 90 percent of all the apples in the basket were Grade A. In other words, we would have moved from the evidence that 90 percent of the apples we observed in the sampling were Grade A to the general conclusion that 90 percent of all the apples in the basket were Grade A. This is obviously a useful method, because no one would want to have to look at every apple in a carload to decide whether they were Grade A.

Because people using statistics are usually dealing with large quantities, they need a device for arriving at a general conclusion without having to investigate every single item. If you were trying to establish television ratings for a program, it would be impossible to ask every person in the United States what show he or she was watching, say, last Tuesday at 9:00 P.M. One must take a limited "sample" (or number of people), ask these people what show they were watching, and, on the assumption that these few are representative of the population as a whole, form a general conclusion about the popularity of the particular program; say, that 70 percent watched the "Movie of the Week."

Everyone must be alert to the dangers of statistical arguments that employ either insufficient or biased statistics. Here is an example in which a conclusion is based on *insufficient statistics*:

> Our representative, in his speech to Congress, reported that the people in his district were for capital punishment. He claimed he had talked to people at one of the local supermarkets for a half-hour on Monday morning.

Clearly, sampling a few people in one location in a short space of time is not very reliable in determining the opinions of a whole district. This inductive argument fails to be convincing because it employs insufficient evidence.

Now consider the following example of an argument that employs *biased statistics*.

Last night the city council encountered a momentary setback in its attempt to oust the City Planner, George Slacker, on the grounds of neglect of duty and incompetence. The setback occurred when Mr. Slacker argued, on the basis of ten letters attesting to his professional competence, his integrity, trustworthiness, thriftiness, and willingness to do a good deed every day that 80 percent of the people of the city supported him. The members of the council were at a loss how to handle the situation until it was brought to their attention that one of the letters was written by Mr. Slacker's brother, one by his sister, another by a second cousin, and two by his mother (using her married and maiden names).

In this case, Mr. Slacker was advancing a statistical argument that employed statements from close relatives as reasons (premises) for the conclusion that he was competent. The argument is not only deficient in using biased statistical evidence; it also entails fallacious appeals to authority, in that there is no reason to believe that Slacker's relatives are authorities on the duties of a professional city planner.

As these two examples illustrate, you should watch for both insufficient and biased statistics when formulating and evaluating arguments.

ANALOGIES

Another form of inductive argument is the analogy. This form was demonstrated in Chapter 1 in our example of the experimenter testing food coloring. Basically, an argument by analogy compares two or more things or classes of things and argues that because they are similar in certain respects, it is reasonable to conclude that they are similar in a further respect that we have not been able to observe directly.

Consider the case of an agricultural researcher testing new enriched feeds. One group of sheep is given normal feed while another is given an enriched diet. The researcher discovers that all the sheep given the enriched diet are more active, less disease-prone, and have thicker wool than the sheep that received ordinary feed. From this the researcher decides that all the sheep of the farmers in the district would benefit similarly from the enriched diet. When the statements are expressed one by one, the argument involves the following steps:

1. The enriched diet benefitted the sheep in the test group.
2. The farmers' sheep are similar to the sheep in the test group.
3. *Therefore* the farmers' sheep will benefit from the enriched diet.

Premiss 1 was something the researcher discovered directly by observation. Premiss 2 is actually a summing up of a number of known facts about similarities in physiological structure, body chemistry, and environment that exist between the researcher's sheep and the farmers' sheep. Thus we have an analogy that involves a comparison of two different groups that have certain similarities. From a knowledge or observation of *some* similarities between the individuals of the two groups, we argue that they may be similar in other respects. In our example, the further suggested similarity has to do with the animals' thriving on an enriched diet.

Being able to recognize similarities between two or more individuals or classes is an important skill in reasoning. In searching for possible explanations when we have a problem or puzzle, we frequently look for a similar situation that might afford a clue to a reasonable hypothesis. Processes we are uncertain about—such as human thinking—are often considered in terms of analogies: is the mind like a mechanism, such as a watch, or is it like a computer? Such analogies provide us with models that we hope will help us to understand better what we do not at present fully comprehend. By considering thinking processes to be *like* the operations of a computer, we might be alerted to features we should look for and expect in a human brain or in human conscious experience.

It is important to note that not every analogy and not every mention of similarities amounts to the presentation of an argument. We often use analogies merely to illustrate or amplify points or in descriptions and explanations. We can call this a *nonargumentative use of analogy*. To say, "The effect of the hailstorm on the crops was like dropping hundreds of golf balls on a window box of violets" is to use an analogy in an imaginative way to describe an event. This is an example of a nonargumentative use of an analogy.

By contrast, an *argument by analogy* points out similarities between two things and then draws the conclusion—that is, *argues*—that they will be similar in a further respect. Here is an example of an argument by analogy. "The red ball and the yellow ball are exactly alike in weight, texture and diameter; since the red ball can be made to bounce over the wall, therefore it should be possible to make the yellow ball bounce over the wall too." As we pointed out at the beginning of this section, an argument by analogy has premises that state similarities between two things or classes of things and then draws the inference—that is, concludes—that a further property possessed by one will also be possessed by the other. We can express the *structure* of an argument by analogy more precisely in the following way.

1. Thing X and Thing Y have property P.
2. Thing X and Thing Y have property Q.

3. Thing X and Thing Y have property R.
4. Thing X and Thing Y have property S.
5. Thing X has property T.
6. *Therefore* Thing Y also (probably) has property T.

Here we have four premisses—1 through 4—stating relevant similarities between the two items X and Y. Premiss 5 states that we have evidence that X has the further property T. The proposition 6 concludes from these premisses that Thing Y will (probably) also have the further property T. We can see this structure in the case of the example of the red and yellow balls just mentioned. Let "R" stand for "red ball" and "Y" stand for "yellow ball." We then have:

1. R and Y both have the same weight.
2. R and Y both have the same texture.
3. R and Y both have the same diameter.
4. R will bounce over the wall.
5. *Therefore* Y will (probably) bounce over the wall.

There are some famous arguments in the history of Western thought that employ analogies. Two of these are the Argument from Design and the Argument About Other Minds.

The Argument from Design

The Argument from Design centers on the question, Is there a proof of God's existence? Some believe that there *are* clear proofs and that one such proof is offered by the structure and marvelous order of the natural world. The complex order of this physical world demonstrates that there must have been an intelligent, rational God who created it. The Argument from Design proceeds by arguing from analogy. It attempts to show that if we compare the physical universe to manmade, designed objects such as watches, we will be forced to conclude that there is a God. The Scottish philosopher David Hume (1711–1776) presented this argument—as well as criticisms of it—in a lively and useful way. Here Hume introduces the Argument from Design:

> Look round the world, contemplate the whole and every part of it:
> you will find it is nothing but one great machine, subdivided into an in-
> finite number of lesser machines, which again admit of subdivisions. . . .
> All these various machines . . . are adjusted to each with an accuracy
> which ravishes into admiration all men who have ever contemplated

them. The curious adapting of means to ends, throughout all nature, resembles exactly, though it much exceeds, the productions of human contrivance—of human design, thought, wisdom, and intelligence. Since therefore the effects resemble each other, we are led to infer, by all the rules of analogy, that . . . the Author of nature is somewhat similar to the mind of man, though possessed of much larger faculties, proportioned to the grandeur of the work which he has executed. By this argument . . . we prove at once the existence of a Deity and his similarity to human mind and intelligence.[2]

In the first two sentences Hume urges us to note that the world can be seen to be like a machine, and it is easy to grasp the appeal of this. Machines, such as cars, have parts that are designed so that they interact with one another to serve a purpose. And parts of a car, such as a carburetor, are themselves composed of smaller parts. The natural world also seems ordered and purposeful. For example, there seems an order to the relationships between various species. Small animals, such as rabbits, with many natural enemies, breed in great numbers, while the larger animals that prey on them, such as wolves, have few offspring. In this way a balance is maintained, to the end that both species survive.

Similarities between natural creatures and machines are also easy to note. What could be more similar than, on the one hand, the circulatory system of a cat, which has a heart pumping blood through special tubing, and, on the other hand, a water system designed to pump, by means of a gasoline engine, water through pipes? In fact both the cat's heart and the water pump use fuel, although different *kinds* of fuel. Both require oxygen. And so on. Certainly, it is not unreasonable to think of the world as being similar to a watch, a car, or a water system in terms of having parts ordered and organized to perform selected functions and to serve specific purposes.

Having established that there are observed similarities between machines and the natural world, Hume's analogical argument now infers a further similarity. In doing so it goes beyond the content of its premises—the statements of similarities and resemblances—and because it does so this analogy, as any analogy, is classified as an inductive argument. The conclusion is that since we know that watches and water systems are the result of the work of intelligent planners or designers, we can conclude that the order and purpose in the world are the result of the intelligent designing abilities of a rational designer, namely God. In the last sentence Hume points out that the argument has not only shown that God exists but has demon-

---

[2] David Hume, *Dialogues Concerning Natural Religion* (New York: Hafner Publishing Company, 1948), p. 17.

strated that He must be of an intelligence similar to human intelligence.

The Argument from Design displays the same structure as any analogy. Briefly stated, the argument is:

1. The world and machines are similar in certain respects, such as order and interrelationships.
2. Machines have intelligent designers.
3. *Therefore* the world must have had an intelligent designer.

While the Argument from Design has a great deal of appeal and plausibility, it is open to criticism, as Hume readily saw. In fact Hume thought the Argument from Design was not, in the final analysis, adequate for proving God's existence. First, Hume asked whether there were enough similarities and whether they were relevant. (These are key worries about analogies—the similarities upon which an analogical argument is built must be *adequate* to link the items together, and the similarities mentioned must be *relevant*.) For example, Hume suggests that if we think of a house, the design of an architect and house builder, it is hard to think of the universe as being similar to it in design. This makes it less certain that we can reasonably think of the universe as having a builder.

Second, Hume attacks the Argument from Design by arguing that it leads us to a scandalous view of God. For example, human designers of watches and water systems often make mistakes, as we all know from our experience, and so we can also legitimately conclude, by analogy, that God could be capable of mistakes. Perhaps God has tried a number of times to make a perfect world and has failed every time. Surely this is an unacceptable and unorthodox conception of God. Because the analogy used here leads us to this untenable conclusion, the analogy must be rejected. (Here Hume is using a powerful form of critical argument called a *reductio ad absurdum*, or a reducing of things to absurdity. This argument form will be discussed in Chapter 8.)

The Argument About Other Minds

There are a number of beliefs that virtually everyone endorses. We all believe that we live in a world of physical objects and that we are not alone in this world—that there are other beings just like us. These other human beings have similar experiences to ours and react to events much as we do. If another person hits his thumb with a hammer he feels a severe pain in his thumb and will yell, hold the thumb, and perhaps even curse the hammer. We would react in a similar fashion. If you see a flash of white jagged lightning during a thunderstorm, you expect that others around you also see that flash of lightning, provided they are looking in the right direction and have normal vision. There is nothing more natural and common than our belief that the people around us, whom we encounter every day in a variety of situations and contexts, have the same kind of experiences we do. They see the red color of a traffic light, get heartburn from eating too much pizza with hot pepper on it, think of what they will have for dinner tomorrow, get sore feet, have headaches, and take pleasure in being complimented. In short they have all the mental experiences— the pains and pleasures, the fears, angers, and jealousies—that we ourselves have. How could we doubt this?

While we may not doubt that other people have the same kinds of conscious mental experiences we have, it is not obvious how we know they are having experiences similar to ours. If we think about it, a pain, for example, is private. When you hit your thumb *you* feel a pain, but your friend standing beside you does not feel that same pain. Only you *have* the pain caused by the blow of the hammer. Your friend only knows that you are in pain because he hears you yell or sees you jumping around holding your thumb with your face screwed up in agony. In other words, while each of us experiences our own pain in the sense that we actually *feel* the sting of the needle, the warmth of the blush, or the knotting in our stomach, other people *never* feel our stings, warm sensations, or angry knottings. Other people never experience our inner sensations and feelings; they only observe our "outer" side, our behavior, such as yells or exclamations. How, then, do other people *know for certain* that you are in pain when you are, and how do they ever know the exact *kind* of pain you are having? They can never *feel* your pains, so how can they know how you are feeling? Again, if you think about something and don't say anything or betray your thought by your actions, how can anyone ever know what you are thinking about?

The answer to this is that others know about your feelings and thoughts by analogy with their own experiences. They know that when they hit their thumbs with a hammer they feel a pain, because they can and do experience their *own* pains. When they see you hit your thumb with a hammer, they *inductively infer* that you also feel a pain. This conclusion is reached by an *analogy*; other people assume similar reactions and feelings in you because you are similar to them in structure and overall make-up. It is an *inductive* inference because it goes beyond the outward similarities among people to the conclusion that you, another person, have a specific, conscious mental experience.

The nineteenth-century philosopher John Stuart Mill asked the same question. Here is his answer:

> I conclude that other human beings have feelings like me, because, first, they have bodies like me, which I know, in my own case, to be the antecedent condition of feelings; and because, secondly, they exhibit the acts, and other outward signs, which in my own case I know by experience to be caused by feelings. I am conscious in myself of a series of facts connected by an uniform sequence, of which the beginning is modifications of my body, the middle is feelings, the end is outward demeanor. In the case of other human beings I have the evidence of my senses for the first and last links of the series, but not for the inter-mediate link. I find, however, that the sequence between the first and last is as regular and constant in those other cases as it is in mine. In my own case I know that the first link produces the last through the intermediate link, and could not produce it without. Experience, there-fore, obliges me to conclude that there must be an intermediate link; which must either be the same in others as in myself, or a different one: I must either believe them to be alive, or to be automatons: and by believing them to be alive, that is, by supposing the link to be of the same nature as in the case of which I have experience, and which is in all other respects similar, I bring other human beings, as phenomena, under the same generalizations which I know by experience to be the true theory of my own existence.[3]

This is an analogical argument. Its structure is:

1. Other people are similar to me. (This would be backed up with several claims about relevant similarities in terms of physical, biochemical, and behavioral organization.)
2. In certain circumstances, when I yell out "It hurts!" I actually have a *feeling* called a pain.
3. *Therefore* when other people yell out "It hurts!" in appropriate circumstances, they too *feel* a pain.

You can see that this conclusion is reasonable but only probable, as are all inductive conclusions. Obviously, you cannot *always* count on someone's being in pain just because they *act* as though they are in pain or *say* they are. Actors behave as though in pain when they are not, and people sometimes pretend to be in pain in order to get a day off from school, to be excused from an onerous task, or for a variety of other reasons. People also sometimes mask pain even though suffering intensely.

[3] J. S. Mill, *An Examination of Sir William Hamilton's Philosophy*, 6th ed. (London: Longmans, 1889), pp. 243–244.

The examples cited provide reason enough to be cautious in making inductive inferences about the mental life of other people. However, there is one criticism of this argument from analogy that you may think undermines it completely. Remember the hazard of making a hasty generalization, of drawing a conclusion from inadequate or insufficient evidence. The health inspector who looks at only one room of a large hotel can hardly form a satisfactory judgment about the way the hotel is run. Someone who meets one Scot and then assumes that all Scots must have the characteristics of the one he met has jumped to a conclusion—has made a hasty, unwarranted generalization. In the case of judgments about other minds, it can be argued that the inferences are not acceptable because they are based on only *one* example. We only know about the connections between behavior and mental states and events in our *own* case; so in making inferences about other people, we are assuming that all other people are like ourselves. We are moving from *one* example—our own experience of certain relationships—to the conclusion that these relationships hold for *all* people.

In defense of the argument it has been claimed that we are not inferring fallaciously from one case because each of us has several—indeed, hundreds—of firsthand experiences of these relationships. The critics will hardly be deterred by this, however, for their point remains that no matter how many cases within *her* experience Jones can cite, it remains that when talking about others Jones must formulate conclusions about them *solely* on the basis of *one* person's experience, namely her own.

WAYS TO EVALUATE INDUCTIVE ARGUMENTS

In looking critically at an inductive argument, you should always ask three basic questions:

1. Is the evidence *sufficient*?
2. Is the evidence *biased* or specially *selected*?
3. Is the evidence *relevant*?

A great danger with both statistical and analogical arguments is that there may not be adequate or sufficient evidence. A statistical sampling may be too small to warrant the conclusion. The similarities upon which someone bases an analogy may be too few.

Evidence must also be unbiased. It is not uncommon for people to select facts specially in order to prove a point or conveniently to "forget" points of dissimilarity while telling you about similarities.

And evidence must be *relevant*. In comparing the performance of a new kind of ski with a known type, the length and material are relevant to drawing conclusions about how the new pair of skis will perform under real-life conditions; but the *color* is not. Only a fool would conclude that the new skis will perform as well as the old ones *because* (and only because) they are the same color. Relevance, here, is clearly defined in terms of the *purpose* or *use* of the argument; some things affect how an item can be used, others do not. The color of a ski or the color of the stringing in a tennis racquet do not affect how they perform—unless the athlete using them has psychological hang-ups about certain colors or has a "lucky" color, neither of which has anything to do with the performance of the equipment as such.

In presenting or analyzing an argument from analogy, one must pay particular attention to the question of whether the situations are sufficiently similar to allow comparison. This point is illustrated by correspondence that appeared in a newspaper column devoted to solving consumer problems. The reader writes to the newspaper columnist stating a problem, and the columnist communicates with the company or government office concerned and tries to help work out a solution for the reader. The reader's initial letter plus the columnist's response and findings are subsequently published. The following letter and response involve comparisons and analogical reasoning:

TIMEX REPLIES

I have run across a Timex watch that did not stand up to their torture test advertising. During March, a gentleman was visiting his wife at the hospital where I work, and had taken off his watch to hold his newborn baby. While putting on the watch at the elevator, it slipped from his hand and fell down the elevator shaft. When the engineer retrieved it he jokingly commented this was one Timex watch that had not stood up to the torture test. I asked if I could have the watch to send to the company. I wanted to know why it didn't stand up as this was two floors only and the advertising of the diver and water skier indicated much more of a force. I also sent them a stamped addressed envelope to ensure a reply. Instead, they fixed the watch, which I had not asked them to do, and sent it back with a bill minus the 12 cents postage and no explanation. I wrote them again, because everyone I talked to thinks they should at least have had the decency to explain the difference of this Timex and the ones they use for their advertising tests. I sent them the money for repairs but I still would like an explanation about the torture test. I also want to know why they didn't write first before fixing the watch.

E. L.
Saskatoon

Timex has replied to our inquiry: " . . . true that in our advertising we authentically depict our watches being used in many shock and water testing situations . . . unless [she] is an engineer it would be impossible for her to compare the result of dropping a watch two floors down an elevator shaft to those demonstrated during one of our diving torture tests. The two situations are simply not comparable, since there is no way of determining what the watch hit at the bottom of the elevator shaft. In our advertising we attempt to demonstrate that our watches will withstand a great deal more than what the normal consumer would expect and we feel that the thousands of unsolicited testimonial letters from our customers who have experienced their own Timex torture tests certainly authenticate our claim to producing an extremely rugged watch at a very reasonable price. We do not, however, make any claim that our watches are totally shock proof; they are, however, highly shock resistant in normal use situations."[4]

The reader, E. L., is arguing that since the watch that fell down the elevator shaft is the same as the ones used in the famous torture test, it should have stood up to the "torture" of being dropped down an elevator shaft. That is, on the basis of the similarity between this watch and the ones in the torture test (all are Timex watches), she reasons, by analogy, that this watch should withstand shocks. Notice that since this watch did not survive its trip down the elevator shaft, she wonders whether there is a difference between it and the watches they use in the torture test. Again, she is arguing well by considering the possibility that there is not the similarity requisite for drawing the analogy and, therefore, for expecting the same endurance in her watch. Implicit in this is her worry that the torture test ads are misleading if they use special watches.

On the other side of the question, the person responding for Timex makes clear the intent of the torture test advertisements and tells of letters from consumers confirming the ability of Timex watches to withstand shocks in everyday situations. The Timex representative also argues that it is not possible to compare the torture tests to dropping a watch down an elevator shaft. This claim is an attempt to defeat E. L.'s argument by showing that the analogical conclusion— that the watch that fell down the shaft should have withstood the drop—cannot be drawn.

The difficulty in this dispute seems to be that there is a gradation of possible abuses that a watch might suffer. While you are asleep, your watch is not likely to suffer any shock, especially if it is lying on your dresser. This is one extreme. The other extreme would include abuse such as being put in a cement mixer or run over by a

[4] Dene Creswell, "Trouble Shooting," *The Saskatoon Star-Phoenix*, May 10, 1977, p. 20. Quoted by permission.

steamroller. No one expects a watch to be damaged while it is on your dresser; everyone will expect it to be severely damaged by the steamroller. The debate in our example is about the points between such extremes that are represented by falling down a shaft or being subjected to a torture test. The writer thinks the two are at the same point between the extremes. The Timex agent thinks a drop down an elevator shaft is more like an encounter with a steamroller, while the torture tests are clearly far down the scale toward the other extreme. Here there is clearly a problem about language of the sort discussed in Chapter 1: What constitutes "torture"?

In addition to keeping alert to the above dangers and possible areas of criticism, you can also attack inductive arguments if you can find *another* conclusion that might follow from the premisses. This weakens the inductive argument by showing that the stated conclusion is not the only possible conclusion, and it will be destructive of that argument if the alternative conclusion is contrary to the purposes of the person advancing the argument.

Perhaps an illustration will make this point clearer. In attacking the Argument from Design, Hume suggested that there were a number of "extra" conclusions we might draw once we had established the similarities between the order of the natural world and the order of man-made objects such as watches and houses. To take one, Hume suggested that it is possible, on the basis of the analogy set up, to conclude that the Divine Designer (God) makes mistakes, the way human house builders and watchmakers sometimes do. This conclusion, Hume claims, is just as legitimate as any other conclusion, in that establishing these similarities licenses us inductively to infer a further point of similarity. So why not that God is imperfect? This is a good attack on the Argument from Design because it offers a reasonable conclusion drawn from the same premisses (the statements of the similarities), but a conclusion that no one advancing the Argument from Design would ever accept. So it presents the propounder of the Argument from Design with a difficult choice: either give up the argument and, with it, the proof of God's existence, or else accept an additional, unacceptable conclusion.

EXERCISES

I. This exercise is designed to help you recognize inductive arguments. In each of the following examples, premisses are given from which a conclusion follows, but the conclusion is not stated. In each case you are to state the conclusion that follows from the given premisses.

Here is an example:

All swans ever seen before the discovery of Australia were white. In Australia, black swans were found.

The conclusion we can inductively infer from these statements is "All swans are either black or white." Beware the temptation to draw conclusions you are not warranted to draw from these premises. For example, you cannot conclude that "All Australian swans are black," because, even if true, the premises neither say nor imply it. The first sentence says that many swans have been observed to be white, while the second says many swans have (in Australia) been observed to be black. All we can conclude is that all swans are either black or white, as opposed to some other color.

Try the following on your own:

1. A recent survey interviewed people suffering from colds who had taken Dr. Good's Patented Cold Syrup. Over 90 percent of these people reported that their colds were gone within a day or two.
2. All the hillbillies we met on our trip were pretty dumb, which is not surprising since they all drank corn whiskey.
3. Professor Smart did exhaustive studies of subjects who had temporary or permanent amnesia. In each case he found that there was some form of brain damage or malfunction. Many temporary cases were restored by use of drugs or surgical procedures, which confirmed his findings.
4. Experiments done this year showed that no viable crop of citrus fruit could be grown in this area. Similar experimental attempts over the last 15 years produced similar results.
5. The students in Professor Smith's section of introductory biology had a 37 percent failure rate. Professor Jameson's two sections had failure rates of 36 percent and 37.7 percent respectively. The students of the other professors had failure rates of 36.2 percent, 38 percent, 37.3 percent, 36.4 percent, and 37.9 percent.

II. Each of the following is meant to appear to provide adequate premisses for a sound inductive inference. However, some do not, and some of them are questionable for specific reasons. In each case you are to decide whether a conclusion follows or not. Also, mention any conclusion that the imagined arguers might be hoping we would accept as implied by the premisses; indicate why that conclusion is not justified.

Here is an example:

George and Fred are both poor. And they both use vulgar language.

No inductive conclusion follows. Remember that an inductive conclusion goes beyond the content of the premisses, so it is *not* a conclusion that "Fred and George are poor *and* use vulgar language," because that just repeats the premisses.

Presumably, the arguer here hopes we take the conclusion "All poor people use vulgar language" or "All people using vulgar language are poor." But neither of these is justified, because the evidence, being based on just two examples out of millions of people, is insufficient. So nothing follows in this case.

Try the following on your own:

1. Bill is skeptical about going to the theatre tonight. He says that the last two plays he saw were terrible and he has no reason to think this one will be any better.
2. Now is the time to bet on tails coming up. The last 15 times it has come up heads, so the coin is due to come up tails.
3. After she discovered that most of the wine had gone bad, Samantha went to the police to tell them her story and her theory about the wine. They suggested that the people she suspected might have another explanation for the state of the wine, but agreed to investigate.
4. I don't care what the studies show. Aunt Bessie had treatments involving Laetrile and was cured of cancer. And Billy's friend in Omaha also took Laetrile and she didn't die of cancer either. The same for my grandmother.
5. The prince said that he did not want to go on his planned North American tour because every time he had left home in the past, there was an attempted coup.

III. Here are some more complex inductive arguments. Analyze each, stating the premisses and conclusion. Evaluate the arguments in terms of the criteria of relevance; adequacy; and selectivity of evidence, or bias.

1. Recently, there has been much concern about the increasing number of male nurses in geriatric hospitals. A spokesman for one group of doctors has claimed that elderly patients respond better and recover more quickly when cared for by female nurses. He said this was because the elderly are very like children in terms of their needs and attitudes and that women are, by nature, more suited to the care of children.
2. Lowering highway speed limits will not only save gas; it will save lives. The Traffic Research Council reported that in each of the three years when lower speed limits were in effect in

35 states, the number of deaths from automobile accidents was reduced at least a full 20 percent from the previous annual rate. This was true in every year in every one of the 35 states surveyed.

3. Female nurses are "molested" by male patients—grabbed or pinched—not because they encourage it or are seductively attractive but simply because of something in the male attitude. A questionnaire completed by female nurses in all the hospitals in the city clearly indicated that even women who were homely (by their own description) and who had not encouraged interest in men were sexually molested in the course of performing their duties. Over 90 percent of those who handed in the questionnaire had been the victims of such an indignity on at least one occasion.

4. The game "Death Race," in which one drives a simulated car in an attempt to "kill" as many make-believe pedestrians as possible in a given period of time, should be banned. Just as football shapes character by encouraging the positive attitudes of personal courage and support for a group effort, "Death Race" will foster the negative attitude of disregard for people and will associate this with driving a car. The result will be to encourage bad driving and dangerous driving on our streets and highways.

5. I don't agree, General. We cannot trust Smithers to lead the detail against that machine gun position. Why, he couldn't even pass his class in English literature. And half the time his locker is a mess. No, we must trust this to someone else.

8

Some Perplexing Arguments: The Dilemma and the Reductio

THE DILEMMA

We all know what it is to be in a dilemma. Suppose Len has promised his wife that he will go on a rigid diet. A few days after starting the diet he and his wife visit his kindly Aunt Mary. They stay for tea and Aunt Mary offers Len a piece of her justly famous chocolate cream pie. What is he to do? If he refuses to have a piece of pie, Aunt Mary will feel insulted. If he has a piece of pie, Aunt Mary will be pleased, but his wife will be disappointed in him for going off his diet. Which way can he turn? No matter what he does, he will displease either Aunt Mary or his wife. This is a genuine dilemma.

The above example points out the key to a dilemma: it *forces* someone to choose between two alternatives, both of which are unpleasant. Since there usually are but two alternatives available in a dilemma, and no other choices, the situation has been described as similar to being faced with a charging bull. Each of the bull's horns represents one of the alternative choices. The idea is that, no matter what, you will be caught by one of the two horns of the dilemma.

It is a devastating technique in an argument to place one's opponent in this position. To highlight this point, imagine a debate among members of the Federal Reserve Board about inflation. One group is proposing to introduce high interest rates on loans and mortgages in order to slow down or halt the inflationary spiral. An opponent of this proposal argues against higher interest rates on the grounds that they will either be worse than useless or will increase unemployment. In other words, either higher interest rates will not succeed in holding down inflation—in which case they will create needless hardship for borrowers—or, if they do succeed in holding down inflation, it will be at the expense of people who are put out of work. The opponent puts this argument in the form of a dilemma:

> If higher interest rates do not curb inflation, then a lot of suffering by those with mortgages and loans will have occurred for nothing. If having higher interest rates does lower inflation, then it will cause greater unemployment. The proposal either will not produce the desired result or else it will have an additional bad consequence. Therefore, we ought not to accept the proposal for higher interest rates.

To develop the dilemma, we point out two possibilities: either (1) the proposed new interest rates will curb inflation or (2) they will not. These two alternatives exclude any other choices. The next step is to establish that an undesirable consequence results from either of the alternatives. On the one hand, we have hardship for borrowers and no effect on inflation; on the other hand, we have suffering in the form of unemployment. Since the alternatives were exhaustive, we are *forced* to accept, with either alternative, one or the other of the unpleasant consequences.

If we then set out the above example according to the structure appropriate to a formal dilemma we have:

1. Either the proposed new interest rates will curb inflation or they will not.
2. If they curb inflation, then unemployment will increase.
3. If they do *not* curb inflation, then needless hardship will be caused for borrowers.
4. *Therefore* either suffering caused by greater unemployment or useless hardship to borrowers will result from adoption of the proposed new interest rates.

In analyzing a dilemma, it is usually helpful to set it out according to this model. Assumed premises are made clear. Since the dilemma always starts with a statement of the alternatives and then draws an unacceptable or unpleasant consequence from each alternative, the structure of a dilemma can be put schematically in the following way (letting A stand for "alternative," C for "consequence," and numbers to indicate different alternatives):

1. Either A_1 or A_2.
2. If A_1, then C_1.
3. If A_2, then C_2.
4. *Therefore* either C_1 or C_2.

Also note from this schema that the constructions "if . . . then," and "either . . . or," or any other phrases that could substitute for these while performing the same functions, are *cues*. They signal the premisses of a dilemma and, thereby, serve as crucial aids to *finding* arguments of this form when analyzing reports, articles, and the like.

Two further points should be borne in mind when you are developing an argument in the form of a dilemma. First, a dilemma is most effective if it begins with two alternatives that are contradictories and therefore admit to no other possible alternative. For example, if you are alive, you are not dead. Second, a dilemma need not work from the two alternatives to two different unacceptable conclusions. Instead, it may work from two alternatives to *one* conclusion, thereby illustrating that no matter which alternative is adopted, the same (unacceptable) conclusion follows. If traveling with Fly-by-Night Airlines means you have a choice of crashing into a mountain or of drowning in the sea, then the end result is the same in either case.

One of the most famous uses of a dilemma occurs in discussion of the religious puzzle known as the problem of evil. The presence of evil in the world has always been a source of difficulty for theists, and many have thought that it is the most persistent of theological problems. That there *is* evil in our world can hardly be denied. Human pain and suffering, crime, violence, immorality, dishonesty in high and low places, all attest to the fact of evil in our world. Not all of it is caused by human beings nor visited upon the guilty, for natural disasters such as earthquakes and floods kill young babies as often as they do hardened criminals. For the most part, it is only in the pages of romantic novels that we find nature meting out justice in terms of selective disasters.

But how are we to interpret the evil in our world? Is it somehow part of a divine plan, perhaps a trial of the faith of the people? Or is it part of divine cosmic justice? or an elaborate warning system? Or is evil simply evidence that there is no God or—worse—that God is uncaring and hostile, like a malicious child who delights in causing death to a fly?

Those critical of religious belief have argued that the fact of evil shows conclusively that our world could not be the creation of an all-powerful, and loving God; nor could it be in the care of such a Being. This argument is usually put in the form of a dilemma. Consider the following version and, before you read beyond it, try to set out the steps of the argument.

God is supposed to be both all-powerful and loving. But this cannot be so; for He obviously allows evil to exist in our world, which means either that He is unable to do anything about it or that He just doesn't care.

The first sentence states two of the properties usually assigned to God; most theists consider God to have limitless power and to love every living creature. The second sentence states the conclusion: "This cannot be so"—that is, the claim in the first sentence must be false. Next come premises signaled by the cue word "for."

If we put this out in a schema of premises and conclusions, we have:

1. There is evil (pain, human misery) in the world.
2. *Either* God cannot prevent this evil *or* God does not wish to prevent this evil.
3. If God *cannot* prevent the evil, then He is not all-powerful.
4. If God does not *wish* to prevent the evil, then He is not a loving God.
5. *Therefore* God either is not all-powerful or is not loving.

(Strictly speaking, the dilemma is presented in steps 2 through 5. Premiss 1 is a fact that is really contained in 2, so it is redundant to add it as a separate premiss. However, it does no harm to spell things out fully by introducing this as a separate premiss.) The conclusion presents a dilemma for the theist, who believes that God is *both* all-powerful *and* loving—as the first sentence of the original version of the argument states. The dilemma, as set out, is pointed and strong because the conclusion of the argument contradicts this belief.

In passing, you might note that we could make this argument even more complex by introducing God's purported infinite wisdom, or omniscience. We could then add a premiss stating that even if God cares and has the power, perhaps He does not *know* about the evil in the world. This would add a further alternative to the conclusion, namely that God is not all-knowing or infinitely wise—which, again, would be unacceptable to orthodox belief. However, arguments constructed on the basis of dilemmas usually contain only two alternatives, because the aim is to provide exhaustive alternatives in the first premiss.

One might find someone building onto a dilemma, though, in order to create a means of escape. One obvious defense against the above argument, for example, would be to deny that these are the only alternatives. Another possibility might be that while God knows and cares and has the power to alter things, He is just, thereby allowing evil as punishment for sin.

Here is an example of a dilemma in which each initial alternative is shown to lead to one and the same consequence. The English philosopher and political theorist John Stuart Mill—whose work has been quoted earlier—was an advocate of free speech. He argued that a government has no right to silence anyone, nor does any group have the right to try to coerce people or refuse to let them speak out, no matter how wrong the majority might consider their opinion to be. Here is part of Mill's argument:

> The peculiar evil of silencing the expression of an opinion is that it is robbing the human race, posterity as well as the existing generation— those who dissent from the opinion, still more those who hold it. If the opinion is right, they are deprived of the opportunity of exchanging error for truth; if wrong, they lose, what is almost as great a benefit, the clearer perception and livelier impression of truth produced by its collision with error.[1]

The repeated cue word "if" signals premisses of a dilemma. Set out according to the schematic model for a dilemma, the argument is:

1. Any silenced opinion is either right or wrong.
2. If it is right, we lost a chance to hear the truth.
3. If it is wrong, we lose a chance to see the truth better as contrasted to the erroneous view.
4. *Therefore* by silencing an opinion we lose (either because the opinion is true or because hearing it expressed gives us a better view of the truth by contrast).

Mill's point is that no matter which alternative is true, the same consequence will result—namely that we will have lost something by not allowing someone to voice an opinion.

As you can see, dilemmas are valid deductive arguments, which is one reason they are so bothersome. If the conclusion does validly follow from the premisses, one *must* accept the conclusion. Yet the conclusion of a well-constructed dilemma is often something we do not wish to endorse.

Here is a final example that illustrates these features. It is known as the dilemma of determinism and free will.

Whenever something happens we expect that there is some *reason* why it happened. If plaster falls from the ceiling we know there must be a cause—perhaps moisture leaking in or the house settling. Likewise, if a close friend speaks harshly to you one day, you believe there is a reason or cause for such behavior; perhaps he or she had a sleepless night or learned some bad news. Trucks and cars do not just

[1] J. S. Mill, *On Liberty* (New York: Bobbs-Merrill, 1956), p. 21.

stop running for no reason at all. People do not change their positions on crucial issues for no reason at all. It seems clear that every event, human or otherwise, is determined, or brought about, by causes or sets of causal factors. (Note that we are here using "cause" in a wide sense, to include physical causes *and* psychological causes such as anger, desire, or fear.)

Now consider your own actions. If you go to the cafeteria for lunch, you might well choose an egg salad sandwich. Ask yourself whether you *freely* choose this sandwich rather than a fruit salad or vegetable soup. Again, you probably freely chose your clothes this morning; most likely no one made you pick a white rather than a blue shirt. Of course, other people and events do sometimes affect such choices. If you are to buy lunch in the cafeteria, you can't decide to eat something that is not on the menu; and going out for Sunday dinner usually requires dressier clothes than those needed for a trip to the laundromat. But at least on *some* occasions we believe that we freely select what we will eat or wear.

One could provide further examples, but these will suffice. The point to note is that we have two beliefs, as outlined in the preceding two paragraphs, which we might express by the following propositions:

D: All events have causes sufficient to explain why they happened.

F: Some events, namely certain human actions, occur freely.

These have been labeled D and F because D is a statement of the thesis of universal determinism while F is a statement about human free will. To say that some actions occur freely, or are not determined, is to say that human beings have free will.

We can immediately see that these beliefs are incompatible. If D is true, then all actions are determined and so none can be free; hence F is false. And if F is true, then *not* all actions are determined and so D is false. We thereby have a paradox. The two assumptions that we normally make, labeled D and F, both seem to be true. Yet they will lead to results that are inconsistent, because D entails that F is false while F entails that D is false.

Determinists, people who deny that human beings have free will, sometimes put forward their argument in the form of a dilemma. It is first argued that any event or action is determined by prior causes or else it is not. Any uncaused action or event, however, is said to be a random or chance event. It would also be argued that to adopt F, is to admit that there are uncaused events or actions—random or chance events. But an action that is random or that happens by chance is not one that any person does or can control by an act of will; rather, that event just happens. Expressed schematically, the dilemma presented by the determinist is as follows:

1. All human actions are either determined by causes or are chance (uncaused) events.
2. If all human actions are determined by causes, then there is no free will.
3. If all human actions are chance (uncaused) events, then there is no free will.
4. *Therefore* there is no free will.

By interpreting F to be an admission that human actions are uncaused and therefore random or chance events, the determinist would claim to have shown conclusively by this dilemma that to adopt either D or F is to be committed to the conclusion that there is no human free will. From the alternatives in the first premiss, the determinist validly *deduces* the consequence in the fourth proposition. That conclusion is *entailed* by the premisses.

After reading the next section about defenses against the dilemma, you might like to consider whether there is a way to avoid the consequence of this dilemma. It will be difficult to find an escape, though. Given that chance and random events have been equated with uncaused events, the first premiss contains exhaustive alternatives, thereby making it a strong dilemma.

DEFENDING AGAINST THE DILEMMA

Earlier we mentioned that the dilemma has often been viewed metaphorically as a charging bull. The unfortunate opponent of the bull is subsequently impaled on one or the other of the horns. Hence it is common to refer to the alternatives provided as the "horns of a dilemma." Continuing this metaphor helps us to visualize and remember ways to avoid being caught by one of the horns of a dilemma. The following are defenses that will sometimes work:

Going Between the Horns

We can often escape a dilemma by "going between the horns" and finding a *third* alternative. If there is such a possible alternative, it will allow us to avoid the unpleasant conclusion. In the above example *The Problem of Evil*, one could go between the horns at premiss 2 by arguing the third possibility that God created human beings with free will and it is we who have caused the evil. Hence, it is not that God cannot do anything about evil or doesn't want to; He values free human choice, and human beings are responsible for the evil because they have chosen sinful actions.

This technique for evasion will, of course, not work if the alternatives do not admit of a third possibility. If you start a dilemma by saying, "Either it will snow or it will not snow tomorrow," there are only these two choices, so one cannot go between the horns in such a case. The best dilemmas are constructed in terms of alternatives that are exhaustive and do not admit of other possibilities.

Grasping a Horn

One can also "grasp the horns of the dilemma," by attacking one of the conditional premisses—one of the "if . . . then" statements. For example, we might defend against the dilemma about interest rates and inflation by arguing that the premiss "If they [higher interest rates] curb inflation, then unemployment will increase" is false (provided we could show that it *is* false).

Charging the Bull: Constructing a Counterdilemma

Another way to deal with a dilemma is by "charging the bull." The idea here is to construct another dilemma around the initial situation or set of facts, but one that leads either to the opposite conclusion or to an equally unacceptable pair of consequences.

First, let us consider an example of the latter. Imagine someone has argued that voting is not worth the effort, because whether you vote or not, you have no effect on the result. The dilemma presented to you could be:

1. Either you vote or you do not vote.
2. If you vote, you have no effect on the outcome (because your vote is only *one* in *thousands*).
3. If you do not vote, you have no effect on the outcome.
4. *Therefore* you have no effect on the outcome.

And your opponent might conclude that if you can have no influence on the outcome, voting is a waste of time.

You can oppose this dilemma by considering the opposite point of view. Your opponent has talked of voting as useless, so ask about the consequences of not voting. Your opponent has ridiculed the results of voting; but what are the results of *not* voting? You could then construct another dilemma by considering *why* someone might not vote and what not voting says about that person's character. Here is a possible counterdilemma constructed along these lines:

1. Someone who does not vote is someone who simply does not take the trouble to vote or who does not think voting is important.
2. If the person does not take the trouble to vote, then that person is lazy and morally reprehensible.
3. If the person does not think voting is important, then that person is ignorant and uncaring about democratic freedom.
4. *Therefore* those who do not vote are *either* lazy and morally reprehensible *or* ignorant and uncaring about democratic freedom.

Here the tactic has been to construct *another* dilemma having unpleasant consequences. It is a *counterdilemma* because it confronts and provides an argument against the position of the opponent who presented the initial dilemma. It is, in this example, constructed partly on the opponent's conclusion (that voting is a waste of time).

A case of a counterdilemma that reaches the opposite conclusion of the original is the famous case of the lawsuit between Protagoras, a teacher of the art of rhetoric and of arguing in ancient Greece, and one of the pupils, Eulathus. Protagoras told his pupil that he was so confident of being able to teach him how to argue well in court that Eulathus need not pay him if he lost his first court case. If Eulathus won his first court case, however, he would then pay Protagoras for the lessons.

Eulathus took the course of lessons but never appeared in a law court to prosecute or defend a case. So Protagoras eventually sued him to recover the unpaid fees for the lessons in arguing. But in court, Eulathus presented the following dilemma:

1. Either I win this court case or I lose it.
2. If I lose, then I do not have to pay the fee (because Protagoras agreed to waive the fee if I lost my first court case).
3. If I win the court case, then the court will have judged that I do not have to pay Protagoras's fee.
4. *Therefore* I do not have to pay Protagoras.

What a crushing dilemma! But Protagoras had a trick up his sleeve and argued by presenting the following counterdilemma:

1. Either *I* win this court case or I lose it.
2. If I lose, then I get paid by Eulathus (for he will have won his first case and by our agreement must then pay).
3. If I win, the *court* will have judged that I am to be paid.
4. *Therefore* Eulathus must pay me.

This case must surely have taken more than a little head scratching to decide. The oddity lies in having a court case that involves the original agreement between the teacher and the pupil, which agreement *in turn* refers back to the same court case—since it is the *first* court case the student becomes involved in.

A little thinking about this puzzle shows that it involves a contradiction not immediately apparent. This can be seen if we look at the pupil's situation. As the court case begins, Eulathus is in a position where *both* the following statements are true:

1. *According to law*, if Eulathus wins this case, he does *not* have to pay the teacher's fee.
2. *According to the agreement between the pupil and the teacher*, if Eulathus wins this case, he *does* have to pay the teacher's fee.

You can see that 1 and 2 together involve contradictory consequences. In fact, the contradiction results from one and the same event; that is, the contradiction that Eulathus has to pay and does *not* have to pay follows directly from his winning the court case he is engaged in.

Because the original agreement in a sense contains this hidden self-contradiction, the dispute *cannot* be settled. When the pupil and the teacher originally agreed that fees were to be paid only if the pupil won his first case, neither of them considered the possibility that the first case might be one involving both of them and the question of paying the fees. And when this situation occurs, the court cannot decide the issue until all terms of the original agreement are met—which means that the case before the court will have to be *already* decided before the judge makes a decision. Yet the terms of the original agreement will not be fulfilled *until* the judge settles the court case. The court cannot decide the issue nor can the agreement settle it, because neither can operate in independence of the other—yet this is what is demanded by the dilemma and counterdilemma originally presented. Protagoras and Eulathus are therefore able to move back and forth between the legal question and the terms of the original agreement. Depending on which is appealed to at any point during the court case, Eulathus does or does not have to pay. In fact, at any point *both* possibilities can be predicted, depending on whether one considers the court or the agreement.

This example shows the importance of knowing the conditions and issues being argued about and what is entailed in an agreement. Don't be caught in a self-contradictory situation, from which there is no escape!

THE REDUCTIO

Consider the following conversation:

SMITH. Punishment ought always to be judged according to how effective it is in deterring people from doing illegal acts.

JONES. Surely not. If we justified punishment in that way, we would be justified in hanging a man for stealing a loaf of bread.

Here Jones has shown that an obviously absurd consequence follows from Smith's position. Because this unacceptable, absurd consequence can be validly deduced from Smith's statement, it follows, Jones claims, that Smith's statement must be false.

An argument of this form is called a *reductio*; the full Latin name for it is *reductio ad absurdum* (reduction of something to an absurdity). This kind of argument is effective as a weapon against an opponent, for it provides a method of illustrating that an assumption, belief, or theory of an opponent is erroneous. As illustrated by Jones's response to Smith in their debate about punishment, the technique involves showing that the belief or theory in question leads to or entails an absurd conclusion or consequence. The *absurdity* is usually a contradiction or an obviously false statement.

Here is an example of a *reductio* that appeared in a newspaper editorial:

A REAL JUDGE, OR NONE AT ALL

Hours before Charles Bick, optometrist and reeve [president of the town council] of Forest Hill, was appointed to the Metro Police Commission he went through a little charade. He was appointed a provincial judge.

He had never served as a judge, he had never fulfilled the role of impartial arbiter of public disputes, and he never would. He was appointed a judge solely to get around the law that called for the presence of a provincial judge on the board of police commissioners.

It was a silly arrangement. If appointment of judges to police commissions has any validity at all—and we say it has none—that validity comes from the argument that judges bring with them the impartiality of their office and the skill they have gained as jurists in mediating disputes.

What Toronto got with Mr. Bick was something less than it was entitled to. There is more to being a judge than just the name.[2]

The editorial went on to discuss what should happen given that Charles Bick was about to retire. The part quoted above is a fine piece of arguing. It suggests that the only reason for appointing a judge would be that a judge has learned to adjudicate disputes in a fair and impartial way (paragraph 3). Charles Bick, however, never served as a judge, and so he had never had a chance to develop the skill and diplomacy required to be an effective and impartial mediator of disputes. To appoint Bick a judge was to do something ridiculous that defeated the purpose of having a judge on the commission. Making him a judge in name only merely emphasized how absurd the situation was.

The strategy of a *reductio* is to show that an absurd conclusion follows from a given statement. In brief, the schema of a *reductio* can be put in the following way, letting S and T stand for any propositions at all:

1. *Assume* statement S.
2. *Deduce* from S either:
   a false statement
   a contradiction (not-S)
   a self-contradiction (T and not-T)
3. *Conclude*, therefore, that S must be false.

This will also allow you to conclude that since the original assumption, S, is false, the contradictory, not-S, must be true. In the example about the judge the argument, schematically represented, is:

1. *Assume* Bick should be appointed to the commission as the required judge on that commission.
2. *Deduce*: The only reason to have Bick (as the required judge) is that Bick would have the qualities of a judge.
   But Bick is an optometrist by training and experience, *not* a judge.
   Hence Bick does *not* have the special qualities of an experienced judge.

[2] The *Toronto Globe and Mail*, May 24, 1977, p. 6. Reprinted by permission.

Hence Bick will not *necessarily* be a good mediator, impartial arbiter, and so forth.
3. *Conclude*, therefore, that Bick should *not* be appointed as the required judge. That is, the original assumption in 1 is false.

Clearly this argument is used in the editorial to prove the *opposite* of the assumption in 1.

In some cases dilemmas and *reductio*s appear together, with the absurdity reached by a *reductio ad absurdum* argument being a dilemma. An example of such an argument occurs in the following passage from an article on child abuse:

There is also abuse of children in another situation—where the child is audience rather than subject. Here television is the prime subject of concern; children are overexposed to what comes through the tube. It will not do to say the family should exercise control. Pious introductions warning of "mature theme" and advice to exercise "parental guidance" are stupid, unless they are cleverly meant to be self-defeating, and in either event they are revolting. If the children are not watching, the caveat has no purpose; if the children are watching, the caveat is a lure.[3]

Here the position that families should control children's television viewing is reduced to an absurdity. The consequences of parents' controlling the children with the aid of a warning (a caveat) preceding a "mature" television show are pointed out, leading to the dilemma that illustrates the absurdity of that position. The *reductio* begins with the third sentence, "It will not do to say . . ." The dilemma announcing the absurdity deduced from the initial position occurs in the last sentence. That dilemma is a fine example because it begins with exhaustive alternatives. Spelled out, the dilemma is:

1. Either the children are watching or the children are not watching (implicit).
2. If they are *not* watching, then the caveat is useless.
3. If they *are* watching, then the caveat is a lure.
4. *Therefore* the caveat is either useless or a lure.

The conclusion in 4 points out the absurdity of the initial recommendation. In other words, to follow *that* advice would either be a useless exercise or would work *against* a solution of the problem by luring children to watch "mature" material.

[3] Charles Rembar, "Obscenity—Forget It," *The Atlantic Monthly*, May 1977, p. 40. Reprinted by permission of the author and the author's agents, Scott Meredith Literary Agency, Inc., 845 Third Avenue, New York, N.Y. 10022.

A famous example of a *reductio* argument appears in Plato's *Republic*. Early in that work the characters are discussing the true nature of justice and of right action. What, they ask, is a just or right act? Cephalus suggests that right action consists in telling the truth and repaying all debts. Here is Socrates's response to this view expressed by Cephalus:

> You put your case admirably, Cephalus. . . . But take this matter of doing right: can we say that it really consists in nothing more nor less than telling the truth and paying back anything we may have received? Are not these very actions sometimes right and sometimes wrong? Suppose, for example, a friend who had lent us a weapon were to go mad and then ask for it back, surely anyone would say we ought not to return it. It would not be "right" to do so; nor yet to tell the truth without reserve to a madman.[4]

Socrates has shown that an absurd consequence can be deduced from Cephalus's position. So he concludes that one cannot correctly define right and just action as being truthful and repaying all debts of all kinds.

Reductio ad absurdum arguments are often useful in helping us decide which of a number of rival theories is true, because we can occasionally eliminate a particular theory on the strength of a *reductio* argument. An example of this can be found in connection with what is traditionally known in philosophy as the mind-body problem.

This example is more difficult than some of the previous ones. We might best begin by thinking about ourselves for a moment. If we were asked to report the basic facts about ourselves, we might well reply that we have bodies and that we have minds. Our bodies are extended in space and can occupy chairs or parts of a room. By and large, our body is just a kind of physical object, in that it will fall if unsupported, cannot be in two places at once, and can be bumped and pushed about by other objects. A stone can be kicked around by someone's boot; we can be jostled in a crowd or knocked down by a car.

Our mind, by contrast, is not a spatial entity, but is the private place that harbors thoughts, feelings, and emotions. Others do not feel our personal pains or think our private thoughts; only we do that. And it is our minds, not our bodies, that perform such tasks.

Moreover, we would add to this picture the fact that our minds and bodies interact with one another. If our body is injured, perhaps

---

[4] F.M. Cornford, ed. and trans., *The Republic of Plato* (London: Oxford University Press, 1941), p. 7.

because a hand has touched a hot object, this causes a pain (a mental event) that will, in turn, cause us to remove the hand. Sometimes we think about a problem and plan, in our mind, what we will do, after which our mind informs the body to get on with the necessary tasks. If you plan to celebrate someone's birthday by baking a cake, this plan cannot remain only a thought in your mind but must be carried out by bodily actions such as sifting flour, measuring milk, and so on.

However, some people have been uncertain of this ordinary picture of each person as a combination of a mind and a body. As medical science progresses and increasingly more is learned about the brain and its functions, greater numbers of people have come to wonder whether all of us are not just complicated *physical* bodies without minds. One way such a position could be supported is negatively, by showing that the traditional picture of persons as interacting minds and bodies is not acceptable. Here, introduced step by step, is a *reductio ad absurdum* argument to present this view:

1. The ordinary view of persons is that (a) each person has a mind that is different from the body in terms of being not extended in space, and (b) minds act upon bodies and vice versa. (One name for this position is *dualistic interaction*: dualistic because each person is construed as a *duality* of mind and body; interaction because a person's mind and body are said to *interact* with each other.)
2. In order for any physical object to be causally affected by some other thing, that thing must be an extended physical object having mass and acceleration. For example, a billiard ball can be caused to move *only* if it is hit by some other object that can come into the same general spatial location and affect it by impact.
3. This point, 2, means that if the mind is to cause the body to do something, then the mind must be an extended object that can be in a spatial location and that has mass and acceleration so it can move through space and interact with the physical body or a part of it.
4. But the mind, according to the original thesis in 1, is not extended in space; so the mind cannot have mass or be in a spatial location.
5. *Therefore* the interaction of the mind with the physical body or parts of it would require that the mind be extended in space and capable of motion. But this *contradicts* the original definition of a mind and so, by *reductio*, has been shown to be unacceptable.

The thrust of this *reductio* is to show that one must give up some part of the original position in 1. In fact, something of a dilemma results: if the mind is nonspatial, then we cannot conceive of interaction with the body being possible. And if there *is* interaction, then the mind cannot be nonspatial.

DEFENDING AGAINST THE REDUCTIO

Since a *reductio* advanced against your own belief or position will begin with a statement of your belief as a premiss, you must either attack the *logic* of the argument presented or you must be ready to endorse the conclusion. The former is simple and involves checking for logical errors; if the logic is faulty the *reductio* fails and can be rejected. The latter is harder because the conclusion is supposedly absurd and no one wishes to endorse absurd, false, or contradictory positions. But sometimes one can defend the conclusion—which comes down to confronting the other person on the question of what is absurd. Again, this may be impossible if the absurdity is a formal contradiction. You have no defense if your position logically leads to the claim that "All people are over 60 and all people are *not* over 60 at the same time." You do, however, have a defense if the *reductio* is said to lead to a false statement. If someone said that your astronomical theories were ridiculous and must be abandoned because they lead to the conclusion that the earth is not flat, you can counter this by denying the falsity of the conclusion, since it *is* false. In other cases issues might be more difficult to settle, and so one might again be able to defend oneself by endorsing the conclusion. For example, if someone ridicules your theory of art because "It means you must hold that a plaster duck is as good as a Picasso painting," you may feel that you can accept this conclusion without embarrassment. The moral is that when you are faced with a *reductio* against yourself, at least consider whether you can and should stick to your guns.

Imagine yourself in the middle of a conversation in which you are attacking free enterprise because you feel that it allows a corporation to take inordinate profits at the expense of consumers. Your opponent states:

> If you *don't* have free enterprise, then there will be no incentive for making profits. If you have no profits, there will be no money for investment, which will mean less industrial expansion and an increase in unemployment. Without free enterprise, then, you have no investment, which we need so badly.

Your opponent clearly intends this as a *reductio* of your belief that we should not have a free enterprise system. You could attack the *reductio* by accepting the conclusion that there would be no investment; perhaps because the role played by investment in a free market could be played just as well by a government planning agency. Here you are disagreeing that the conclusion is absurd. You can then move back up the ladder of your opponent's argument and deny the truth of the initial premiss—the premiss that one needs free enterprise to have profits.

Always keep in mind that if an argument is valid yet the conclusion false, one of the premisses must also be false. If in attacking a *reductio*, you can plausibly reject the conclusion, then you know that the opponent who advanced the argument began from a false claim (provided the argument has the proper logical links). Also remember that if you are faced with a *reductio*, you may be able to turn it to your advantage—as the above example illustrates.

BACKING SOMEONE INTO A CORNER

A variant on the technique of the *reductio* argument form is "backing someone into a corner." Here the opponent is led to an untenable conclusion because of having agreed to certain things. The person is backed into a corner and then shown that it is an unpleasant corner to be in. This technique is illustrated dramatically by the TV lawyer's cross-examination of a witness:

LAWYER.   You said earlier that you saw Jones at the scene of the crime on the night of April 10.

WITNESS.   Yes.

LAWYER.   Had you ever seen Jones before?

WITNESS.   No.

LAWYER.   But weren't you and Jones members of the same golf and country club?

WITNESS.   Yes.

LAWYER.   Then you must have seen Jones sometime before.

WITNESS.   No, I didn't.

LAWYER.   Mr. Witness, would you look at this picture, Exhibit A, and tell me who is in it?

WITNESS.   That's me on the right.

LAWYER.   And who is the person you are talking to? Is it not Jones?

WITNESS.   Yes.

LAWYER.   So you *did* know Jones before the day of the crime!

Here the lawyer has backed the witness into a corner by forcing an admission of perjury. The lawyer, suspecting the witness of lying, has forced him to say that he did not know Jones and then has gotten him to admit that he did, thereby catching the witness in a contradiction. This proves that the witness had lied in his earlier testimony. (You can see that this merely illustrates a variant of the *forcing* attack that is the backbone of the *reductio*.)

EXERCISES

In each of the following, state the kind of argument involved. Outline the argument briefly, and then indicate how one might try to refute or counter it.

I. If we ban erotic films, we are denying people the freedom to make their own choices about what they see. But if we do not ban erotic films, our children will be encouraged to engage in sexual activities. We must either ban or not ban erotic films. We must either deny some people one of their freedoms or we must encourage our children to engage in sexual activities.

II. The purpose of going to school is to get help from a teacher. But a good student does not need the help of a teacher, while a poor student cannot learn even with a teacher's help.

III. Although you said that Threadbare was not in town, you cannot have really believed Threadbare was out of town since you phoned his office several times and were seen at his house.

IV. It is best to believe in God. If He doesn't exist, you have lost nothing by your belief. If He does exist, you have saved yourself from the damnation that would have been your lot for refusing to believe in Him.

V. I don't know what we should do: if we surrender, they will take all our lands; if we fight, many will be killed.

VI. By the term "God" we mean the most perfect being you can think of. But if God did not exist, then we would have to admit that we could imagine a more perfect being—one who had all God's perfect properties *plus* existence. But we *cannot* think of a more perfect being than the most perfect being. So God *must* exist.

VII. Everyone can pay plenty of taxes; for they either live in fine houses, which demonstrates that they clearly have wealth to spare, or they live in poor houses, which shows that they are hoarding their wealth instead of spending it on a pretentious dwelling.

9

Connecting Your Thoughts: Alternatives and Causes

Up to this point we have distinguished two basic types of thinking: deductive and inductive. We have also introduced some argument forms that illuminate the logical structure of these thinking, or reasoning, processes. On the one hand there is *deduction*: deductive inferences are always meant to *draw information out* of premisses. This information is already implicit in the premisses, but it is not openly stated as such. By drawing out the implications and consequences of premisses, a deductive inference *deduces* a conclusion from the premisses given. Since the conclusion is *entailed* by the premisses, a deductive conclusion *necessarily* follows from its premisses. The categorical syllogism (Chapter 5) is one example of a deductive argument form. The dilemma (Chapter 8) is also a deductive argument form reflecting a thinking process that draws out, or deduces, consequences from stated premisses.

On the other hand we have *induction*: inductive inferences always *go beyond* the information given by the premisses. On the basis of certain facts stated by the premisses we conclude that it is reasonable to expect some further fact to hold. Since inductive conclusions go beyond the content of their premisses, they are not entailed by the premisses but are only probable. Statistical arguments and analogies (Chapter 7) are examples of argument forms that reflect inductive reasoning.

While there are many other features to logical reasoning and sound arguing, most thinking processes and most argument forms will be either deductive or inductive. Some arguments, such as those about cause-and-effect relationships, are hard to classify—but even these sometimes are clearly deductive.

DEDUCTIVE REASONING

In this chapter we are going to discuss two new types of reasoning processes and argument forms. The first type involves the presentation of alternative choices and the elimination of one or more of the choices. The second type employs hypothetical reasoning ("if . . . then"). Many of the latter concern cause-and-effect relationships. Both types are instances of deductive reasoning.

Consider an example. Imagine picking up your evening newspaper and reading the following report:

> Last night the police began to question employees of Spinner's Record Shop in connection with the theft of over $4,000 last weekend. Mr. Garnet Spinner reported that when he opened his store on Monday morning, he discovered the money was missing. Chief detective Alan Ketchum said that police detectives are questioning Spinner's employees, because there was no sign of a break-in and the theft had to have been either the work of someone who broke into the store over the weekend or else an inside job.

In the last part of this fictional report we are presented with the chief detective's reasoning about who might have committed the robbery. He knows that *someone* stole the money, provided Mr. Spinner is not lying. How does money get stolen from a store? It gets stolen by someone breaking into the store or walking in with a gun and demanding it or else by one of the clerks taking it out of the till. The chief detective knows that this case is either a break-in or a theft by an employee; he has formulated two alternatives. He then decides that there is no evidence of break-in: there are no forced doors or windows, no smashed locks, no broken glass. Thus he concludes that the money must have been stolen by one of the employees. Hence he is now questioning the employees to try to confirm his deduction that it was an inside job.

The point to note is that Chief Detective Ketchum's thinking process involved *considering possible alternatives* and then *eliminating some alternatives* until he was left with the most likely one. (There are other possibilities, of course; for example, the theft might have been the work of outside thieves who somehow had gotten hold of a key.) In the imagined newspaper report Ketchum's argument stated the alternatives as a premiss, stated why one possible explanation was ruled out, and then concluded that the remaining alternative was the one they were checking.

A conclusion is deduced in this example from an argument with a complex premiss involving alternatives. This gives us a sentence with two thoughts connected by "or": "someone broke in *or* some employee did it." It might be best to pause briefly to make a few general remarks about this type of reasoning and this type of argument form.

It is always helpful to note the building blocks of arguments. Arguments such as the categorical syllogism, you will remember, are built of a series of simple propositions. Each proposition has two terms, is either affirmative or negative, and is either universal or particular. For example, the argument

1. Sloppy eaters are disgusting.
2. Fred is a sloppy eater.
3. *Therefore* Fred is disgusting.

is composed of simple categorical assertions which state unequivocally that certain things are true.

In contrast to this kind of proposition, we are now about to move into arguments involving hypothetical claims, such as "If Fred comes near me, I'll punch him in the nose"; or alternatives, such as "Either you leave the room at once or I'm going to call the police." You can see that these sentences using "if . . . then" and "or" are really complex sentences made up of combinations of simpler sentences, plus a connecting word such as "or." The statement

Bill is usually on time or has a good excuse

is merely two simpler sentences,

1. Bill is usually on time,
2. (Bill) has a good excuse (for not being on time),

connected by the word "or."

Words such as "and," "or," and "if . . . then" are called *logical connectives* when they link propositions together in various logical ways. "And" is merely the putting together of two propositions. "Or" is used when we think of two statements as alternatives. "If . . . then" is used when we express connections in terms of cause and effect (as in "If the fire reaches the dynamite, then the cabin will blow up") or when we predict a sequence of related events ("If you put the mouse in the maze, then it will find the cheese in 3.78 seconds").

All arguing involves putting together thoughts or ideas. The syllogism is used when we logically connect the thought that one thing is classified in a certain way ("Fred is a sloppy eater") with another thought about a related classification ("Sloppy eaters are disgusting"). Hypothetical arguments, which we are to discuss in this chapter, connect thoughts together in terms of one event being the cause of another or of one possibility being an alternative to another. The connectives—"and," "or," "if . . . then"—allow us to join simple propositions together in a variety of ways to form arguments that are more complicated than the syllogism.

While hypothetical arguments are more complicated, in that they involve both simple propositions and logical connectives, they occur frequently in everyday life and are often easy to analyze. For example:

1. If you went to the drive-in movie last night, then you did not have time to do your homework.
2. You went to the drive-in movie last night.
3. *Therefore* you did not have time to do your homework.

This is clearly a valid argument. Premiss 1 uses "if . . . then" to connect two simple propositions: (a) "You went to the drive-in movie last night" and (b) "You did not have time to do your homework." In the rest of the chapter we build on this principle of logically connecting propositions to provide you with more skills in arguing.

ELIMINATING ALTERNATIVES: THE DISJUNCTIVE SYLLOGISM

Here is a familiar situation. You have misplaced your car keys. First, you look in the usual places—on the kitchen shelves, in your overcoat pocket—with no success. Then you decide to be more systematic: "Where," you ask yourself, "could the keys possibly be?" You mentally list all the possibilities: they could still be in the car or in the kitchen or in your coat pocket. Next you check off possibilities you have eliminated: you searched the kitchen thoroughly and looked in your coat pocket, thereby assuring yourself that these possibilities can be discarded. Therefore you conclude that the keys must still be in your car. You go out to the car and there they are!

This is a familiar reasoning pattern. It involves thinking of alternative possibilities or choices and then eliminating alternatives until there is just one possibility. Using our example of the misplaced car keys and assuming just *two* possibilities, the deductive argument reflected by the reasoning process in that example can be put out in terms of the following premises and conclusion:

1. The keys are in my coat *or* the keys are in the car.
2. The keys are *not* in my coat.
3. *Therefore* the keys must be in the car.

This argument form is known as a *disjunctive syllogism*. "Disjunctive" is the name given to compound propositions using the logical connective "or"; and the argument is called a syllogism because it has exactly two premises and a conclusion. The structure is easy to remember if we put it into schematic form, using A to stand for "alternative" and numbers to designate different alternatives:

1. A_1 *or* A_2.
2. *Not* A_1
3. *Therefore* A_2.

The disjunctive syllogism is a valid *deductive* argument form. This means that the conclusion is *drawn out* of the premises; and it means that if the premises are true, the conclusion *necessarily* follows. If you are sure that the keys must be either in the car *or* in the coat pocket, and if you know for sure that they are *not* in the coat pocket, then they *must* be in the car. Of course, this reasoning may fail if there are other possibilities that are not taken account of by the argument. For instance, the keys might really have fallen on the floor behind the bed, in which case the conclusion that they must be in the car would be incorrect.

The logical reasoning involved in the disjunctive syllogism is straightforward. You most likely have not found it novel but have merely gained a fancy name for a type of argument you have often used. Some ancient logicians purportedly said that the reasoning of the disjunctive syllogism was so patently obvious that even dogs could use it. A dog chasing a rabbit, when it comes to a fork in the road, will sniff up the road in one direction; if it does not find a scent the dog will immediately go back and proceed in the *other* direction *without further sniffing*. So the dog apparently reasons:

1. The rabbit went *this* way or *that* way.
2. It did not go *this* way (since there is no scent here).
3. *Therefore* it *must* have gone *that* way.

The fact that the dog goes in the alternate direction without sniffing again indicates that the dog recognizes that the conclusion *necessarily* follows! Knowing that the rabbit went in one of the two directions, and eliminating one by sniffing for the rabbit's scent, the dog concludes that the rabbit *must* have gone the other way. And if it must have gone that way there is no point in further checking by sniffing for a scent. Whether dogs can reason in this fashion, we are not prepared to debate. But if they do, they are certainly to be praised for their logic. No self-respecting dog would ever be caught barking up the wrong tree.

In Chapter 8 we discussed J. S. Mill's argument in favor of free speech. There we showed his use of a dilemma to illustrate the unacceptable consequences of *not* allowing free speech. Since Mill is in favor of free speech his argument is more complicated and involves a dilemma within a disjunctive syllogism. This is simpler than it sounds. In skeletal form Mill is arguing:

1. Either we allow free speech *or* we do not allow free speech.
2. It is unacceptable *not* to allow free speech (the dilemma proves this premiss).
3. *Therefore* there should be free speech.

So Mill starts with exhaustive alternatives in premiss 1, eliminates one alternative in premiss 2 by means of the dilemma he constructs, and concludes that we *must* accept the remaining alternative. This is a perfectly valid deduction and a good example of two different argument forms being used together: one provides the overall logical structure of the general argument being advanced, while the other provides an argument for one premiss.

VALID ARGUMENTS USING "IF...THEN"

One of the most frequent connections we make in our thinking and arguing is expressed by sentences using "if . . . then." Some of the basic and key uses of "if . . . then" in ordinary language are as follows:

Causal Connections

Our experience of the world teaches us that things are interdependent; some things cause other things to happen. Bumping one's shin causes a pain and a bruise. Connecting wires to complete an electrical circuit, which is what turning on a wall switch does, causes the lights in the room to go on.

With enough experience of how things work—of what causes what—we can predict events. Consider, for example,

If the cut becomes dirty, then it will become infected.

Here a causal connection is claimed to hold between dirt and infection. Dirt in a cut causes infection.

Counterfactuals

We sometimes claim that there are or might have been connections between things or events even though one of the things doesn't exist or one of the events didn't come about. In such cases we are making claims that go against the facts—or we are supposing that things might have been different than we know they are:

If unicorns were real, they would look a lot like horses.

If the pitcher had played better, then the Giants would have won.

If the king had been alive, there would not have been a riot.

In each of these we are saying that *had* one situation been the case or *had* one event occurred (even though it had not), then something else would have followed as a consequence.

Tentative Connections

We also use "if . . . then" to express a likely connection that we are not certain about, as in "If the nail is long enough, then it might hold the boards together."

Conditional Claims

Often "if . . . then" introduces a conditional statement, such as "If you eat up all your spinach, then you may have some dessert," which claims that one event is conditional upon another's happening first.

Hypothetical propositions are not usually difficult to pick out; the cue word "if" and the cue phrase "if . . . then" are normally present. There are some exceptions, however. Frequently "then" is omitted, as in "If you do that, I'm going to scream"; but it is clear that this is intended to be a hypothetical claim telling you that *if* you do "that," *then* screaming will result. Sometimes we have more difficult cases, such as, "Do that, and I'll scream." Here the *intent* is clearly to tell you that, *if* you do that, *then* screaming will ensue. Close attention to the meaning of a spoken or written sentence will usually make clear whether the speaker or writer really *intends* an "if . . . then" claim.

More difficult cases involve sentences using "unless." It is clearly a hypothetical statement (an "if . . . then") that is intended by,

He will kill you *unless* you give him the money.

But what exactly is the conditional proposition that is being expressed? It must be,

If you do not give him the money, then he will kill you,

because the original sentence says that you *are* going to get killed if you do not hand over the money. This is easier to see if you consider a *progressive* change of the original through four stages:

1. He will kill you *unless* you give him the money.
2. *Unless* you give him the money, he will kill you.
3. *Unless* you give him the money, *then* he will kill you.
4. *If* you do *not* give him the money, *then* he will kill you.

The problem with this specific example is that it tempts us to draw the further inference that if you give him the money, he will not kill you. But this inference is not warranted. The original does *not* give you any information about what might happen if you do give him the money. Perhaps he will go away; perhaps he will kill you anyway. The only legitimate meaning we can assign to the original is that if you do *not* give him the money, you will be killed.

When you see the cue word "unless," you can be sure you are dealing with a conditional statement ("if . . . then"). Here is another example:

I will go camping unless it rains.

This means:

If it does *not* rain, then I will go camping.

Again, the easiest way to sort out such sentences is to put them down with the "unless" first. Having done that, the translation into a proposition using "if . . . then" becomes obvious. This can be illustrated by a further example:

Fred will come *unless* he has a flat tire,

becomes

Unless he has a flat tire, (then) Fred will come.

This, in turn, becomes

If he does *not* have a flat tire, (then) Fred will come.

There are three basic valid deductive argument forms employing "if . . . then." We will present an example of each, then set out the argument in terms of premisses and conclusion, and, finally, indicate schematically the structure of the argument.

Affirming the Antecedent (Modus Ponens)

The traditional, Latin, title for the form of argument that we call *affirming the antecedent* is *modus ponens*.[1] Here is an example of such an argument:

Jones believes that we could test his theory by using a rat and a maze. The theory claims that the drug will alter the rat's learning procedure so that it will learn to run the maze successfully after only one exploratory trial run. So, if the rat runs the maze successfully—with *no* errors—on the second run, then the theory is correct. We put the rat into the maze and let it work its way out. We then put it in a *second* time and the rat successfully ran the maze without an error. So Jones's theory must be correct.

There is considerable information in this example and much background material, but the statement of the test procedures provides the following argument about the method. Put in premisses with a conclusion, it is:

1. *If* the rat runs the maze successfully on the second occasion, *then* the theory is correct.
2. The rat ran the maze successfully on the second occasion.
3. *Therefore* the theory is correct.

Premiss 1 states the hypothesis, or theory, under investigation—that if one claim is true, we can expect another to be true. In a conditional the first proposition, following the "if," is called the *antecedent*; the second proposition, following the "then," is called the *consequent*. So premiss 1 is a hypothetical proposition that states a relationship between two simple propositions. It tells us that if the antecedent is true, then the consequent will be true as well. Premiss 2 asserts that

[1] The Latin word *modus* means "way," as in *modus operandi*, or "way of operating." *Ponens* is a form of the Latin verb *ponere*, which means "to place." So *modus ponens* means "way of placing—or *establishing* or *affirming*—the antecedent."

the antecedent *is* true, thereby allowing us validly to deduce the consequent in the conclusion.

This argument form is deductive and you can probably obtain an intuitive grasp of it without much trouble. Using A to refer to "antecedent" and C to refer to "consequent," we can represent this argument by the schema:

1. If A, then C.
2. A.
3. *Therefore* C.

Arguments using the valid deductive form of affirming the antecedent, or *modus ponens*, occur in contexts where someone is attempting, first, to demonstrate either that there is a causal relationship between two events or situations or that one is dependent upon the other in some way. That is, the relationship can be expressed by a hypothetical, or conditional, proposition using "if . . . then." That person is frequently attempting, secondly, to show that given the conditional situation expressed by the hypothetical proposition, and assuming that certain facts would come into play, a predictable result can be inferred.

In a discussion of the energy crisis a few years ago, it was argued that the crisis resulted not so much from shortages of reserve energy resources, but from the difficulty of making those resources available at an acceptable economic and ecological cost. The article ended with these two brief sentences:

> But there is a huge step between potential reserves and currently available fuel. Covering the distance takes time, money and technology, and this is why the short-term outlook is nowhere near as sanguine.[2]

This is merely a brief summary conclusion of a fairly lengthy article. Nevertheless, the *form* of the argument can be seen to be that of affirming the antecedent (*modus ponens*):

1. If there is a difficult step between potential reserves and available fuel, then the short-term outlook is not hopeful (sanguine). [Unexpressed premiss.]
2. There *is* a difficult step between potential reserves and available fuel.
3. *Therefore* the short-term outlook is not hopeful (sanguine).

[2] *The Saskatoon Star-Phoenix*, April 28, 1973, p. 42.

The phrase "that is why" cues a conclusion. The second premiss is supported on the grounds that money, time, and technical know-how are required. The argument is clearly valid.

There is an old joke, known in several variants, which works because it employs the logical deductive form *modus ponens*. Picture Nancy and Fred seated at a table with a deck of playing cards. Nancy selects three cards at random from the deck and places them face down on the table.

> "How many do you see?" she asks.
> "Three," Fred says cautiously.
> Nancy moves them around on the table and asks again, "How many?"
> "Three," Fred says, with a little more confidence.
> Another bit of moving around, and Nancy says, "*Now*, how many are there?"
> "Still three," Fred says.
> "No," says Nancy, "there are four."
> Fred looks closely and sees only three, and says so.
> "A-ha!" says Nancy, "there are four."
> "Only three," Fred says, with full confidence now.
> "Well," says Nancy, "I say there are four. But I'll tell you what. *If I'm wrong*, will you buy me lunch?"
> "Certainly!" Fred cries, being sure Nancy *is* wrong.
> "O.K.," Nancy says, "I *am* wrong. And now you owe me a lunch."

By saying "If I am *wrong*," Nancy made Fred believe he should agree with what she was saying (because Fred knew she was wrong). But the argument she caught Fred with was a plain old *modus ponens*. Here it is:

1. If I am wrong, then you must buy me lunch.
2. I am wrong.
3. *Therefore* you must buy me lunch.

Nancy foxed Fred by getting him to agree to the "if . . . then" proposition. Once Fred did that his goose was cooked. Nancy had only to "assert the antecedent" by admitting she was wrong and a faultless logic decreed that the consequent followed logically and that Fred owed her a lunch.

Advertisements frequently play on our ability to reason logically by stating something in a way that encourages us to draw a conclusion from that statement. In this way the advertiser leads us to accept something without really coming out and asking us to do so. This device is not necessarily deceptive, but it could be intentionally misleading. It is a subtle way of persuading us to buy a product.

Everyone has seen movie ads worded something like this:

If you want to see at least one good movie this year, see *The Red Hot Cowboys*.

Clearly this claims, indirectly, that *The Red Hot Cowboys* is a good movie. Undoubtedly everyone would agree with the antecedent; everyone wants to see good movies. Once that agreement is given, the conclusion follows. The reasoning process this is meant to trigger is:

1. If you want to see at least one good movie this year, (then) see *The Red Hot Cowboys*.
2. I want to see at least one good movie this year.
3. *Therefore* I will see *The Red Hot Cowboys*.

This kind of advertisement makes us agree to a logical line of argument that already, in itself, has us almost on the way out the door to the theater. We are so distracted by agreeing to the obvious truth that we want to see a good movie that we forget to question the hypothetical statement (the first premiss in the above argument). We neglect to ask, "Is this movie really good just because this ad says so?" The example also uses the phrase "at least one" to suggest that the other movies we might have seen so far have not really been all that good. But the key to its success is in initiating the reasoning process that leads us to conclude that we should see the movie being advertised.

Argument forms are also frequently used in everyday life to test out propositions or hypotheses. This is not surprising: people regularly use sound logical thinking, so we should expect all aspects and employments of logical reasoning to be displayed in ordinary contexts.

Here is an example of the use of this skill. It involves two children who are discussing whether they will become Roman Catholics, which in turn leads them to a discussion of what Roman Catholics believe. After the citing of some actual beliefs, we are presented with this conversation:

"They believe if you don't go to mass you'll turn into a wolf."
"Will you?" I said.
"We don't go," he said, "and we haven't."[3]

Presumably, if the belief that failure to go to mass causes one to change into a wolf is true, the following inference should be allowable:

[3] Margaret Atwood, *Surfacing* (Toronto: McClelland & Stewart, 1972), p. 56.

1. If we do not go to mass, then we turn into wolves.
2. We do not go to mass.
3. *Therefore* we turn into wolves.

This argument is valid—it is an instance of affirming the antecedent (*modus ponens*). But the first speaker in the quoted conversation feels he has shown that the belief he cites is a *false* belief. In this, he is correct. If an argument form is *valid* it must preserve the truth of the premisses. A valid argument *cannot* have true premisses *and* a false conclusion. In the argument premiss 2 is true, and the argument is valid because it is a proper instance of *modus ponens*. But the conclusion is *false*, which *must* mean that the remaining premiss —premiss 1—is false also.

Remember that if you have a *valid* argument but a false conclusion, one of the premisses must be false. The children did not turn into wolves, even though the belief stated by the hypothetical proposition, "If you don't go to mass you'll turn into a wolf," would logically lead one to expect that they would (since they do *not* attend mass). This means that the original belief expressed by that hypothetical proposition must be false (unless, of course, the process of turning into a wolf is a more complicated and *longer* process than the children expect and their days as wolves are yet to come). We have suggested this rule before: if the conclusion is false, go back and check the premisses.

Denying the Consequent (Modus Tollens)

The traditional name for the valid deductive argument known as *denying the consequent* is *modus tollens*.[4] Here is an example:

The Dutch boy had his finger in the hole in the dike, and I told him to keep it there until I returned with help. "The dike will not break *so long as* you keep your finger in," I told him. But when I got back the dike had broken, so he must not have kept his finger in.

First recognize that the statement "The dike will not break *so long as* you keep your finger in" means the same as "If you keep your finger in, then the dike will not break." Put in premisses and conclusion the argument is:

---

[4] As mentioned in footnote 1, the word *modus* means "way." *Tollens* is a form of the Latin verb *tollere*, which means "to take away." Hence *modus tollens* is "the way of taking away," which gives the sense of denying (taking away) something—namely the consequent of the hypothetical.

1. If you keep your finger in, (then) the dike will not break.
2. It is *false* that the dike did not break.
3. *Therefore* you did *not* keep your finger in.

Premiss 2 could appear as simply "The dike broke," since that means the same as "It is *false* that the dike did *not* break." The present wording is merely double negation; just as "not-not-happy" or "not unhappy" mean simply "happy," and just as, in mathematics, "minus minus 4" equals "4."

The form *modus tollens* involves denying the consequent of a hypothetical and concluding the *denial* of the antecedent. The schema for it is:

1. If A, then C.
2. *Not* C.
3. *Therefore* not A.

Encountering the cue phrase "if . . . then" or some stand-in for it will not by itself tell you whether you are dealing with a dilemma or some other kind of deduction. But "if . . . then" in conjunction with "not" or "it is false that" is a good clue that you should suspect and look for an argument of the form *modus tollens*, or denying the consequent.

Imagine someone reacting to a government ban on the use of saccharin in soft drinks by saying,

> If I am to get cancer from using saccharin, I will have to drink over 500 bottles of diet soda a day! Not even *I* can drink *that* many; so I will *not* get cancer from saccharin.

"So" in the last part of the last sentence indicates a conclusion. The "if" in the first sentence is a cue word alerting you to the presence of *one* of the argument forms using "if . . . then." And the uses of "not" make it almost certain that the argument is *modus tollens* (denying the consequent). The argument is:

1. If I am going to get cancer from using saccharin (then) I must drink 500 bottles of diet soda a day.
2. I *cannot* drink 500 bottles of soda per day.
3. *Therefore* I am *not* going to get cancer from using saccharin.

Here the arguer has stated the connection between cancer and saccharin use; namely, that great quantities of saccharin over a long period of time will cause cancer. The first premiss expresses this connection. The second premiss is a statement of fact that *denies* the consequent. This allows the arguer to conclude, validly, that he or she is not going to get cancer from use of saccharin.

It is worth noting that one must *not* be tempted to draw illicit inferences from hypothetical statements. The temptation to do so can often be strong. If you were told that "If you drink large amounts of diet soda, then you will get cancer," it might be tempting to think that if you do *not* drink large amounts of diet soda, then you will *not* get cancer. That is, it is tempting to accept the following structure as an acceptable argument form:

1. If A, then C.
2. Not A.
3. *Therefore* not C.

In the example just stated, this would be:

1. If George drinks large amounts of diet soda, then George will get cancer.
2. George does *not* drink large amounts of diet soda.
3. *Therefore* George will *not* get cancer.

This last argument, however, is *invalid*. Premiss 1 *only* indicates what will happen if one drinks large amounts of diet soda; it does *not* say what will happen if one does not. George may still get cancer from some other cause even if he does *not* drink large amounts of diet soda. Drinking diet soda is one cause of cancer (if the studies relied on are correct), but it is not the only cause.

In arguments about causes it is often important to distinguish *necessary* from *sufficient* conditions. A condition is *necessary* if a specified result *cannot* occur without that condition coming into play. For example, oxygen is a necessary condition of fire. If there is no oxygen, a fire cannot start. Nor could a fire continue to burn without oxygen, which is why chemical foams or wet blankets can smother it.

A condition is *sufficient* if it is one possible cause or agent that can bring about a result, but not the only one. Such a condition is *sufficient* to cause the effect but *not* necessary. In the example just cited, drinking large amounts of diet soda was given as a sufficient cause of cancer. But it was not a necessary, or sole, cause. And it is a sufficient condition of getting a flat tire that the tire is punctured by a large nail. But this, alas, is not a necessary condition, because one could *also* get a flat tire by hitting the curb too hard, thereby knocking the tire off the wheel rim—or by having a younger brother let out the air.

Hypothetical Chains (The Hypothetical Syllogism)

It has been noted that reasoning often occurs in "chains" of connected moves. Categorical syllogisms occur in chains when one set of premisses provides a conclusion and then that conclusion is used as a premiss in a *new* argument. We can also connect two hypothetical statements together in a chain of reasoning. Consider this case:

Smith was adamant. He argued that if we let Jones join the club, Jones would use his club membership to lobby other club members about the new land development. And if Jones uses his membership to lobby the members, then we, the executives, will be criticized and our judgment questioned. We may even be asked to resign our executive positions, much to our collective and individual embarrassment.

The main line of Smith's argument is clear; it involves two hypothetical propositions. In the argument Smith is trying to convince his colleagues that a proposed course of action—admitting Jones to membership—will ultimately result in criticism of them (the executives of the club) and also may result in the demand for their resignations. In brief, the argument is:

1. If Jones is admitted, then Jones will lobby members.
2. If Jones lobbies members, then we will be criticized.
3. *Therefore* if Jones is admitted, then we will be criticized.

This argument form is called a *hypothetical syllogism*: "hypothetical" because the premisses and conclusion are each hypothetical (conditional) propositions; "syllogism" because it has exactly two premisses and a conclusion.

You have probably noted that there really is more implied in Smith's argument about admitting Jones to membership. The hypothetical syllogism is used by Smith to connect the admitting of Jones to the subsequent disgrace and embarrassment of the executives. But Smith most likely *assumes* that the executives do not wish to be disgraced and is assuming that if they accept his reasoning—his hypothetical syllogism—they will then agree to reject Jones as a member. So there seems a hidden, implicit *further* argument here:

And if we do not want to be criticized and asked to resign, we must not let Jones join the club.

If we take the conclusion of the hypothetical syllogism and add the first part of this sentence as a premiss and the last as a conclusion, we get:

1. If Jones is admitted, then we will be criticized.
2. Do *not* let us be criticized.
3. *Therefore* do *not* admit Jones.

This is a case of *denying the consequent (modus tollens)*. While Smith's argument explicitly presents a hypothetical syllogism, the tone suggests that Smith also wants the other executive members to accept this *implicit* argument *modus tollens*, since the point or intent of his speech is to convince them that Jones ought *not* to be admitted.

The reasoning that occurs in chains of hypothetical propositions is common to cases in which one is *drawing out* the consequences or implications of facts at one's disposal. Suppose your best friend phones to tell you that she has bought a new car. "Guess what color it is," she says. You think for a minute and guess silver. "Right," she replies, "but how did you know?" "Well," you say, "every time you buy a car, you buy a Guzzler V-8 hardtop with mag wheels, 440, overhead cam, and power steering. These cars are only made in silver, so yours must be silver." Here you have connected buying a new car to its being a Guzzler V-8 and silver in color by means of an implicit hypothetical syllogism:

1. If she has bought a new car, then it is a Guzzler V-8.
2. If it's a Guzzler V-8, then it is silver.
3. *Therefore* if she bought a new car, (then) it is silver.

Although you didn't use explicit "if . . . then" statements, you used statements that function in the same way: to say "Every time she buys a car, she buys a Guzzler V-8" means the same as "If she buys a car, then she buys a Guzzler V-8." These sentences both express the same proposition. Hence the argument is implicit in your reported reasoning, and it relies on the deductive inference permitted by the hypothetical syllogism.

IF AND ONLY IF

Sometimes we argue not only in terms of "*If* you do this, *then* I'll do such and such," but also in terms of "I'll do such and such *if and only if* you do this." Such statements are called *biconditionals*. Imagine the union leader saying to the management negotiators,

> We will lower our demand for a pay increase to 8 percent *if and only if* you change the normal work week from 40 to 35 hours.

Here the negotiators are presented with two items conditionally linked to one another: *if* the work week is changed to 35 hours, *then* the pay raise can be lowered to 8 percent; but *also, if* the pay raise is lowered to 8 percent, *then* the work week *must* be lowered to 35 hours. Each of the two is a condition of the other. We must have *both* or none.

FINDING CAUSES

When "if . . . then" occurs in arguing, it usually introduces a causal connection. When the weatherman says, "If the low pressure area moves to the edge of the northerly high pressure area, we will get rain," he is assuming a causal relationship between certain meteorological events and rain. To be told that "If you smoke in bed, then you will burn the house down" is to be informed, indirectly, of the causal relationship between smoking in bed and house fires.

Many things in our world are causally related. Puncturing the skin with a pin causes an unpleasant sensation and perhaps bleeding. Praising someone's work may cause the person to work even harder to achieve similar or better results. Holding a lighted match to a paper sets the paper on fire.

However, our world is complex—especially in the realm of human motives and behavior—and often events have more than one cause or are the effects of a complex interplay or sequence of causal factors. This frequently creates a problem: how do we select or find the cause of something? Since the ability to work out causal connections is an integral part of our ability to reason about and understand the world and the people around us, it is important to have some way of finding causes.

In actual experience we seldom have trouble deciding that some things are relevant and count as the cause of an event, while others are not. For example, if Green accidentally drops a brick on Brown's toe, we do not count the action of the person who sold Green the brick as the *cause* of the accident, even though Green could not have dropped the brick on Brown unless he had bought or obtained bricks somewhere. Yet we might well decide that the cause of the accident was the fact that Green had an injured wrist or was not paying attention to what he was doing. Clearly, we do place a special importance on the *voluntary actions* of people in such cases. For the things people do are often the causes of events; and the things they do voluntarily, or of their own free will, are things we feel we can hold them responsible for.

There are two rules that will help you determine the cause of an event. The first rule is: *Look for the relevant factors.* Usually the situation or context of an event dictates what will be relevant. In explaining an automobile accident, it is relevant that the car was in the wrong lane, that the car was hit by a bus, and that the bus was speeding. It is *not* relevant that the car was hit by a *yellow* bus rather than by a *green* one.

To some extent we are dependent on our previous experience to provide clues about what the relevant possibilities are. Our experience shows us that people die from falls and from being hit by cars, by other heavy objects, or by lightning; experience also shows that no one is likely to die from being hit with a down pillow. Circumstances will also eliminate some possibilities. The possibility that someone lost consciousness from being struck by lightning will be dismissed if there were no thunderstorms that day and no lightning was seen.

Having looked for the relevant, the second rule is: *Look for the unusual.* In our accident example, after we have discovered what facts are relevant to causing the accident in which the automobile collided with a bus, we must next ask whether there was an unusual break in the normal course of events that was the major cause of the accident. Perhaps the driver had just been given new allergy pills by her doctor and these pills had made her drowsy. She then fell asleep at the wheel, went over the center line, and hit the bus.

A *new*, unusual, or abnormal factor in a situation can cause novel events to occur, so these events can often be explained by finding a novel causal factor. If a scientist has done an experiment with a certain liquid a hundred times and then, on the hundred-and-first time, raises the temperature of the liquid by 10°, this temperature increase *must* be the cause of the new gas that is produced in the experiment for the first time. If only one new factor is at work, it is almost certainly the cause of a new effect. However, if there are several variables all changing at once, no one can be certain which is the cause. For this reason, physical scientists and social scientists try to control experiments and studies so that only one factor is changing at a time.

Explanation in terms of unusual causal factors is a common form of reasoning. For example, recent increases in rates of violent crime have often been blamed on increased showing of violence on television. Here the fact to be explained, the increase in crimes of violence, is related to an unusual and novel factor, the recent increase in the presentation of violence on television.

Here is another example:

Chief Dogood told reporters that he believes there is no doubt that women's fashions that emphasize the "nude look" are the reason for the increased number of sexual crimes against women in the city. He cited statistics to show that in the three years previous to the introduction of the nude look there were an average of 53 reported sexual crimes per year. Last year, after the nude look became popular, this figure had risen to 129. "The conclusion is obvious," said Chief Dogood.

We have all encountered similar arguments. The principle behind it is this: When trying to explain something, you must look at all relevant factors which are antecedent to the event or events needing explanation; if this does not provide the answer, you must move on to the second principle. If you can find some *unusual* feature—some *abnormality* in the normal course of events—then this unusual feature will be *the* cause of the event requiring explanation. In the example, Chief Dogood is trying to explain the rise in sexual crimes. The only new and unusual factor, he claims, is the now-popular nude look; so he concludes that *that* must be the cause of the increased rate of sexual crime.

Such reasoning was also the basis for legislation that was enacted in a province of Canada a short time ago. The legal age for drinking alcoholic beverages had been 21 and was then lowered to 18. A couple of years later, the government of the province introduced legislation to *raise* the drinking age again, this time to 19. The reason given was that among 18-year-olds there was an increase in alcohol-related accidents. It was argued that the unusual condition, the newly gained ability of 18-year-olds to obtain alcohol legally, had caused the higher accident rates. Hence, to reduce the accident rate, the selected cause was going to be eliminated (or at least partially eliminated) by raising the drinking age again.

The point to note is that we can often find causes by looking for relevant factors and by looking for unusual events and reasons. In both these procedures you are being both logical and creative: logical because you are relating factors to the event in a reasoned fashion; creative because you are looking for the unusual and thinking divergently.

MILL'S METHODS OF FINDING CAUSES (MILL'S CANONS)

John Stuart Mill presented some general rules about experimental inquiry in his *System of Logic*, which provides the classic account of various types of inductive inferences.[5]   Since the object of inquiry is to establish connections between things in terms of laws, Mill sees any inquiry as a search for causes. Hence we might also call these rules for establishing causes. Mill outlines four distinct methods, but since he believes we can also combine the first two to provide an additional method, he ends up with five "canons," or rules. Since Mill's points are fairly easy to grasp, we shall briefly present each of the five. For the most part, we shall start with an example and follow it with explanatory comments. Mill is fairly accessible, so anyone wishing to read further about these methods would do best to consult his text directly.

The Method of Agreement

Imagine space travelers landing on a strange planet and setting out to explore it. After returning to their ship, several complain of numbness in their hands and arms and a chilly feeling in those regions. The medical officers agree that these symptoms must be caused by something on the planet. Upon questioning the dozen or so sick people, it is discovered that each of them handled some purple, fernlike plants. Therefore the medical officers conclude that the cause of the illness is a substance found on the plants.

The key point Mill makes about the *method of agreement* is that once we find a common feature or element surrounding repeated instances of something we want to explain, then we feel that we have found the cause—or at least an *essential* causal factor. If all the people who got headaches rode in your car, then the cause very likely has something to do with your car—perhaps an exhaust system needing repair.

Of course this method is harder to apply if the causes are many or complex. If the space travelers had to touch three distinct types of objects in a certain sequence before becoming ill, it would very likely take much greater effort to see the point of agreement and, therefore, much longer to establish the cause of their ailment.

[5] J.S. Mill, *A System of Logic*, Book III, chs. 8 and 9, *in* Ernest Nagel, ed., *John Stuart Mill's Philosophy of Scientific Methods* (New York: Macmillan, 1974).

The Method of Difference

Imagine that you manufacture golf balls and wish to test a ball made from a new synthetic fiber. You have a machine that allows every ball tested to be hit with precisely the same force, at the same angle, and so on. The new ball is found to travel approximately ten yards farther than conventional balls. You repeat the experience numerous times with the same results. So we could produce the accompanying table.

	New Ball	Conventional Balls
Size	1.68 inches in diameter	1.68 inches in diameter
Weight	1.6 ounces	1.6 ounces
Surface	pitted, hexagonal	pitted, hexagonal
Surface Material	Synthex 12	rubber (natural)
Core	steel	steel
Average Distance Travelled	173.8 yards	164.1 yards

The only difference between the types of balls is the surface material. So, by applying the *method of difference*, we can claim that the new surface material, Synthex 12, is what causes the balls made with it to travel about ten yards farther than other types of balls.

The Joint Method of Agreement and Difference

As its name suggests, the *joint method of agreement and difference* merely combines the previous two methods.

Another example will make it clear: If all the passengers on a flight from New York to New Orleans become ill except *one*, we have discovered a candidate for the cause once we learn that the only point of agreement among the ill passengers is that they all ate the sour cream with their baked potatoes (the method of agreement). We have further evidence when we learn that the one well passenger differed from the ill ones in that she did not eat the sour cream (method of difference).

Jointly, these circumstances greatly increase the probability that the sour cream is the cause.

The Method of Residues

We discussed the *method of residues* earlier—although we did not use this name—so there is no need to discuss it at length here. Basically, this method involves removing from consideration all normal or known causes and effects. This allows us to infer that the remaining phenomenon (the residue) will be the cause of the remaining effects or effect. The new antecedent factor in a situation will be the cause of the new effect.

The Method of Concomitant Variation

The rule in Mill's *method of concomitant variation* is that if one phenomenon always varies whenever another changes in some specified way, then the first phenomenon is either a cause or an effect of the second. Or, at least, the phenomena are connected causally in *some* way. The beginning horn player who learns that as he tightens his lips together, the pitch of the resulting note becomes higher is applying this rule.

Of course, causes may be complex. Often several factors influence the behavior of an object. A penny dropped from the top of a building is influenced by gravity, by wind currents, and by its shape and markings. Mill also discussed difficulties and limitations of using these methods, and he pointed out situations in which several causes might act concurrently or in conjunction with one another. Nevertheless, Mill believed that the methods were useful in almost any scientific inquiry. He saw them as having two roles:

> If discoveries are ever made by observation and experiment without deduction, the four methods are methods of discovery; but even if they were not methods of discovery, it would not be the less true that they are the sole methods of proof. . . . The great generalizations which begin as hypotheses must end by being proved and are, in reality . . . proved by the four methods.[6]

You can see that the question of establishing causes is related to the topic of Chapter 6, finding explanations and establishing hypotheses.

[6] Mill, *op. cit.*, Bk. III, ch. 9, p. 237.

CAUSAL FALLACIES

We have outlined useful reasoning processes and arguments concerning *causal connections*. But some kinds of bad argument also involve causal analysis.

No Connection

It is a fallacy to assume that just because one event follows upon another (happens after it), the one caused the other. There may have been *no connection* between them. Suppose, for example, that Jeff drank a bottle of soda on Monday and that on Tuesday he discovered a bunion on his toe. It would be silly to argue that the soda caused the bunion just because Jeff drank it *before* the bunion appeared.

The Cart Before the Horse

Beware of *putting the cart before the horse* by confusing causes and effects in a given situation. Suppose Professor Dull noticed that university students who were industrious and sober got good grades while those who were lazy and sat around drinking beer most of the time got terrible grades. What if he then proposed to the university president that good grades be given to the lazy students in order to make them sober and industrious? Surely he would have mistaken the causes for the effects, and vice versa.

In her novel *Surfacing*, Margaret Atwood writes of a child who makes a similar mistake. The child is obviously learning that events constantly occurring in succession are frequently causally related. But the child does not always understand the nature of the causal connection. In the story the character, now an adult, remembers her childhood perception:

> There used to be a barometer on the porch wall, a wooden house with two doors and a man and a woman who lived inside. When it was going to be fair the woman in her long skirt and apron would emerge from her door, when it was going to rain she would go in and the man would come out, carrying an axe. When it was first explained to me I thought they controlled the weather instead of merely responding to it.[7]

[7] Margaret Atwood, *Surfacing* (Toronto: McClelland & Stewart, 1972), p. 24.

Occasionally you will encounter an argument that attempts to establish a cause-and-effect relationship between two things when it is not clear from the context which is the cause and which is the effect. In a sense, this is a variant of the fallacy of confusing cause and effect.

For example, a psychiatrist, Dr. Roderic Gorney, spoke to the American Psychiatric Association in Miami in 1976 on the topic of censorship of television violence. In discussing the relationship between watching violent television programs and other viewer behavior, he claimed that a study he had conducted demonstrated a direct link. A story carried in many newspapers reported Gorney as saying that "results showed those who primarily watched police and detective shows were significantly more aggressive . . . than those who saw nonviolent . . . programs."[8] This survey finding was taken by Gorney and others to show that viewing violence on TV caused aggressive behavior.

However, this relationship is not clearly shown—at least from what Gorney is reported to have said. It could be that aggressive people choose police shows to watch and that nonaggressive people choose nonviolent shows. One needs more evidence in order to decide in which direction the causal link occurs. Does viewing violence *cause* aggressive behavior and shape aggressive characters? Or does the aggressiveness of certain people *cause* them to choose violent programs to watch? Be careful, therefore, when two events appear to be related, in deciding which is the cause and which is the effect.

Common Cause

When you discover two events that appear to be related, be aware that there *might* be a third factor—a *common cause*—affecting both. Suppose we note that every time the barometer falls, the river rises soon after. It would be fallacious to think that the fall in the barometer *causes* the river to rise. The real cause of both is a change in atmospheric conditions that causes pressure changes (affecting the barometer) that, in turn, bring rain (causing the river to rise). Remember that things are often complex, so be cautious.

[8] From *The Saskatoon Star-Phoenix*, May 14, 1976; the story was an Associated Press release.

EXERCISES

I. Write out each of the following in terms of premisses and conclusion. State the type of argument used in each case.

1. Since good pitching is so important, it means that either Oakland or Cincinnati should win the pennant. But Oakland will not have good pitching now that Brownstone has injured his arm, so they will not have a chance to win. Thus Cincinnati will win.

2. If the governor pardons him, we will be the laughing stock of the nation. Because if the governor pardons him, he will go on television arguing that the state is soft and unprincipled, and if he says that on television we will be the laughing stock of the nation.

3. She was told that she must either come to the meeting or forgo her voting privileges. Since she did not come to the meeting, she has forgone her voting privileges.

4. China will not back down, because if China backs down she will lose face and China will not do anything that will make her lose face.

5. You would have to be a naive fool to be unaware that the carnival operator was conning the public. Yet Jones is neither naive nor a fool about such things, so he must have been aware of what was going on.

6. It's no wonder his daughter left home. I told John that if he continually nagged his daughter, then she would up and leave; yet he continued to nag her anyway.

7. If I buy a new cello I must buy a humidifier; otherwise my cello will crack. But if I buy a new humidifier, I can't get the new car I want. However, my musical career is more important than having a new car. So I must accept the consequence that if I buy a new cello, then I just cannot get a new car.

8. When it got loose the horse must have gone to some place it was familiar with, which means it went either to its old paddock or it went to Orkney's farm. We have already checked the old paddock and it's not there, so it must be at Orkney's.

II. Each of the following provides premisses for a conclusion that is *not stated*. In each case state the type of argument involved and supply the conclusion that follows from the given premisses in terms of that argument form.

1. If she comes home late she will miss supper, and if that happens her mother and father will be upset.
2. If Johnny brings the mouse into the house his parents will scold. However, he is bringing it into the house anyway.
3. Mary is doing badly in her schoolwork. Students who do badly are either stupid or lazy and her past performance assures us that Mary is not stupid.
4. If there were going to be a thunderstorm, then the barometer would be falling right now. But the barometer is not falling.
5. Either old MacDonald had a farm or Simple Simon met a pieman. From what I heard, old MacDonald didn't really have a farm *after all.*
6. Victoria is not going to Chicago; yet if the stocks go up, Victoria always goes to Chicago.
7. What a mess! If Jones goes to Wales he misses the party, and if he misses the party we cannot present him with his award.
8. He is coming and Sharon promised that if he *does* come she will give him back his book.
9. They never get it quite right. Either the string beans are overdone or the potatoes are hard. However, I see that the string beans are *not* overdone this time.
10. The orchestra's favorite finishing number is either an overture or an orchestral suite. But the trumpet player told me they are not doing an orchestral suite at all tonight.

FOUR

EMPLOYING THE TOOLS

10

How to Find and Evaluate an Argument

In the previous chapters we examined various argument forms, identified fallacious kinds of arguments, and showed how to analyze and formulate arguments. Now the emphasis will be on practical application. We shall offer techniques that will help you to *find* an argument in a report, article, or speech, and to *evaluate* the argument.

Not all writings and speeches are arguments leading to a conclusion. Some are stories and descriptive reports that merely list events. Therefore, one of the first questions to ask yourself when you are faced with a report, article, or speech is, What is the author or speaker attempting to do here? Is the passage merely describing an incident, or telling a story? Is the speech an attempt to persuade the listener to adopt a certain point of view?

Once you have decided that the writer or speaker is, indeed, presenting an argument, you are ready to use the techniques outlined in the following sections.

FINDING THE ARGUMENT: WHAT IS THE SCORE?

To help you remember the principles to be followed in finding an argument, we have arranged them so that, with a letter to represent each one, we can spell a word. The word, or acronym, is *SCORE*. In trying to find an argument you are trying to find out what the SCORE is. What is the writer or the speaker attempting to show? What is he or she up to? The principles represented by the letters of the acronym *SCORE* are outlined in the accompanying table.

S	Search	*Search* for cue words or anything that will help you to *break up* the argument into its parts.
C	Conclusion	Find the *conclusion*. First, discover the main point, or conclusion, and *then* work back to the supporting reasons of premisses.
O	Order	Find the logical *order* of the *reasons* given for the main conclusion. Arrange
R	Reasons	the argument so that these reasons (premisses) are first and the conclusion last.
E	Evidence	Decide whether any further *evidence* is provided to support the main premisses. If so, what is it? Are there secondary arguments used to support those premisses?

In applying the SCORE technique, keep in mind the lessons of earlier chapters. For example, arguments sometimes are not fully stated and therefore you must supply missing premisses. Even a conclusion is sometimes omitted. At times you must be prepared to rearrange sentences (provided you do not alter their meaning) in order to show the logical connections.

The SCORE technique is used to detail the stages through which the argument progresses. Once this has been done, the argument can be evaluated by the FATE technique.

EVALUATING AN ARGUMENT: WHAT IS ITS FATE?

We again use a letter to represent each of several basic principles for critically evaluating an argument. These form the acronym *FATE*. In evaluating, we are deciding the *FATE* of the argument.

F	Fallacies	Are there any *fallacies* or errors in the logical connections?
A	Alternatives	Are the supporting premisses the only possible ones? Are there *alternatives* that come to mind? Are there additions or counter-examples you can think of as you question the premisses?
T	Truth	Are the premisses *true*?
E	Evidence	This is similar to step E of the SCORE technique. In the *FATE* test, your interest lies in evaluating the *evidence* presented to support the main premisses.

Counterexamples

Counterexamples, mentioned under step A of the FATE table, call for special attention. The technique of counterexample is an important critical tool. Consider the following:

"We must clamp down on the players," said the chief referee. "Every game we begin by being lenient ends in violence."

"But," responded referee Krackshaw, "the game last week between Atlanta and New York was not like that, nor were the previous games involving New York. Maybe it's got more to do with the nature of the players on the various teams than with the degree of leniency we exercise in refereeing."

Here the chief referee claims that whenever the referees are lenient the game ends in violence. From this he wants to conclude that it is thereby necessary to "clamp down." Krackshaw has provided some counterexamples to this claim, thereby destroying the chief referee's position. At the very least, the chief referee must revise his claim to "*Some* games beginning with lenient refereeing end in violence." The technique of counterexample, used by Krackshaw, has demonstrated that the chief referee's argument is based on a faulty premiss and, as such, is not acceptable. Once Krackshaw has shown that the chief referee's generalization is not true, he goes on to provide an alternative explanation in terms of the characters of the players on different teams.

SCORE-FATE METHODS AT WORK

The following sections contain arguments to be analyzed and evaluated according to the SCORE and FATE techniques. Before reading the discussion that follows each argument, try applying the techniques on your own. You may find it helpful to underline or encircle cue words found in your search. (For a brief list of common cue words, refer back to the table in Chapter 6.) You can also cross out phrases such as "I feel strongly that . . .," which do not contribute to the content of the argument but are merely emotional. Numbering the key statements as they are revealed by your search will also help. After you have worked each example on your own, check your analysis and evaluation with ours.

EXAMPLE 1. THE THANKSGIVING DINNER CONTROVERSY

Imagine two students, Gloria and Vivian, who share an apartment, in the middle of a heated discussion. The topic is whether they should invite Gloria's friend, Wilma, for the Thanksgiving weekend. So far, Gloria has based her appeal on her friendship with Wilma. But Vivian has claimed that Gloria and Wilma do not really get along and that she (Vivian) does not have time to entertain on this particular weekend, given that midterm exams are only a week away. Finally Vivian says:

> The real problem will be in the kitchen. Maybe Wilma will mind her own business and leave the cooking to us; or maybe she will want to "help." Given past performances, it's a certain bet she *won't* mind her own business. She'll want to butt in. Oh, she'll call it "helping," but within a day she'll have taken over.
>
> Then what will happen? If I insist she get out of the kitchen, she'll be insulted and then *you'll* get mad at *me* for upsetting her. Yet if I let her take over the meals, no one will eat them. You and I both *hate* her cooking.
>
> There's no way out—*except* not to invite her in the first place.

What Is the SCORE?

S: The Search. The search points out an "or" in sentence two, which indicates alternatives and alerts us to a possible disjunctive syllogism. "Given," at the beginning of sentence three, signals a premiss. In the second paragraph "if . . . then" signals a hypothetical and alerts us to a possible dilemma *or* a valid argument form using "if . . . then."

C: Conclusion. There are two conclusions. One occurs at the end of paragraph one: " . . . she'll have taken over." The other occurs at the very end, in the short last paragraph: " . . . not to invite her in the first place."

O and R: Order and Reasons. The order of the reasons (premisses) is as follows:

1. Wilma will mind her own business and leave the cooking to us or she will interfere and take over the kitchen (that is, "help").
2. Wilma won't mind her own business.
3. *Therefore* Wilma will interfere and take over the kitchen (that is, "help").

The conclusion, 3, is reached by a disjunctive syllogism.

The next part is *another* argument following as a consequence of the conclusion in 3:

4. *Either* I insist that Wilma get out of the kitchen *or* I let her take over (implicit).
5. If I insist she get out of the kitchen, then she will be insulted and you will get mad.
6. If I let her take over, then no one will eat her meals.
7. *Therefore* either she will get insulted and you will get mad or no one will eat her meals.

Steps 4 through 7 provide a dilemma. Since the alternatives in the conclusion, 7, are both undesirable, Vivian suggests that the whole problem be solved by not inviting Wilma in the first place. This solution *will* work—because if Wilma is not invited, the alternatives in 1 do not become possible and none of the other consequences will actually occur. In a sense this destroys the initial disjunctive syllogism by providing another alternative ("or Wilma stays at home"). And with that extra alternative, the conclusion in 3 does *not* necessarily follow.

E: Evidence.   Premiss 2 is supported by the evidence of past experience: Vivian alludes to Wilma's "past performances." The fact that no one eats the meals is evidence that they all hate Wilma's cooking.

Presumably, these premisses are to be accepted as true, although an extended debate might show Gloria disputing these claims. If that happened, the premisses would be questionable and the whole chain of arguing weakened accordingly.

What Is the FATE?

F: Fallacies.   There are no fallacies or logical errors.

A, T, and E: Alternatives, Truth, and Evidence.   No alternatives, questions of truth, or counterexamples arise here. (In a slightly different, extended, example, though, Gloria might question the truth of the premisses by citing counterexamples—that is, by introducing instances of meals everyone has liked, and so on.)

All in all, this argument rates highly. It is logical, and the key premisses are supported with evidence. It is hard to evaluate, though, apart from praising its logic, because we do not know the truth of the evidence. But assuming that Vivian is right about how Wilma will act and about how much the meals will be disliked, it is a sound argument.

EXAMPLE 2. THE OVERWEIGHT MAN

In Chapter Four we introduced an example in which someone infers that an overweight person is a heavy eater. Here is a slightly extended version of that example:

> Look at that man. He is so overweight, he must eat a lot. And he is ordering pie and ice cream! Since all that overweight people have to do if they want to lose weight is cut down on their food intake, he must not want to lose weight.

What Is the SCORE?

S: The Search. "Must" in the second sentence suggests a conclusion; "since" signals a premiss; and "if" alerts us to a possible dilemma or argument form using "if . . . then."

C: Conclusion. There are two conclusions. *First,* "he eats a lot"; *second,* "he does *not* want to lose weight." The "not" in the second conclusion, coupled with the cue word "if," suggests we look for an argument *modus tollens* (denying the consequent).

O and R: Order and Reasons. The first argument is a categorical syllogism:

1. All overweight people eat a lot (assumed premiss).
2. He is overweight.
3. *Therefore* he eats a lot.

The second argument is an argument *modus tollens*:

4. If he wants to lose weight, he will cut down on his food.
5. He is *not* cutting down on his food.
6. *Therefore* he does *not* want to lose weight.

E: Evidence. Premisses 2 and 5 are based on observations.

What Is the FATE?

F: Fallacies.   There are no fallacies or logical errors. A Venn diagram will show that the categorical syllogism is valid.

A: Alternatives.   There is a possible alternative to 1, namely that *some* overweight people have glandular problems.

T: Truth.   Premisses 2 and 5 are true because they are based on observations.

E: Evidence.   Premiss 4 can be challenged by a counterexample: someone may *want* to lose weight but *may not be able* to cut down on food intake because of psychological problems.

All in all, this set of arguments is logical but has questionable premisses. Given those questionable premisses, the argument is *not acceptable*, or beyond reproach. In a sense it is good *as far as it goes*, because it employs valid deductive argument forms. But it fails to rate highly because its premisses are not certain and may be easily challenged by finding alternatives or counterexamples.

EXAMPLE 3. THE LETTER FROM DEATH ROW

The following is a real, rather than a fictional, example. Caryl Chessman was to be executed at San Quentin on February 19, 1960. At the last moment he was granted a 60-day reprieve by Edmund G. Brown, Sr., who was at that time the Governor of California. Chessman then wrote a long letter to the governor stating his views on capital punishment, on its effectiveness in reducing crime, and on his days in a death cell. Here is a small part of that letter to Governor Brown, written on February 26.

> As long as the death penalty is on our statute books, there will be too much emotionality and circus atmosphere tainting our administration of justice. And for those who doubt this, there is a ready and rational test at hand: Let a moratorium be ordered on the supreme penalty for a period of, say, five years. I am certain during that period there will be no rise in the per capita crimes. Rather, I am convinced the crime rate will drop appreciably and that justice will function in a far more even-handed and fair way. The sensationalism inevitably attending capital crimes will vanish.[1]

[1] From Caryl Chessman, letter written from San Quentin Prison, February 26, 1960, to Edmund G. Brown, Sr., Governor of California; *in* H. K. Girvetz, ed., *Contemporary Moral Issues*, 2nd ed. (Belmont, Cal.: Wadsworth, 1968), p. 147. Chessman was executed on May 20, 1960.

What Is the SCORE?

S: The Search.   There are no *obvious* cue words. However, the tone of the writing does suggest that the first sentence is a conclusion. The later sentences clearly are claiming that certain things will happen as a *consequence* of other events. So we should expect some "if . . . then" propositions.

C: Conclusion.   The conclusion advanced is "If we have the death penalty, then there will be emotionality."

O and R: Order and Reasons.   The conclusion plus Chessman's proposed "rational test" suggest that he is arguing:

1. If we have the death penalty, then there will be emotionality.
2. Let us *not* have the death penalty (that is, let us have a moratorium).
3. *Therefore* there will *not* be emotionality.

While this appears to be the main thrust of Chessman's argument, he also seems to be arguing for connections between crime rates, capital punishment, and sensationalism. It is hard to feel absolutely certain, because Chessman just *states* a number of things in the last half of this quotation. Nevertheless, it seems his intention to argue:

1. If we have no death penalty (have a moratorium), then the crime rate will drop and justice will be more fair.
2. If the crime rate drops and justice is more fair, then sensationalism will vanish.
3. *Therefore* if we have no death penalty (have a moratorium), then sensationalism will vanish.

E: Evidence.   The second argument is evidence for the second premiss of the general argument.

What Is the FATE?

F: Fallacies.   The second argument is a valid hypothetical syllogism. The first is *invalid* because it denies the antecedent. In other words, the first argument uses the *invalid* form:

1. If A, then C.
2. Not A.
3. *Therefore* not C.

In fairness to Chessman, though, we can reorganize the argument into the valid form of denying the consequent (*modus tollens*), as follows:

1. If we have the death penalty, then there will be emotionality.
2. There should *not* be emotionality.
3. *Therefore* we should *not* have the death penalty.

Besides being valid in this form, the argument expresses what Chessman clearly wishes to say. However, by suggesting a moratorium, he presents his argument in such a way that the normal reader will take it as we did. Put in that way, it is *not* a valid argument.

A: Alternatives.   Alternative possibilities include the worry that a moratorium will increase murders *because* there is no longer the deterrent of capital punishment.

T: Truth.   There is a genuine difficulty here because Chessman merely states things boldly: "I am certain that . . ." "I am convinced . . ." Such claims are highly contentious, and much of the current debate on capital punishment centers on these issues.

E: Evidence.   The passage itself provides no evidence for the truth of Chessman's claims. (Of course this is only a *very* short quotation from a long letter that does provide more.) Against Chessman, one could argue that people *are* deterred by the thought of punishment and that *only* the fear of capital punishment will deter potential murderers. Could we ever know how many potential criminals *have* been deterred by the threat of capital punishment?

The main point to note about the example is that had Chessman listed his reasons and conclusions more *clearly* and provided more *clues* to his thinking in this passage, he could have constructed a very good argument. In fact, except for his implicit use of the invalid argument form in the overall scheme, most of the argument is good.

EXAMPLE 4. THE CAUSE OF IDEAS

Human experience involves a continual presentation of images, impressions, or ideas. Walking down a busy street one encounters colors, shapes, noises, and smells. In dreams and in the fantasy world of imagination we also have numerous and varied ideas and images.

In his book *A Treatise Concerning the Principles of Human Knowl-*

edge, written in the first part of the eighteenth century, Bishop George Berkeley asks what *causes* these ideas. In answer he provides the following argument.

> I find I can excite ideas in my mind at pleasure and vary and shift the scene as often as I think fit. It is no more than willing and straightway this or that idea arises in my fancy . . . But whatever power I may have over *my own* thoughts, I find the ideas actually perceived by sense have not a like dependence on my will. When in broad day-light I open my eyes, it is not in my power to choose whether I shall see or no, or to determine what particular objects shall present themselves to my view . . . There is, *therefore* some other will or spirit that produces them.[2]

What Is the SCORE?

S: The Search.   The last sentence contains a "therefore," so we can expect that "some other will or spirit that produces them [ideas of sense]," which follows, is the conclusion.

The third sentence presents two alternatives: that ideas are self-produced; or that ideas are *not* in our power, so are *not* self-produced. The third and fourth sentences *deny* (note the "not" in each) one alternative, so we should anticipate a disjunctive syllogism.

C: Conclusion.   The last sentence does indeed contain the conclusion, which is "Ideas of sense are caused by another will or spirit."

O and R: Order and Reasons.   The order of the reasons is a *valid* disjunctive syllogism.

1. *Either* ideas of sense are self-produced and created by an activity of my will, *or* ideas of sense are caused by another will.
2. It is not the case that ideas of sense are self-produced or created by an activity of my will.
3. *Therefore* ideas of sense are caused by another will.

E: Evidence.   The first two sentences mention common facts in support of the first alternative stated by premiss 1. Here Berkeley is establishing, as we will all agree, that sometimes *we* create or produce ideas when willing or imagining. The fourth sentence suggests, again a common fact, that in certain cases ideas seemed *forced* upon us and we have no feeling of willing them or choosing them, thereby supporting premiss 2.

[2] George Berkeley, *A New Theory of Vision and Other Writings; in* A. D. Lindsay, ed. (London: J.M. Dent, 1910), pp. 126–127.

What Is the FATE?

F: Fallacies.   The argument is not fallacious but is a *valid* deductive argument. It is a disjunctive syllogism.

A: Alternatives.   There is one further alternative to those offered in the first premiss. Our ideas of sense could be caused by something external to us that was not another will or mind: they could be caused by physical objects. (While this alternative is not suggested in the quotation before us, Berkeley does in the larger context consider and reject this possibility.)

T: Truth.   The question of truth is harder to decide in this case, because we are asked to accept appeals to introspective evidence. While it certainly *seems* that we can often distinguish cases in which we control our ideas from other cases in which ideas are forced on us, it is not implausible to hold that sometimes ideas we believe we control are in actuality forced on us.

Such ideas could, for example, be caused by other ideas stored in our memory or by chance associations that bring them to mind. For example, seeing your friend's guitar might bring her to mind. Hence we could *feel* that we were choosing and controlling our thoughts when in reality they were determined by events around us and other associated ideas in our memory. You might *believe* that you freely chose to have a chocolate sundae; but in fact you might be responding automatically to a sign at the ice-cream shop showing happy people eating chocolate sundaes. The idea has been put into your mind, yet you feel you freely willed that idea.

These considerations suggest that we ought to be cautious of Berkeley's argument.

E: Evidence.   The alternative imagined when we discussed step T actually provides a possible counterexample.

Our analysis shows a deficiency in this argument. However, the reader should note that we have taken an isolated portion of Berkeley's text to illustrate the SCORE-FATE techniques. Elsewhere, Berkeley considered other possibilities—for example, that our ideas are caused by direct contact with material objects. Hence, to provide a final overall assessment of Berkeley, we would have to analyze his other arguments as we have analyzed the one just considered. But this leads us to philosophical problems and controversies that are beyond the scope of this text.

EXERCISES

Using the SCORE and FATE guidelines, analyze and evaluate each of the following arguments. Some are valid; others are invalid or fallacious for one reason or another.

I. There are only two ways to deal with murderers: either send them to prison or execute them. Obviously, we must execute them, for sending a murderer to prison is just a waste of the taxpayers' money since no criminals are reformed by spending time in prison (as the recidivism rate shows). And if no murderer is to be reformed by being sent to prison, then we are just wasting our money by sending someone there.

II. At first Mary was apprehensive. But then she began to feel better, after which she thought she might be able to eat a little of the cake. It was *delicious*! She had another slice, after which she began to feel nauseous again. Deciding that she had had enough of the party, she went home.

III. Communists have always claimed that communism is a philosophy. A philosophy is a system of thought which attempts to furnish the ultimate answer to the reason for man's existence and man's relationship to this existence. By definition, it seeks ultimate truth. Hence, every philosophy must continually question all premises, conclusions, judgments, values, and principles. However, the validity of the basic theoretical premises of communism cannot be questioned by its adherents, for these premises must be accepted as facts.

   Communism does not permit an objective search for truth. Communism tolerates only efforts to justify the validity of its alleged "scientific" principles. The current conflicting interpretations of Marxism by the leading communist countries—the Soviet Union and China—demonstrate that communism is not "scientific." Therefore, communism is not, and cannot be, a philosophy in the strict sense of the word. It is, rather, an ideology—an interpretation of nature, history, and society which is developed with some logic from premises which are demonstrably false but which are not open to question or criticism by its adherents.[3]

IV. "No, Sir," [said Dr. Johnson]; "medicated baths can be no better than warm water: their only effect can be that of tepid moisture." One of the company took the other side, maintaining that medicines of various sorts, and some too of most powerful effect, are introduced into the human frame by the medium of the pores; and, therefore, when warm water is impregnated with salutiferous substances, it may produce great effects as a bath. This appeared

[3] J. Edgar Hoover, *J. Edgar Hoover on Communism* (New York: Warner Paperback Library, 1970), pp. 62–63.

to me very satisfactory. Johnson did not answer it; but talking for victory, and determined to be master of the field, he had recourse to the device which Goldsmith imputed to him in the witty words of one of Cibber's comedies: "There is no arguing with Johnson; for when his pistol misses fire, he knocks you down with the butt end of it." He turned to the gentleman, "Well, Sir, go to Dominicetti, and get thyself fumigated; but be sure that the steam be directed to thy head, for that is the peccant part." This produced a triumphant roar of laughter from the motley assembly . . .[4]

V. At the recent Democratic rally the main speaker argued that it was clear that his party will win Tuesday's election. "Our record speaks for itself," he said. "Since the last election our party has fulfilled all its promises made at that election. We have increased social benefits, we have lowered personal income taxes, and we have cut government spending by 15 percent. This is a good record! And the people always vote for a party with a good record. Because of this, people from every walk of life—business executives and union members, husbands and wives, professionals and hourly workers—will vote for us next Tuesday, election day."

VI. "Oh brethren, don't you *know* the Bible says that man was made in the image of *God*! Then how *can* he be made in the image of a monkey?

"Brothers, judges," gasped the divine, pausing to mop his dripping face, "you know that our school books are full of this damnable doctrine [the theory of evolution]. What air you goin' to *do* about it? Air you goin' to let the deceivin' agnostic, hell-bound college perfessers send our children to *hell*?"[5]

VII. No civilized people want public censors, because civilized people want freedom of expression and public censors do not allow freedom of expression.

[4] James Boswell, *The Life of Samuel Johnson* (New York: Random House, 1952), pp. 165–166.
[5] T.S. Stribling, *Teeftallow* (Garden City: Doubleday Page, 1926), p. 25.

11

How to Construct and Present an Argument

In the last chapter we discussed techniques for analyzing and evaluating existing arguments that you might find in a newspaper, a magazine, a talk, a company report, a school essay, or wherever. In this chapter we shall show how the same techniques can be applied in making up and presenting arguments of your own.

No one doubts that the ability to present convincing and persuasive arguments is important. A committee report must provide logical reasons for the recommendations being made by the committee. A student's essay must be organized in a logical way and the conclusions backed up by sound arguments and examples. But how do you develop the skill to present your opinion on a topic in a logical and convincing manner? To know what sort of language will be most effective? To choose the argument form that will be the most useful?

As with so many other skills in life, these are developed by practice. A book can tell you how to finger a trumpet and how to shape your lips when you blow into it; but only hours of practice can produce silvery musical tones instead of the moose-calls and wind-whistles of the budding musician's first attempts. It is the same with arguing: you must practice. Ideally, you should practice with someone else— especially someone who can recognize good arguments and respond to yours in a challenging way. But many people learn a great deal about arguing from the give-and-take of everyday situations in which one discusses politics, religion, sports, or other topics. This kind of "thinking on your feet"—advancing and defending a position against criticism, considering the beliefs and assumptions of other people, and trying to decide how to bring others around to your point of view —is invaluable practice in developing good arguing skills.

CONSTRUCTING THE ARGUMENT: PREPARING TO SCORE

In constructing an effective argument, you can again use the SCORE technique that was explained in Chapter 10. We introduced SCORE as a method of finding an existing argument. The same procedure can be followed in deciding how to present your own argument. Here is the SCORE technique as you apply it to constructing an argument:

Search

S: Search. Once you have selected the topic, you must ready yourself to present a winning argument. First, prepare your case well by *searching* for all the facts and possible views. Ask yourself, What opinions are commonly held about the subject? What do most people believe? Why do people have the opinions they do? Do whatever research you can, provided time allows. While in the middle of an argument, you cannot leave your friends in the coffee shop and run to the library to read up on silent movies. You *can* do this type of research, though, for a report, speech, or essay.

The key to good preparation is to *look at both sides* of an issue. Good lawyers prepare both sides of a case, thereby not only thinking through ideas and arguments for winning the case but also thinking of the way their *opponents* will try to win in court. They ask what facts they would introduce and which witnesses they would call if they were on the opposite side. In preparing your argument ask yourself these questions:

1. Do I have *all* the *relevant* facts?
2. What positions are possible? What opinions are commonly held on this subject?
3. Do some people take a certain position because of *other beliefs* they have? For example, is someone a pacifist because of religious convictions?
4. What is *my* opinion on this subject? *What* do I believe, and *why*?

C: Conclusion. Decide the *conclusion* you wish to present. What is your belief, your position, on the topic?

O and R: Order and Reasons. In what *order* should your *reasons* be arranged to lead most persuasively to your conclusion? Once you have decided what premisses (reasons) you will use to lead to your conclusion, decide how to order these logically so that the conclusion does follow and so that your argument will be convincing.

E: Evidence.   What *evidence* and *examples* can you provide to support your premisses?   Are there studies, facts, or authoritative sources you can quote?

EXAMPLE 1. WIRETAPPING

Let us apply the SCORE steps to a specific example: wiretapping. Imagine that you are to write something or present a talk about whether the police or the F.B.I. should be allowed to tap telephones in order to listen in on the calls of individual citizens. Very briefly, here is how to use the SCORE technique in preparing your argument:

S: The Search.   In the search step, you should ask yourself the following questions:

1. What are the relevant facts?   These would include the right of individual citizens to privacy.   They would also include the reasons law-enforcement agencies have for wishing to use wiretaps—averting threats to national security and controlling organized crime, for instance.
2. What positions are possible?   Presumably, one could be completely for or completely against allowing law-enforcement agencies the legal right to use wiretaps.   Or one could believe that the practice would be acceptable only in certain clearly specified circumstances, such as a real danger to national security.
3. What are the underlying issues and beliefs that would affect views on this topic?   On one side we would have the belief in each person's constitutional right to civil liberties, including the right to conduct one's life without undue scrutiny and to conduct private, personal business without fear of coercion. Someone might argue that civil liberties are threatened if wiretapping is legal, because many people will be inhibited by the fear that others may learn about their personal business.   For example, a person might be reluctant to voice an opinion about a job applicant if there were reason to fear that these remarks might get back to the applicant.   A construction company president would not want details of a contract revealed to the com-

petition. Nor would one feel free to discuss family problems with relatives over the telephone.

On the other side, we would have the belief that national security is of greater importance than the privacy, or even the civil liberties, of a few individuals. If terrorists are a threat to the peace and security of all, then every measure should be taken to stop them, even to the extent of sacrificing the civil liberties of a few. If wiretapping is one of these needed measures, it is to be accepted.

C: Conclusion.   For the sake of argument let us assume the stance of someone who believes that wiretapping is justified in certain circumstances. Our conclusion will therefore be, "Wiretapping by law-enforcement agencies, in the interest of national security, is justified and should, therefore, be legal."

O and R: Order and Reasons.   Our initial working through of this problem at the *search* stage led us to think of measures that insure national security as being legally justified and to think, further, of wiretapping as one possible way to protect national security. Clearly, we are involved in classifying in both instances. And since the syllogism is an argument form dealing with classes we might consider constructing the main line of our argument in terms of a syllogism. Here is a suggestion:

1. All measures intended to insure national security are justified.
2. All wiretapping by law-enforcement agencies is intended to insure national security.
3. *Therefore* all wiretapping by law-enforcement agencies is justified.

E: Evidence.   Having set out the main structure of our argument, complete with ordered reasons (premisses) leading to a conclusion, we should go on to provide evidence in support of these main premisses. As evidence for premiss 1, you might argue that the national interests supersede the rights of individuals, in that some civil liberties and individual rights must occasionally be sacrificed for the national good. Moreover, it could be argued that one basic purpose of a nation is to protect its citizens, so that failure to preserve the state and protect it is failure to protect the individuals of that nation.

While a discussion of premiss 1 undoubtedly leads us into theoretical issues about the relationships between a nation and its citizens and about the nature of social and political organizations, the second premiss centers on points of fact. Does the legal right to tap phones help law-enforcement agencies apprehend terrorists or others who threaten national security? Is there misuse of these powers in countries that have legalized wiretapping by such agencies? This is a large topic that could profitably be discussed at much greater length.

EXAMPLE 2. POLLUTION

Let us try the SCORE method for constructing an argument on *another* topic. Imagine you are asked to give a talk on what should be done to companies that pollute the environment. We cannot pretend to be exhaustive in our treatment. We will, however, take a position for the sake of argument.

S: The Search. The search reveals such facts as: pollution contaminates sports and recreation areas, it interferes with the life cycle of fish and plants, and it's unpleasant.

On the other hand, we find that pollution is a necessary by-product of modern industry. We also find that antipollution devices are expensive. They would, therefore, add to the cost of products and they might drive many companies into bankruptcy, thereby increasing unemployment.

During your search remember to note all the evidence and examples you can, for later use.

C: Conclusion. The conclusion we arrive at is that pollution is so detrimental to the environment that it must be stopped. The only way to insure this is to have antipollution laws, enforced with stiff fines.

This conclusion involves two points that we wish to make: (1) stop pollution, and (2) impose fines. So we construct a separate argument in support of each of these points and then link the arguments together.

O and R: Order and Reason. One reason for wanting to stop pollution might be that pollution will ruin the environment for future generations. This suggests a *causal link* between polluting and future events, so one of the premisses will be: "If we pollute, then we will contaminate the world for future generations."

The conclusion we want to reach is that we should *not* pollute. This negative claim plus the "if . . . then" suggests we order the argument in terms of "denying the consequent" (*modus tollens*). So we have:

1. If we pollute, then we will contaminate the world for future generations.
2. We should *not* contaminate the world for future generations.
3. *Therefore* we should *not* pollute.

We next have to connect stiff fines with stopping pollution. This clearly requires that we believe that stiff fines will influence the actions of companies. Since this, again, suggests a cause-and-effect relationship, we can express that belief by "if . . . then" statements:

1. If stiff fines are imposed, then the actions of companies will change.
2. If the actions of companies change, then pollution will decrease.
3. *Therefore*, if stiff fines are imposed, then pollution will decrease.

The logical order of this argument is that of a hypothetical syllogism.

E: Evidence.   As evidence for the claim that we should not contaminate the world for future generations, we might argue that we have obligations to all people, whether present or future. By preserving the environment, we can make the world a better place for future generations than it otherwise will be.

People will have no trouble seeing the relevance of this point once they realize that their children and grandchildren will be part of the future generations.

Analyzing these examples has shown how to use the SCORE method for constructing an argument. You will also have noticed that as you set out your conclusion and your reasons, you begin to find clues about how to order your argument effectively. If your reasons involve causes, "if . . . then" arguments are appropriate. If they involve negative claims, then argument forms such as denying the consequent (*modus tollens*) or the disjunctive syllogism (eliminating the alternative) can be profitably used.

You can now see the benefit of learning to recognize a variety of good argument forms. Knowing them provides useful ideas about how to order your own thoughts logically. In the wiretapping example it was clear that we were *classifying* wiretapping as a measure contributing to national security; and classifying suggested at once that we use a syllogism to present the argument in a sound and convincingly logical way. In the pollution example, our thinking was in terms of *causes* and *effects*. Recognizing this immediately made it clear that a winning argument would be one using "if . . . then" to connect the thoughts.

EXAMPLE 3. SCEPTICISM

Let us take one final example, related to the philosophical problem of scepticism about sense perception. In this case we will present some introductory material on the problem, ending with a brief argument for the sceptical position. This will make it slightly different from the preceding examples, for the challenge will be to try to construct an argument that *counters* the one presented. Consider the initial argument carefully and, before reading our suggestion, try to decide how you might construct an argument *against* the sceptic's position.

We naturally believe that we learn many things about our world through our senses. We see colors and shapes; we hear musical notes, bird calls, train whistles, and so on. On the basis of such sense experiences we make judgments about the world. You experience a blue, spherical shape in your visual field and judge that there is a blue ball on the table in front of you. You put your hand into a bucket and experience a wet, warm sensation, whereupon you judge that there is lukewarm water in the bucket.

However, let us imagine meeting someone who is sceptical about relying on sense experience. This person points out that we are often fooled by our senses. A white object seen through tinted glass may appear pink. If our hands are extremely cold, a pail of cool water may feel lukewarm to us. The sun only *looks* to be the size of a half-dollar but is, we know, in reality much larger than the earth. Dreams often involve vivid experiences that make us *believe* we are someplace other than in bed when we are not. Such illusions and deceptions should teach us to be cautious, says the sceptic. If we go around making judgments about the world simply on the basis of the experiences we have, we will make numerous errors. Indeed, says the sceptic, we can never be absolutely *certain* that *any* experience we are having is *not* illusory

Let us express the sceptic's argument in a simple form:

1. There are sense experiences that are illusory or deceptive in some way.
2. It is possible for *any* sensory experience to be illusory, and we have no way to detect such illusions on the basis of sense experience itself.
3. *Therefore* we can never count on, or be certain of, the evidence of our senses. That is, a judgment based solely on the evidence of the senses could always be erroneous.

How can an argument be constructed to offset this sceptical conclusion? Here is a suggested line of attack, using the SCORE method.

S: The Search.   In one sense the search stage is simple, because in this example we are *given* a position to oppose. The problem is to think of possible lines of assault.

There are some counterarguments that will clearly not work. We might, for instance, suggest that we often appeal to the experiences of *other* people or check something against other experiences we ourselves have had. But the sceptic will reject this, rightly claiming that such reasoning begs the question. If the other experiences appealed to are sense experiences too, how can we be certain of *them?* If the reliability of sense perception is in doubt, we cannot dispel that doubt by simply appealing to more sense experience.

Can we attack the first premiss? Ask whether there are any so-called facts being accepted that are actually false or any assumptions being made here that we might question. If we look closely at premiss 1, it appears to be based on an assumption. The argument claims that there are in fact actual examples of illusion or deception. But what is required for us to be able to detect an illusion or a deception? Surely, what is required is that we must be able to distinguish deceptive cases from nondeceptive cases. Here, then, is our clue for a possible counterargument.

C: Conclusion.   The conclusion we are to reach, according to the task we assigned ourselves, is to show that the sceptic is wrong, that the sceptical position is not acceptable.

O and R: Order and Reasons.   Our search suggested an attack on premiss 1. In particular, we might begin by looking at the assumption pointed out above and the two possible alternatives it suggests: either we can detect illusions and deceptions or we cannot. These alternatives immediately suggest that we order our reasons in terms of either a dilemma or a disjunctive syllogism. Since the alternatives are contradictories, to argue for the elimination of one alternative will simply be an argument for the other, so a disjunctive syllogism would be out of place. Let us, therefore, try a dilemma. We shall state the alternatives and then present consequences of each. Briefly stated, we can argue:

1. *Either* the sceptic can detect illusions and deceptions *or* he cannot detect illusions and deceptions.
2. If the sceptic can detect illusions and deceptions, then his second premiss and his conclusion are false.
3. If the sceptic cannot detect illusions and deceptions, then his first premiss is false (or meaningless).
4. *Therefore either* the sceptic's second premiss and his conclusion are false *or* the sceptic's first premiss is false or meaningless.

E: Evidence.   We could provide further discussion to strengthen our arguments by showing that our dilemma is based on a strong conceptual point about the meanings of "illusion" and "deceit." Namely, these terms are meaningless unless they have a contrast in "nonillusory" and "nondeceitful." That is, if the role of such terms is to pick out or refer to certain types of experience, they can only do this by identifying such types of experience in contrast to other types. "Deceitful" describes *this* deceitful act as opposed to or in contrast to *that* nondeceitful act. Similarly, a color term such as "red" identifies red objects as opposed to objects that are green, yellow, and so on. If we lived in a monochromatic world, we would have no color terminology.

At this point we might consider a possible counterargument to ours. What are we to say if someone constructs a counterdilemma on the basis of our first premiss? It might go like this:

1. Either we can detect illusions and deceptions, or we cannot detect illusions and deceptions.
2. If we can, then we would never be fooled by our senses, which is false.
3. If we cannot, then the sceptic is right that we cannot count on our senses to give us truth.
4. *Therefore* either we must believe something that is false or we must agree with the sceptic.

Against this, we should perhaps prepare to argue about premiss 2. To say that we can have means of detecting errors, a criterion by which to distinguish sensory deceptions from nondeceptions, is *not* to claim that at no time and under no circumstances will we ever be fooled. You might very well be in possession of clear criteria for distinguishing genuine Van Gogh paintings but on occasion be fooled for a short period by a clever fake. A successful attack on premiss 2 of the counterdilemma will save our original argument against the sceptic.

DOUBLE-CHECKING YOUR ARGUMENT

After you have constructed your argument, check it to make certain you have not made any errors. For this, you can use the FATE technique that was detailed in Chapter 10. Consider your argument coolly and objectively. Imagine you are an opponent looking at it with an extremely critical eye, searching for any little weakness or slip. Ask yourself:

F Have I committed any fallacies or used any invalid logic?

A Are there alternatives to my position that I missed?

T Are my premisses true?

E Are there any counterexamples or other evidence that might weaken my argument?

As you examine your argument for fallacies and logical errors, you may wish to refer to earlier chapters that treat these subjects. Fallacies, for instance, are discussed at length in Chapter 3. And they are all listed and briefly defined in the Glossary, at the end of the book.

PRESENTING THE ARGUMENT

Having constructed and checked the argument you wish to advance by using the SCORE and FATE techniques, you must next pay attention to how you present your argument. You must decide the *tone* of your presentation. Should emotively charged language be used, for example? Here you would do well to review the discussion of words and language in Chapter 2, to remind yourself about the various uses of language.

In deciding on the tone of the presentation, the work you did at the search stage, when you were preparing, will be important. For example, in the wiretapping case it sounds positive to call the practice of wiretapping a "step taken in the interests of national security." Moreover, such a phrase appeals to a basic belief most people will endorse—namely that everyone should be interested in national security and place a high value on it. By contrast, to call wiretapping "prying" gives it a clearly negative tone. Naturally, one chooses words to achieve psychological advantage—as every good politician and advertiser knows. In this way your argument will be more persuasive.

MEETING CHALLENGES

After using the SCORE technique to arrange your argument in a persuasive, logical way, and after attending to the tone of your presentation, you must prepare to meet challenges to your argument. A good argument, like a good military campaign, allows for the unexpected.

Whether it is being presented by a lawyer in court, an interviewer on television, or a student at a committee meeting, nothing upsets an argument more than a *surprise* fact or an *unexpected* challenge. The successful arguer guards against surprise by thorough preparation. Part of this preparation is to anticipate possible developments during a debate and possible responses to your speeches or writings. However, you cannot always anticipate everything; often the unexpected *does* occur, regardless of how well you have prepared.

Let us consider that you are now defending yourself in an argument. What should be your tactic? Using the wiretapping example one more time, imagine someone challenging the position we took earlier. There the argument was set out in the form of a syllogism:

1. All measures intended to insure national security are justified.
2. All wiretapping by law-enforcement agencies is intended to insure national security.
3. *Therefore* all wiretapping by law-enforcement agencies is justified.

Someone might challenge the second premiss by arguing that abuse of power by those in authority, including law-enforcement officials, is not unheard of. So to accept wiretapping is to accept similar future abuses of the authority to tap telephones.

In response, you could argue that there is an important difference between the question of whether a practice is justified and should, therefore, be allowed by law and the question of whether some people might somehow abuse or disobey that law. You could also draw an analogy between the objection to wiretapping and an objection to licensing carnival operators on the grounds that similar operators have cheated the public before. Again, there are two questions. One is about the wisdom of permitting the sale of goods and services of a certain type. The other question is about the possible actions of carnival operators, who should not be treated as guilty before they have done anything wrong.

One last point should be mentioned about meeting challenges. Frequently you can anticipate a challenge and cut it off when you first present your argument. In fact, it is usually a good tactic— especially in writing, when you often have more space in which to develop your argument—to include a critical attack on the opposite view.

In trying to anticipate challenges and to meet possible challenges in advance, you can profitably use SCORE to make up an argument for your opponent. Pretend you are in the other person's shoes. Use SCORE to construct an argument, and then see how the argument can be attacked. Remember, successful lawyers prepare *both* sides of a case, so that they not only know their opponents' arguments but also are ready for what the other side will argue.

EXERCISES

In each of the following exercises you are given a topic and a position on that topic. Using SCORE, provide a brief argument for the position stated. (Our answers in the Solutions section will provide *one* possible way to do this. You may think of other ways.)

   I. Argue that euthanasia should be legal.

  II. Argue that we ought not to use animals in laboratory tests.

 III. Argue against the preferential hiring of minority groups.

 IV. Argue for a government-sponsored heroin-maintenance program.

  V. Argue for the abolition of nuclear power plants.

12

How to Write a Paper or a Speech

In everyday life we make use of reasoning skills while conversing with a neighbor, writing a term paper, giving a talk, preparing a committee report, or writing to a member of Congress. Not only do we want to express our ideas clearly and effectively in these communications; we also want to be forceful: to convince others of the logic of our arguments.

This chapter will aid you in achieving these goals of argument, particularly as they apply to writing a term paper or preparing a speech. Do not, however, lose sight of the fact that what we say about organizing a paper or speech can also be applied to any other form of arguing. We are *not* going to emphasize the technical aspect of good writing and speaking. Topics such as spelling, punctuation, grammar, and preparation of manuscript are treated well elsewhere.[1] What we are focusing on here is organization and logical flow of arguments as these apply to your essays, letters, reports, or speeches.

STEP 1. PREPARING YOUR ARGUMENT

Whatever you are preparing, begin by searching out material on the topic you have chosen or have been assigned. Your instructor, librarian, or friends will lead you to resource material. Then take care to read only articles or books that are relevant to your topic. Make notes as you read about or discuss your theme.

It is during this *search* phase that you decide on the specific sub-

---

[1] See the bibliography for Chapter 12.

ject you are going to treat. Most people tend to choose a theme that is too broad and difficult to cover adequately. If you are to prepare a paper of 1000 to 1500 words, you cannot hope to deal with all aspects of a topic such as "Unemployment" in this one assignment. More realistically, you might focus on "High Crime Rate and Teenage Unemployment in Our City" or "Unemployment and Senior Citizens in Mainsville."

At some point you must establish your exact position, or *conclusion*. We suggest you write out your conclusion concisely, because this will clarify your thinking. Remember that a sound argument—which is what your paper or talk is to be—is the directing of your readers or audience to a sound conclusion. If you choose the topic "High Crime Rate and Teenage Unemployment in Our City," you might be concluding that the high crime rate in your city is the result of unemployment among teenagers.

The next stage is to put together your arguments or findings from your readings, discussions, or thinking. This is the stage of giving *order* to your *reasons*. At this point you are marshaling all the main premises that support your conclusion and that indicate why you believe the conclusion is true. List all the reasons that you have decided support your conclusion. Then begin to arrange them so that they connect to provide the most logically persuasive argument you can devise.

Finally, you will want to support your premises with *evidence* and examples. You must have facts or data to convince your readers or audience. This evidence will be collected during your searching. Examples might also be gathered at that stage. Now you must incorporate this material into your main argument.

STEP 2. OUTLINING YOUR PRESENTATION

Once you have collected your materials and decided on the view you wish to present and how you will support it, make an outline. The outline will be a picture of the logical order of your essay or speech. You will work out the final product from this summary outline.

There are two main points to note about outlining. *First*, since the conclusion is the most important part of the argument, you should state it clearly. Later, when you come to writing the essay or delivering the speech, putting the conclusion first will catch the reader's or listener's attention and *focus* it on *your* topic and *your* viewpoint.

Second, there are only three ways in which an extended argument in an essay or speech can be organized:

1. There may be *one main argument* with secondary arguments supporting the premisses of the main argument.
2. There may be *chain arguments*, in which the conclusion of one argument provides a premiss for another.
3. There may be an *independent series of arguments*, each of which supports one and the same conclusion.

An example of each type of argument follows.

One Main Argument

In this group of sentences the ideas are organized in the form of a single argument:

1. If he is likely to brag, then Joan will not enjoy a date with him.
2. He is likely to brag.
3. *Therefore* Joan will not enjoy a date with him.

This might have the following for support of premiss 2:

4. All Texans are likely to brag.
5. He is a Texan.
6. *Therefore* he is likely to brag.

A *main argument* structure can be pictured in outline like this:

1. If A, then C.

2. A. ⟵—————————— { 4. All T are A.
                 5. He is T.
                 6. *Therefore* he is A.

3. *Therefore* C.

This shows the one *main* or central argument to the left. The supporting argument for premiss 2 is on the right, with an arrow showing that the argument in steps 4, 5, and 6 supports premiss 2.

The Chain Argument

Often we wish to present a complex argument that proceeds by distinct steps, through a series of reasons and intermediate conclusions, to a final conclusion. Each step is, therefore, like the link of a chain connecting one thought to another. Here is an example:

Link 1
{
1. All cows are large.
2. All large animals are noisy.
3. *Therefore* all cows are noisy.

4. All noisy things are frightening. }
5. *Therefore* all cows are frightening. }   Link 2

Note that the statement numbered 3 not only is a conclusion following from premisses 1 and 2 but also is used as a premiss in the second link. The last set of exercises in Chapter 5 provided good examples of chain arguments.

The Independent Series of Arguments

Sometimes two separate and independent arguments will support the *same conclusion*. Here are two such arguments.

Argument 1.
1. Either the smoke is coming from the charcoal burner or it is coming from the garage.
2. The smoke is *not* coming from the garage.
3. *Therefore* the smoke is coming from the charcoal burner.

Argument 2.
4. Whenever the Smiths eat on their patio, smoke comes from the charcoal burner.
5. The Smiths are eating on their patio.
6. *Therefore* the smoke is coming from the charcoal burner.

The preparation you did using the SCORE guidelines will indicate which of these basic outlines should be used in writing your essay or speech. Once you have your outline, you can begin to write. Stick to the logical order of your outline so that your presentation is clear and easy to follow. Remember the lessons of earlier chapters about the choice of positive words. Avoid useless emotive language and fallacies, but use the emotive connotations of words to your advantage.

STEP 3. CHECKING YOUR ARGUMENT

There are two things you can do to check your argument. *First*, using the FATE evaluation test, check it for logical errors and false statements and try to think of counterexamples. *Second*, once you have written a draft of your essay or speech, look at your writing objectively and ask yourself, Can a reader or listener *follow* and *under-stand* my arguments? Will someone be persuaded? Here you might use the SCORE guidelines again.

S: The Search. Did you provide enough cue words and phrases so that the reader can easily—in his or her own search—work through your argument?

C: Conclusion. Is the conclusion clearly stated, so that the reader both knows which statement expresses the conclusion and can under-stand the conclusion?

O and R: Order and Reasons. Is the overall logical order of your writing absolutely clear? Can a reader see easily whether it has one main argument or is a chain or series?

E: Evidence. Have you presented all the supporting evidence and examples for premisses so that the reader not only fully understands them, but also sees which premiss is supported by each piece of evi-dence or example?

In writing, you usually have time and space to develop a point of view in a reasonably full way. So remember to anticipate the argu-ments and evidence of opponents and to include a refutation or counter to each. The FATE test, at the *E* stage, should prepare you for this.

APPLYING THE PRINCIPLES

It may be helpful if we work these principles through with an ex-ample. Let us take one mentioned earlier, "High Crime Rates and Teenage Unemployment in Our City." Imagine that you are asked to write an essay or committee report on this topic.

Preparing Your Argument

S: The Search. Part of the search would involve gathering sta-tistics on crime rates in the city, on unemployment, and on the per-centage of teenagers among criminals and the unemployed. You would also gather firsthand reports from police, counselors, and teenagers.

C: Conclusion.   Let us assume that the material gathered in the search suggests a causal link between teenagers being unemployed and their participation in crime.

O and R: Order and Reasons.   The conclusion suggests that the order should follow the logical lines of one of the argument forms using "if . . . then." The premises (reasons) for this conclusion will involve the statistics gathered in the search. Since you are trying to *explain,* you can cast your conclusion as a prediction, in this way:

1. If unemployment increases among teenagers, then teenage crime rises.
2. Unemployment did increase.
3. *Therefore* teenage crime rose.

E: Evidence.   The statistics will support premises 2 and 3.

Outlining Your Presentation

Now that you have set out the argument in the form of premises and a conclusion, you are ready to prepare the outline. Begin by stating the problem:

Problem: To explain the rise in teenage crime.

Then write down your conclusion:

Conclusion: The increase in teenage unemployment caused the rise in teenage crime (a theory or hypothesis to be proven).

Now write down the whole argument in outline form. In doing so, you may use full sentences for the premises and conclusion. Or else, you may simplify—and shorten—the outline by assigning letters to stand for the main points. Here we shall use "U" for "a rise in unemployment among teenagers" and "CR" for "a rise in the crime rate among teenagers":

1. If U, then CR (hypothesis).
2. U.   ← ———————— Statistical Evidence
3. *Therefore* CR. ←

Note that this sets out the main line of the argument and shows the statistics gathered as supporting premisses 2 and 3.[2]

Checking the Argument

We can check this argument using the FATE test.

F: Fallacies.   There are no fallacies and the first argument is a valid instance of affirming the antecedent (*modus ponens*).

A: Alternatives.   The main worry is whether there might be another factor causing the rise in the crime rate. Since our search has presumably shown that the one relevant and unusual event was the increased unemployment among teenagers, this does appear to be the cause. Of course, someone might argue that the crime rate has only appeared to rise because the police became more efficient. Also, in the interviews the teenagers claimed that they vandalized stores and stole because they had nothing else to do.

T: Truth.   Given that the statistical data are accurate and provided the people giving the firsthand reports are reliable, the premisses are true.

E: Evidence.   There are no counterexamples or contrary evidence.

Let us consider another example. In this case we have selected a philosophical discussion about art, which we will outline in the form of a *chain argument*. Imagine that you are asked to write an essay about the nature of art objects[3] and spectators' responses to art. Here is a brief suggestion on how you could use the SCORE technique in preparing to write or speak on this topic.

S: The Search.   On the one hand we have artists and the objects created by artists, and on the other hand there are spectators who

[2] You will probably develop your own special way of organizing your material when you are writing an extended piece such as an essay or speech. One method would be to (a) collect all your material on file cards, one card for each item you want to note; (b) make your outline; (c) number each point in the outline; (d) go through your note cards and number and organize them according to which part of the outline they apply to; (e) arrange your notes in groups by these numbers; and (f) start writing with the first outline point and the corresponding cards.

[3] In esthetics, the branch of philosophy concerned with the study of art, this is often identified as the question of the ontological nature of art.

view and react to the artistic creations. Given the topic we assigned ourselves, you might ask whether art has more to do with the people who create and enjoy it (artists and spectators) than with the physical creations, such as paint arranged in a certain way on a canvas or a bronze cast into a certain shape.

C: Conclusion.   Assume you conclude that art is basically about emotions and creative ideas. Hence the spectator's response must focus on the ideas expressed, rather than on the physical medium. This means that the spectator must try to understand what was in the artist's mind during the process of creating the object.

O and R: Order and Reasons.   Since the topic requires settling two issues and their relationship, and since the conclusion established at stage *C* indicates two related points, you should set up two connected arguments. The *first* would establish that art objects are essentially the vehicles of artistic ideas and emotions. The *second* would argue that, given the first point, the spectator must "get inside the mind" of the artist in order to appreciate the art object iself. This reasoning suggests a *chain argument*, organized in the following way:

1. Either the "real" art object is merely physical, or it lies with the emotions and ideas of the artist.
2. The real art object is not the mere physical object, such as paint on canvas.
3. *Therefore* the real art object lies with the emotions and ideas of the artist.
4. *If* the real art object lies with the emotions and ideas of the artist, *then* proper spectator appreciation requires coming to an empathetic understanding of the artist's mind.
5. Therefore proper spectator appreciation of art requires coming to an empathetic understanding of the artist's mind.

In this chain argument, the *first link* is provided by premisses 1 and 2, which allow the conclusion, 3, by the valid deductive form, the disjunctive syllogism. The *second link* leads us to the final conclusion, 5, by means of an argument *modus ponens*, based on premiss 4 and on the proposition stated in the conclusion, 3, of the first link.

E: Evidence.   You must ascertain that the alternatives in 1 are exhaustive. Some might claim that they are not, because art objects can be construed as either ideal, physical, or a combination of the two.

Premiss 2 could be supported by comparing art objects with other *mere* physical objects—such as chairs and tables—in order to establish that art objects, *as art*, are not just physical. Rather, their esthetic qualities lie elsewhere—namely, in the feelings and thoughts of the persons who create and appreciate them.

To conclude our discussion of this example, let us create an outline around which an essay or speech could be organized and written. The basic skeleton of the argument would be as follows:

First Link
1. *Either* physical object *or* artist's idea.
2. Not physical object.
3. Therefore artist's idea (from 1 and 2 by a disjunctive syllogism).

Second Link
4. If artist's idea, then spectator must empathetically relate to artist's mind.
5. Spectator must empathetically relate to artist's mind (from premiss 4 and conclusion 3 by *modus ponens*).

Once the evidence is introduced to support these key premisses, the outline becomes more complicated. We then have:

First Link
1. First premiss of first link.
2. Second premiss of first link.←Supporting Evidence
3. Conclusion of first link =
   First premiss of second link.

Second Link
4. Second premiss of second←Supporting Evidence link.
5. Conclusion of second link.

We thus have a chain argument with supporting evidence for the main premisses. This evidence might, of course, consist of further arguments, thereby illustrating a feature of the *one main argument* format.

At this level of complexity it is best to introduce the main premisses of the first link, each with its accompanying support. Then show the first conclusion as following from these premisses. Finally, proceed to the second link and introduce premiss 4, presenting your supporting evidence or arguments for 4. Then clearly draw your final conclusion.

Learning to argue well—whether in conversation, in formal speech, or in writing—takes practice. But you will be off to a good start if you are aware of the basic argument forms and are alert to possible pitfalls. This book has demonstrated that logical thinking and sound arguing are not mysterious processes. They are skills that can be learned by anyone who is willing to invest a little time and effort.

EXERCISES

For each topic listed below, decide on *one* aspect that you wish to cover. Write out your conclusion after you have done your searching. Make an outline of *one* of the topics for a paper of 1500 words or a talk of ten minutes. Follow the models in this chapter.

1. Violence on television
2. Censorship and magazines
3. Treatment of pets in our society
4. Soilless farming
5. The armament question
6. The transportation crisis
7. Banning harmful drugs

Solutions to Exercises

Chapter 1. Introduction

I. 1. Argument.
    2. Argument.
    3. Not an argument; merely a conditional statement.
    4. Not an argument, just a story.
    5. Argument.
    6. Argument.
    7. Argument.
    8. Not an argument, just an emotional statement.
    9. Argument. The first sentence is merely an emotional expression, but the remainder provides an argument.
    10. Argument.

II. 1. b   6. a
     2. a   7. c
     3. c   8. b
     4. b   9. b
     5. a   10. c

Chapter 2. The Trouble with Words

I. 1. a
    2. c (first sentence); a (second sentence); b (third sentence)
    3. a
    4. d
    5. a (informative: claims that not all military leaders were heros)
       b (emotive tone created by terms such as "cheats," "scoundrels," "whimpering," and "cowards")

6. b (first sentence). Some might also argue that it is presenting information as well, and so is an instance of "a" also.

    c (second sentence)

7. d

8. a (first sentence)

    c (second sentence; the second sentence and the third also explain what the consequence of following the advice will be.)

II. 1. a   9. c
     2. c   10. b
     3. c   11. c
     4. b   12. c
     5. d   13. d
     6. b   14. a
     7. d
     8. b

III. 1. This is acceptable. The "they" in the second sentence might appear suspicious, but it clearly refers to "the people" in this context.

     2. In the last sentence, "he" is ambiguous. Does it refer to Jones or to Nixon?

     3. "Revolting" is ambiguous. In one sense it means "in revolt," while to the king it means something akin to "disgusting."

     4. "Good" is ambiguously used in this sentence. What goodness is in teaching is different from goodness as it pertains to military or college performance.

     5. "One," in the second sentence, is ambiguous. Does it refer to the cow or its calf?

     6. "Responsible" is ambiguous. The judge uses it to mean that the conditions necessary for holding a person *legally* responsible and punishable are not met. The juror uses "responsible" in the colloquial sense in which we say, "She did it, she was responsible for the broken window."

IV. 1. b   5. a
     2. a   6. a
     3. c   7. c
     4. c   8. c

V.   1. a   5. b
     2. c   6. c
     3. a   7. b
     4. b   8. a

Chapter 3.   Don't Let Them Fool You: Some Common Fallacies

I. 1. Illegitimate appeal to authority.
    2. Appeal to threats or intimidation (force).
    3. Arguing in a circle.
    4. *Ad hominem* (circumstantial).
    5. Appeal to pity.
    6. *Ad hominem* (abusive).
    7. Arguing in a circle.

8. Appeal to the masses.
9. Appeal to threat or intimidation (force).
10. *Ad hominem* (abusive), on the part of Abercrombie in his second speech.

II. 1. To make her case on the grounds that all others believe she should have a bicycle leaves Susan guilty of the fallacy of appealing to the masses. The first reason, that everyone else has one, could again be a fallacious appeal to the masses or, were the context more clear, and could we *hear* the tone of Susan's voice, it could *possibly* be the fallacy of appealing to pity.
2. Legitimate argument; no fallacies.
3. The prosecuting lawyer commits the fallacy of arguing *ad hominem*. This example is complicated by the fact that the defense lawyer does virtually the same, in a sense, although she does not argue *against* the accused. Part of the difficulty lies with the relevance of facts about the accused person's character or appearance, and in some cases these would be important and admissible. We simply need more information —or a larger context—in order to be able to tell in this case.
4. This argues in a circle, near the end of the passage, and so is fallacious.
5. The first speech by the motorist involves the fallacy of appealing to pity; his second speech involves a fallacious argument *ad hominem*.
6. This is not an argument, but merely a story.
7. This is a *legitimate* appeal to an authority who is making a judgment on a matter well within her competence and professional experience. Hence it is not fallacious. The conclusion is, one might note, a little strong, nevertheless.
8. This fallaciously argues in a circle.
9. This is *not* fallacious.
10. An instance of the fallacy of arguing *ad hominem* (circumstantial).

Chapter 4. How to Classify and How to Draw a Conclusion

I. 1. "so": conclusion
      "since": premiss
   2. "therefore": conclusion
      "since": premiss
   3. "for": premiss
      "and": In this context, the presence of "and" should cause us to check whether *another* premiss is being introduced, since "and" follows "for." As it turns out, there is another premiss following "and."
   4. "because": premiss
      "therefore": conclusion
      "since": premiss
   5. "in view of the fact that": premiss
      "because": premiss
   6. "hence": conclusion
   7. "hence": conclusion
   8. "in view of the fact": premiss
      "given that": premiss
      "we can conclude": conclusion

II.   1. *Premiss*: Some liberals are unrealistic.
         Premiss: All liberals are idealistic.
         Conclusion: Some idealists are unrealistic.
      2. *Premiss*: All horses on our farm are working horses.
         Premiss: All working horses are large.
         Conclusion: All horses on our farm are large.
      3. *Premiss*: Every real baseball fan is a fanatic about the game.
         Premiss: No fanatic of the game fails to buy a season ticket.
         Conclusion: Every real baseball fan buys a season ticket.
      4. *Premiss*: Only people who live in glass houses shouldn't throw stones.
         Premiss: No one in our family lives in a glass house.
         Conclusion: Anyone in our family who wishes to throw stones may
                     do so.
      5. *Premiss*: Every student taking the introductory class in abnormal psy-
                   chology ends up believing that he or she has a neurosis.
         Premiss: Jane is taking the introductory class in abnormal psychology
                   this semester.
         Conclusion: It is not surprising that Jane believes she has a neurosis.
      6. *Premiss*: The last photograph sent by those on the class trip has a
                   kangaroo in it.
         Premiss: Kangaroos only live in Australia.
         Conclusion: Those on the class trip are in Australia.
      7. *Premiss*: Some children are messy.
         Premiss: No messy people are particular about the clothes they wear.
         Conclusion: Some children are not particular about the clothes they
                     wear.
      8. *Premiss*: People who voted for Sandstone expected him to introduce a
                   bill that would lower personal income taxes.
         Premiss: Everyone living in Greystone Heights voted for Sandstone.
         Conclusion: Everyone living in Greystone Heights expected Sandstone
                     to introduce a bill that would lower personal income taxes.

III. 1. serious students
         lazy students
         students who did well
         naturally clever students
      2. Charlie's horses
         horses that speak a language
         horses that speak German
         horses that speak Chinese
      3. battles
         bloody battles
         naval battles
         the Battle of Trafalgar
      4. bread from the local bakery
         bread that is very good
         bread from the supermarket
         bread that is tasteless
      5. penny candy
         licorice braids
         jujubes
         toffees
         jawbreakers

1.

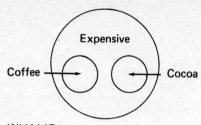

INVALID

2.

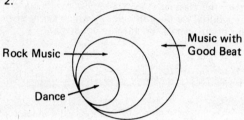

VALID

3.

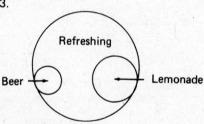

INVALID

4.

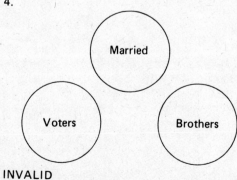

INVALID

5.

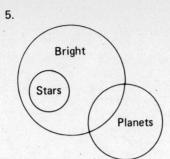

INVALID

(Note that the second premiss only excludes planets from the class of stars, thereby allowing for the possibility we diagrammed, in which *some* planets are bright even though none are stars.)

6.

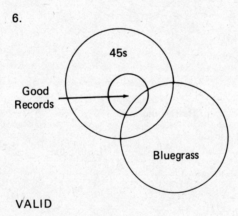

VALID

7.

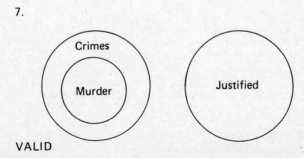

VALID

Chapter 5. Tools for Testing Arguments: Venn Diagrams

I.   1. All roses are red (universal-affirmative).
     2. No violets are red (universal-negative).
     3. All things made by Fred's Bakery are good (universal-affirmative).
     4. No things interesting to eat are free of calories (universal-negative).
     5. Not translatable into standard form.
     6. Not translatable into standard form.
     7. All horses are beautiful (universal-affirmative).
     8. No American is unpatriotic (universal-negative).
     9. No people living in glass houses are people who should throw stones (universal-negative).
    10. All Blamaros are (cars) that go like a bomb (universal-affirmative).
    11. Some (people) who get an A are not super-clever (particular-negative).
    12. All who know the way I feel tonight are lonely (universal-affirmative). (*Note*: This is a tricky case because the original sentence appears to be primarily about the lonely; but it is *not*. It is primarily telling us about "those who know how I feel tonight" and saying that they all fall into the class of lonely people. Similarly, "Only elephants have long memories" is telling us that all things with long memories belong to the class of elephants. It does *not* tell us that every elephant has a long memory; it *does* tell us that if we find something with a long memory it *will* be an elephant.)
    13. All those who tell lies are (people) who are living a lie (universal-affirmative).
    14. No arrogant (people) are (people) who see their faults (universal-negative).
    15. Since this is probably intended to express the claim that "most" tourists are obnoxious, it should *not* be treated as translatable into a standard-form proposition.

II.   *Note*: In these answers we did not attempt to give a complete list of alternatives, so you might be able to discover others. Also, where the original sentence was not already a quantified categorical proposition, we have first restated it in standard form.
     1. All cows dislike children.
     2. No pigs do not squeal.
        = No unsquealing (creatures) are pigs.
     3. All dunces (are people who) stood in a corner.
        = No dunces (are people who) did not stand in a corner.
     4. All dogs chew bones.
        = No dogs do not chew bones.
        = No things which do not chew bones are dogs.
     5. Some boxers are not uncourageous.
     6. All my neighbors are annoyed when I sing.
        = No neighbors of mine are not annoyed when I sing.
        = No human beings that are not annoyed when I sing are neighbors of mine.
     7. Some impolite people are cultured.
        = Some impolite people are not uncultured.
     8. All tolerant people are sensitive.
        = No sensitive people are intolerant.

9. Some unhelpful (people) are friends.
10. No poor (people) are industrious workers.
    = All industrious workers are not poor.

III. 1. Cue words are "since" (twice).
      1. All rare metals are expensive.
      2. No metals used by welders are expensive.
      3. *Therefore* no metals used by welders are rare.
      (Note that you should treat "expensive" and "costly" as synonymous and use only one term to represent this class when you put the argument into standard form.)
   2. Cue words are "so" and "because."
      1. All the delegates were at the reception.
      2. All at the reception were Smith's supporters.
      3. *Therefore* all the delegates are Smith's supporters.
   3. Cue words: "since" and "because" signal premisses; "then" indicates a conclusion.
      1. No neighborhood dog is a growling dog.
      2. All dogs which growl are biting dogs.
      3. *Therefore* no neighborhood dog is a biting dog.
   4. Cue words: "because" signals a premiss; "and" here signals another premiss. (Generally, "and" signals a premiss because it usually introduces an additional fact or claim that provides a reason for the conclusion; occasionally it can signal a conclusion if the writing is fairly colloquial.)
      1. Some astronauts were on the moon.
      2. All people on the moon are able to see all the Earth.
      3. *Therefore* some astronauts were able to see all the Earth.
   5. Cue words are "since" and "and."
      1. Some politicians are people who like to hear themselves talk.
      2. All the people at the party are politicians.
      3. *Therefore* all the people at the party are people who like to hear themselves talk.
   6. Cue words "because" and "and" signal premisses.
      1. No lawyers are socialists.
      2. No labor leaders are socialists.
      3. *Therefore* no lawyers are labor leaders.
   7. Cue words are "because" and "and."
      1. All films seized by the vice squad are pornographic.
      2. No films (and other things) seized by the vice squad are legal to possess (own).
      3. *Therefore* no pornographic film is legal to possess.
   8. "As" signals a premiss.
      1. All completed papers are to be given to a supervisor.
      2. All papers given to supervisors are papers given to someone wearing a name tag.
      3. *Therefore* all completed papers are to be given to someone with a name tag.
   9. "Because" signals a premiss; "and" cues a second conjoined premiss.
      1. Some slaves were not freed.
      2. Some of his ancestors were slaves.
      3. *Therefore* some of his ancestors were not freed.

IV. 1. The cue phrase "or else" introduces a reason and so signals a premiss.
    1. No students in the Grade 9 class were workers on the school project.
    2. All ambitious students were workers on the school project (hidden premiss).
    3. *Therefore* no students in the Grade 9 class are ambitious.

  2. There are no cue words at all in this example, but the conclusion, "There is a gardener," is obvious. This example has another tricky phrase, namely "this garden," which selects a specific garden. You should handle this the same way you handle proper names. That is, treat it as indicating all gardens that are *this* garden (of course there is only one). This will make more sense perhaps if you give the garden a name such as "Quiet Haven"; thus you can say "All Quiet Havens are well kept." That there is only one Quiet Haven garden in town still allows the phrase "Quiet Haven" to pick out that class (which only has one member). If the thought of classes with only one member seems odd, just think of a university class: if all the students in the class of '85 quit except one, then the remaining student *is* the class of '85. Anyway, the answer to 2 is:
    1. All gardens that are *this* one are well kept.
    2. All well-kept gardens are kept by a gardener (hidden premiss).
    3. *Therefore* all gardens that are this one are kept by a gardener.

  3. The cue word "that" signals a conclusion.
    1. Some athletes are users of artificial hormones.
    2. All users of artificial hormones are not competing fairly (hidden premiss).
    3. *Therefore* some athletes are not competing fairly (that is, the athletic competitions are not fair).

(This conclusion captures the intent of the original argument in that if some athletes are not competing fairly, then the competitions or meets in which they appear are not fair competitions. Remember that you must always try to *simplify* matters by recognizing that synonymous terms refer to the same class of things and by recognizing when two differently worded sentences are really just different ways of making the same point.)

  4. 1. All members of the golf club are rich.
    2. Some rich people are people who do not get what they want from the city council.
    3. *Therefore* some members of the golf club are people who do not get what they want from the city council.
    (*Note*: Although the cautious may not have drawn this conclusion, it seems one that the initial sentence *encouraged* us to draw and expected us to draw.)

  5. The cue word "because" signals a premiss.
    1. All school buses are yellow.
    2. No school bus is a downtown bus (hidden premiss).
    3. *Therefore* no yellow buses are downtown buses.

  6. The "and" suggests the linking of premisses, so it is a cue word in this example.
    1. All tasty things are fattening.
    2. All cheesecake is tasty.
    3. *Therefore* all cheesecake is fattening (unexpressed conclusion).

  7. "Since" is a cue word signaling a premiss. The word "must" also provides a reasonable clue that the statement it is embodied in states a conclusion.

       1. Some Armenians are Catholics.

       2. All your relatives are Armenians (hidden premiss).

       3. *Therefore* all your relatives are Catholic.

  8. 1. All who see violent films are corrupted.

       2. All public censors are people who see violent films.

       3. *Therefore* all public censors are corrupted.

  9. 1. All yellow buses are school buses.

       2. No school bus is a downtown bus.

       3. *Therefore* no yellow buses are downtown buses.

       (Note the difference between this example and example 5, above. In 5 the phrase "all school buses are yellow" is taken to mean that the class of school buses falls *within* the class of yellow buses but does not necessarily exhaust that class. In example 9 the phrase "only school buses are yellow" must be taken to mean that all and any yellow bus is a school bus.)

 10. The cue word "so" signals the conclusion.

       1. Some American citizens are drafted into the Army.

       2. Some women are American citizens (missing premiss).

       3. *Therefore* some women are drafted into the Army.

       (Note that since the conclusion was stated in terms of "some women," the missing premiss must employ "some women" too.)

V. The numbering of the following Venn diagrams corresponds to that of the examples in exercises III and IV.

III. 1

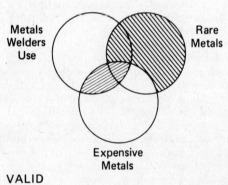

Metals Welders Use

Rare Metals

Expensive Metals

VALID

III. 2

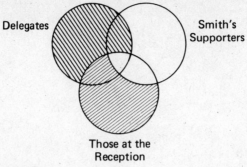

Delegates

Smith's
Supporters

Those at the
Reception

VALID

III. 3

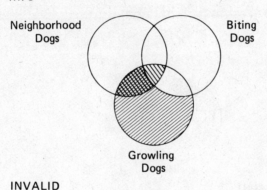

Neighborhood
Dogs

Biting
Dogs

Growling
Dogs

INVALID

III. 4

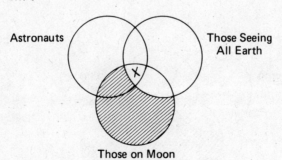

Astronauts

Those Seeing
All Earth

Those on Moon

VALID
(Remember to shade for a universal premiss *first*;
in *this* case shade premiss 2 first.)

III. 5

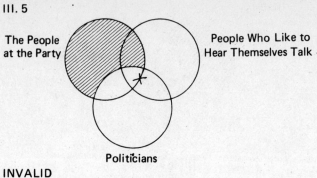

The People
at the Party

People Who Like to
Hear Themselves Talk

Politicians

INVALID

III. 6

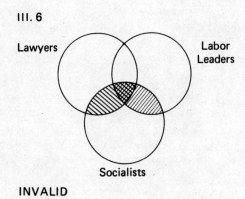

Lawyers

Labor
Leaders

Socialists

INVALID

III. 7

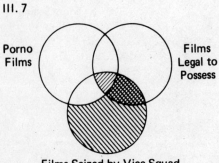

Porno
Films

Films
Legal to
Possess

Films Seized by Vice Squad

INVALID

III. 8

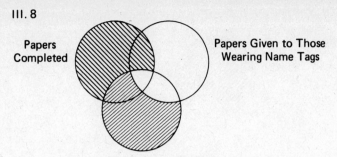

Papers Completed

Papers Given to Those Wearing Name Tags

Papers Given to the Supervisors

VALID
(Note: In this example premiss 2 must be altered slightly
to capture the fact that the whole argument is about papers:
completed papers, papers handed to supervisors, and so forth.)

III. 9

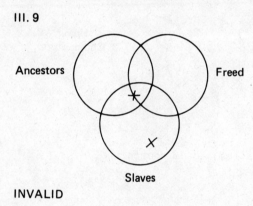

Ancestors

Freed

Slaves

INVALID

IV. 1

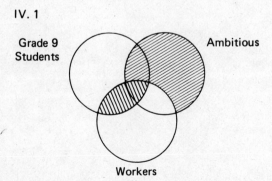

Grade 9 Students

Ambitious

Workers

VALID

IV. 2

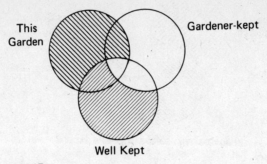

This
Garden

Gardener-kept

Well Kept

VALID

IV. 3

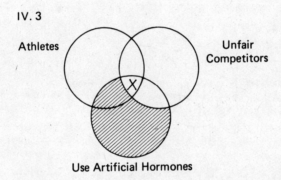

Athletes

Unfair
Competitors

Use Artificial Hormones

VALID

IV. 4

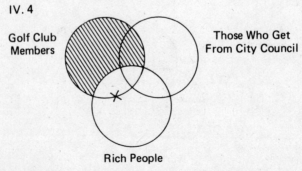

Golf Club
Members

Those Who Get
From City Council

Rich People

INVALID

IV. 5

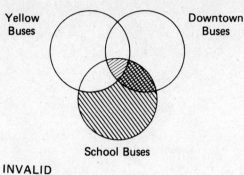

INVALID

IV. 6

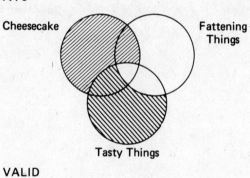

VALID

IV. 7

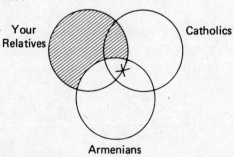

INVALID

IV. 8

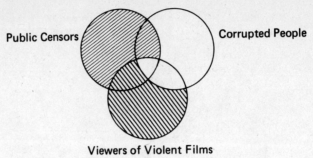

Public Censors Corrupted People

Viewers of Violent Films

VALID

IV. 9

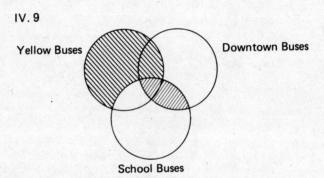

Yellow Buses Downtown Buses

School Buses

VALID

IV. 10

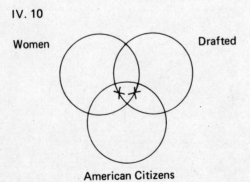

Women Drafted

American Citizens

INVALID

VI. Here we have retained the numbers for the original premisses Carroll began with. We have numbered the intermediate conclusion 4 and the final conclusion 5. In the first one below, for example, 1, 2, and 4 provide one syllogism; 4, 3, and 5 the second.

1. 1. No ducks waltz.
   2. No officers ever decline to waltz (that is, all officers waltz).
   4. *Therefore* no ducks are officers.
   3. All my poultry are ducks.
   5. *Therefore* none of my poultry are officers.
2. 1. All sane people are people who can do logic.
   3. No sons of yours are people who can do logic.
   4. *Therefore* no sons of yours are sane.
   2. All people fit to serve on a jury are sane. (Note how this has been altered to replace "lunatics" while retaining the *meaning* of the original.)
   5. *Therefore* no sons of yours are fit to serve on a jury.
3. 1. All who take the *Times* are well educated.
   3. No one unable to read is well educated.
   4. *Therefore* no one who takes the *Times* is unable to read.
   2. All hedge-hogs are unable to read.
   5. *Therefore* no hedge-hogs take the *Times*.
   (*Note*: Premiss 2 has been put into an affirmative mode in order to avoid having two classes of "those able to read" and "those unable to read.")
4. 1. All unripe fruit is unwholesome.
   3. All fruit grown in the shade is unripe.
   4. *Therefore* all fruit grown in the shade is unwholesome.
   2. None of these apples are unwholesome.
   5. *Therefore* none of these apples are grown in the shade.
   (*Note*: Premiss 3 was put into an affirmative form so that "unripe" would appear in premisses 1 and 3 to link them together; premiss 2 was put into a negative form to exchange "wholesome" for "unwholesome" plus a negation, so that "unwholesome" appeared in 4 and 2.)
5. 1. No colored flowers are scentless.
   3. All flowers grown in the open air are colored.
   4. *Therefore* no flowers grown in the open air are scentless.
   2. All flowers I like are flowers grown in the open air.
   5. *Therefore* no scentless flowers are flowers that I like. (Or, 5 can be expressed as "No flowers that I like are scentless.")

Chapter 6.   Finding Explanations and Making Predictions

I. Cue words: "because" and "they can only."
   1. All dinosaurs are creatures who became extinct.
   2. All creatures who became extinct (at that time) are creatures who must have been killed by a great flood (which was Noah's flood).
   3. *Therefore* all dinosaurs are creatures who were killed in the Great Flood (Noah's flood).

Venn Diagram Test

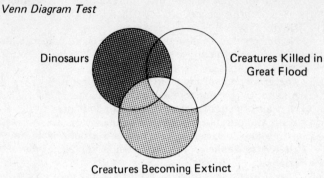

Dinosaurs   Creatures Killed in
                              Great Flood

Creatures Becoming Extinct

VALID

In this analysis we have taken the second sentence to be merely identifying the flood, and we have interpreted the first sentence as licensing the addition of the second, implicit, premiss. This argument explains the extinction of the dinosaurs by claiming that the only possible hypothesis is that they died in a flood, and then deducing the extinction in Noah's flood from that.

Premiss 1 is true but 2 is questionable *if* there are other reasons for which a species might become extinct, such as failing to adapt to its environment. Of course one might argue that the extinction of the dinosaurs and Noah's flood coincided in historical time and so premiss 2 is strengthened. Also, there is a sense in which drowning in a great flood is an extreme example of failure to adapt to a change in the environment.

One must also be cautious of this argument, depending on what it is setting out to prove. As a suggested explanation of the extinction of the dinosaur it has plausibility. In turn, the Biblical account of Noah's flood will be more credible and probable *if* we could independently establish that the dinosaurs died in a flood. The problem occurs when we try to prove *both* points at once. If this is attempted, the argument will become circular immediately.

II. The phrase "lends support to the notion" indicates that the author has a theory or hypothesis in mind—a theory that connects the financial *success* of Western movies with their use of expected social symbolism and expected mythical structure. The author, Will Wright, deduces a *fact* about certain movies from this theory plus a further fact, thereby finding a confirmation of the theory. The last sentence contains three claims:

1. The plots of the two movies (mentioned in the first two sentences) do *not* reinforce the myth of the Western.

2. These two movies failed financially.

3. The success of Westerns is largely determined by the presence of the myths and symbolism of the Western, not just by big stars and advertising.

When the argument is put as a syllogism we have:

1. All financially successful Westerns are Westerns that have the expected myths and symbolism.
2. No films such as *The Big Country* and *There Was a Crooked Man* are Westerns with the expected myths and symbolism.
3. *Therefore* no films such as *The Big Country* and *There Was a Crooked Man* are financially successful Westerns.

A Venn diagram test would demonstrate that this argument is valid. Since the argument form is valid, the conclusion is true, and the second premiss is true, it is almost certain that the initial premiss—the hypothesis Wright is advancing—is true as well. Here Wright has advanced a theory and shown its plausibility by logically deducing a claim from it which in actual fact is true.

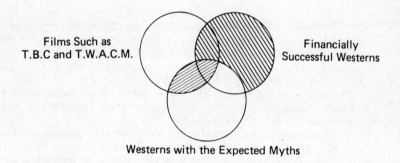

Films Such as
T.B.C and T.W.A.C.M.

Financially
Successful Westerns

Westerns with the Expected Myths

VALID

III. Descartes reasons that there must be one point at which the mind and the body interact. If that point is the brain, it must be in an "unpaired" part of the brain. The only "unpaired" part of the brain is the pineal gland.

One way to express Descartes's reasoning is in terms of a syllogism:

1. An organ having one specific location in the brain is the seat of the soul.
2. The pineal gland is an organ having one specific location in the brain.
3. *Therefore* the pineal gland is the seat of the soul.

(Strictly speaking, the premisses should be put into standard form as universal-affirmative statements. But since they would seem awkward if expressed this way and since the original wording is clearer, we have not put them into standard form.)

A Venn diagram test shows that the argument is valid.

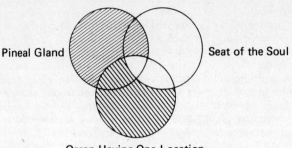

Pineal Gland   Seat of the Soul

Organ Having One Location

VALID

IV. The cue words "my guess" tip you off to an hypothesis, which is that in all situations of anxiety the amount of pain felt may be affected. The argument involved may be put in the form of the syllogism:

1. All situations involving anxiety are situations in which the amount of pain felt may be altered (hypothesis).
2. All cases of going to the dentist are situations involving anxiety.
3. *Therefore* all cases of going to the dentist are situations in which the amount of pain felt may be altered.

In the actual cases cited in the first sentence of the original, the alteration involves a decrease in felt pain. Presumably there can also be cases where anxiety increases pain. All the speaker wishes to explain here is the change in felt pain in a situation in which the physiological cause of the pain—a damaged tooth—is not removed.

A Venn diagram test shows that the argument is valid.

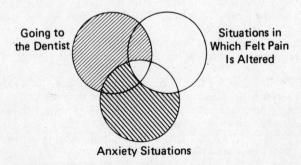

Going to   Situations in
the Dentist   Which Felt Pain
                                        Is Altered

Anxiety Situations

VALID

V. This can best be put in the syllogism:
1. All bodies giving off more heat than they receive from the sun are stars.
2. Jupiter is a body giving off more heat than it receives from the sun.
3. *Therefore* Jupiter is a star.
The last sentence of the original hypothesis about the origin of the heat gives us a further syllogism:
1. Jupiter's heat is heat from nuclear reactions (hypothesis).
2. Heat from nuclear reactions is the kind of heat that stars have.
3. *Therefore* Jupiter's heat is the kind of heat that stars have.
With no *other* alternative explanations or hypotheses about the source of Jupiter's heat, it is conclusive that Jupiter is a star rather than a planet. Of course, the truth of the conclusion also depends on the claim being true that Jupiter is giving off more heat than it receives from the sun.

Venn diagram tests show that both arguments are valid:

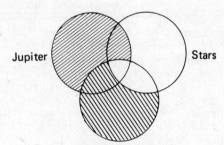

Jupiter   Stars

Bodies Giving off More Heat
than They Receive from the Sun

VALID

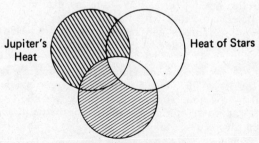

Jupiter's   Heat of Stars
Heat

Heat from Nuclear Reactions

VALID

Chapter 7.   Experience Proves the Rule: Inductive Reasoning

I.   1. Most colds can be cured by taking Dr. Good's Patented Cold Syrup.
     2. People who drink corn whiskey are dumb (or become dumb).
     3. All people suffering memory loss have brain damage or brain malfunction. (*Or*: All memory loss is caused by damage to or malfunction of the brain.)
     4. No citrus fruit can be grown in this area.
     5. The failure rate of students in introductory biology is between 36 percent and 38 percent.

II. 1. Bill intends us to conclude that tonight's play will be terrible. However, the bare fact that the last two he saw were terrible is not conclusive. It would make it likely that the play will be terrible if we knew more—if, for example, it was being done by the same group that did the previous ones Bill thought were terrible.
     2. This is a fallacy gamblers commit. If we are dealing with a "fair" coin —one that has not been tampered with—it has exactly a 50 percent chance of coming up tails on *each* toss. There is no sense in which it is *due* to come up tails, although a *series* of, say, 100 tosses should show approximately 50 tails and 50 heads. (If the coin continued to come up heads, one might begin to suspect that it was a trick coin.)
     3. This is not an argument of any kind, but simply a story.
     4. This is working to the conclusion that Laetrile cures cancer. However it is an inductive inference based on insufficient evidence—only three examples are cited.
     5. The conclusion urged here is, "Every time the prince leaves the country there is an attempted coup." This conclusion depends on how many past instances there are to draw upon. Of course there may be a *cause* one could discover in such a case (for example, that the prince does not rule well). If so, one might be able to establish enough connections to *deduce* for *certain* that a coup will be attempted. But as based just on past experience we have only the *probable* conclusion of an inductive argument.

III. 1. This is an analogy. The first sentence merely sets the stage and does not contribute to the argument. The second states the conclusion, and the cue word "because" in sentence 3 signals the premisses. Basically, the argument is:
        1. Children are like the elderly (in terms of needs).
        2. Females can better care for children (it's part of "nature's plan").
        3. *Therefore* females can better care for the elderly, (and therefore we should have female rather than male nurses in geriatric hospitals).
        Premiss 1 needs more development; not enough is said here to convince us it is sufficient. Premiss 2 is questionable and might be attacked by counterexamples. That is, do we know of cases where men have cared for children as well as or better than women? Perhaps cases of divorced or widowed fathers?
     2. This is a good inductive argument. The premisses are each of the claims about the reduction of deaths in each of the 35 states in each of the three years. (Spelled out, you would have 105 propositions.) The conclusion is that lowering speed limits reduces traffic deaths.

The conclusion is acceptable because each premiss is relevant and there are enough of them to warrant the conclusion.

3. This is a statistical argument. The main evidence is cited in the last sentence. The conclusion is that "most female nurses are sexually molested and through no fault of their own." The claim that "homely women" suffered the same treatment substantiates the part of the conclusion stating that the nurses were not at fault. The evidence that over 90 percent said they had had such an experience substantiates the part of the conclusion that states that *most* female nurses were molested.

4. This is an analogy. "Death Race" and football are compared as games. Although not stated, both presumably require skills, have objectives, and so are certainly games. Given this, the further feature found in football, of engendering attitudes, is *inductively inferred* to be a feature of "Death Race." Since the attitude claimed by this inductive argument is not a good one, the writer is urging that "Death Race" be banned. Presumably this entails a further *deductive* argument with a premiss claiming that all dangerous things and activities ought to be banned.

Against this argument one could claim that there is *another* feature to certain games—namely, we recognize that they *are* just games and not real. Therefore it is not necessarily the case that attitudes learned in games pass over into real life. Of course this is a complicated issue, and the relationship between sports, life attitudes, and skills could be the subject of a very long debate.

5. The speaker is presenting an inductive argument, based on Smither's past performance, to the conclusion that Smithers should not be in charge of the detail to capture an enemy machine gun. As such this is a reasonable way to argue. However, it hinges on the relevance of the evidence. Does failure to pass an English class show *general* stupidity and inability successfully to complete a military task? Does his *messiness* really count *at all*? While the former is *perhaps* relevant the latter is not (unless one could establish a link here, which the speaker does not).

Chapter 8.   Some Perplexing Arguments: The Dilemma and the *Reductio*

I. Dilemma.
OUTLINE
   1. We must ban or not ban erotic films.
   2. If we ban erotic films, then we deny freedom of choice.
   3. If we do not ban erotic films, we encourage children in sexual activities.
   4. *Therefore* we must either deny freedom of choice *or* encourage children in sexual activities.
COUNTER
One cannot go between the horns because the alternatives in 1 are exhaustive. You can grasp either horn by arguing that it is proper to deny freedom on some occasions (versus premiss 2) or by arguing that erotic films do not necessarily encourage sexual activity among children (versus premiss 3).

II. Dilemma.
OUTLINE
1. All students are good or poor (assumed).
2. If good, then a student doesn't need help.
3. If poor, then a student cannot learn—that is, cannot use a teacher's help.
4. *Therefore* a student either doesn't need help or cannot use help.

COUNTER
You can grasp either horn—that is, argue that either of 2 or 3 is false.

III. *Reductio.*
OUTLINE
Phoning someone several times and going to his house are presented as evidence that one believes that the person phoned and whose house is visited can be reached. The person being questioned *did* believe, therefore, that Threadbare was in town. This produces a claim contradictory to the person's statement that Threadbare was *not* in town.

COUNTER
One could imagine reasons for phoning, such as wanting to leave a message, while still believing that Threadbare was out of town. These reasons are likely to be far-fetched, but offering them would be an attempt to break the logical link between certain actions (phoning, visiting) and belief about the availability of Threadbare.

IV. Dilemma.
OUTLINE
1. Either God exists or He does not (implicit).
2. If God exists, believing in Him will save you from damnation.
3. If God does not exist, your belief will have lost you nothing.
4. *Therefore* your belief in God either will save you from damnation or will lose you nothing.

(Note that this is a variant on the dilemma, in that it is an attempt to show that belief in God leads to *good* consequences.)

COUNTER
One can always attack the truth of premises; here it might be arguable that premiss 3 is false because belief does cost something in terms of one's time, finances, and commitment.

V. Dilemma.
OUTLINE
1. Either we surrender or we fight.
2. If we surrender, we lose our land.
3. If we fight, many will be killed.
4. *Therefore* either we lose our land or many will be killed.

COUNTER
One might be able to go through the horns if there is reason to believe that the cavalry (or some similar group) might arrive in time to save the situation. Of course, one could only decide the truth of the premisses if more information were available.

VI. *Reductio.*
OUTLINE
1. God is the most perfect being we can think of.
2. If God did not exist, we could think of a being (call him X) who has *all* God's qualities *plus* existence.

3. Such a being, X, would be more perfect than God.
4. Thus, to think of such a being, X, is to think of a more perfect being than God.
5. *Therefore* to think of X is to think of a more perfect being than the most perfect being we can think of.

COUNTER

One could argue that "existing" is not a quality of things the way "being red" is.

Or else, one could attack the general line of this argument by showing that it allows one to prove the existence of almost anything at all. For example, one could prove that Satan exists:

1. Satan is the most perfectly evil being we can think of.
2. If Satan did not exist, we could think of one *more* evil (call him E), who has all Satan's powers *plus* existence.
3. E would be more perfectly evil than Satan.
4. *Thus* to think of E is to think of a more perfectly evil being than Satan.
5. *Therefore* to think of E is to think of a more perfect evil being than the most perfect evil being we can think of (which is absurd; so Satan must exist).

VII. Dilemma.

OUTLINE

1. Either you live well or you live poorly.
2. If you live well, you can afford to pay taxes (because you *obviously* have money, as all can see from your fine house).
3. If you live poorly, you can afford to pay taxes (because you are obviously holding all your money, since you are *not* spending it on your house).
4. *Therefore* you (and everyone) can afford to pay taxes.

COUNTER

Clearly premiss 3 is false, so one can counter by grasping that horn.

Chapter 9.   Connecting Your Thoughts: Alternatives and Causes

I. 1. Disjunctive syllogism:
    1. Either Oakland will win or Cincinnati will win.
    2. Oakland will *not* win.
    3. *Therefore* Cincinnati will win.
    (Note that the claims about good pitching do not enter into the main line of the overall argument. They are evidence for the *truth* of premisses 1 and 2.)
2. Hypothetical syllogism:
    1. If the governor pardons him, then he will go on TV, and so forth.
    2. If he goes on TV, and so forth, then we will be the laughing stock of the nation.
    3. *Therefore* if the governor pardons him, (then) we will be the laughing stock of the nation.

3. Disjunctive syllogism:
   1. Either attend the meeting or forgo voting privileges.
   2. She did *not* attend the meeting.
   3. *Therefore* she has forgone voting privileges.

4. *Modus tollens*:
   1. If China backs down, (then) she will lose face.
   2. China will *not* lose face.
   3. *Therefore* China will *not* back down.

5. Disjunctive syllogism:
   1. *Either* Jones was unaware *or* he was aware.
   2. It was *not* the case that Jones was unaware.
   3. *Therefore* Jones was aware.
   (The claim about fools and naive people only supports premiss 2.)

6. *Modus ponens*:
   1. If John nags his daughter, then she will leave.
   2. He nags his daughter.
   3. *Therefore* she leaves (or, she left him).
   (Remember that when we are dealing with the logical structure of an argument, we can often ignore the tense of the ordinary English sentence. So we are free to express this conclusion as either "She leaves him," or "She left him.")

7. Hypothetical syllogism:
   1. If I buy a cello, then I buy a humidifier.
   2. If I buy a humidifier, then I cannot buy a car.
   3. *Therefore*, if buy a cello, (then) I cannot buy a car.

8. Disjunctive syllogism:
   1. The horse is at the old paddock *or* the horse is at Orkney's.
   2. It is *not* at the old paddock.
   3. *Therefore* the horse is at Orkney's.

II. 1. Hypothetical syllogism. Conclusion: If she comes home late, (then) mother and father will be upset.
   2. *Modus ponens*. Conclusion: His parents scolded.
   3. Disjunctive syllogism. Conclusion: Mary is lazy.
   4. *Modus tollens*. Conclusion: There is *not* going to be a thunderstorm.
   5. Disjunctive syllogism. Conclusion: Simple Simon met a pieman.
   6. *Modus tollens*. Conclusion: The stocks did *not* go up.
   7. Hypothetical syllogism. Conclusion: If Jones goes to Wales, (then) we cannot present his award to him.
   8. *Modus ponens*. Conclusion: Sharon will give him back his book.
   9. Disjunctive syllogism. Conclusion: The potatoes are hard.
   10. Disjunctive syllogism. Conclusion: The finishing number tonight will be an overture.

Chapter 10. How to Find and Evaluate an Argument

I. S: The "for" of the second sentence signals a premiss (reason); "since" signals a premiss. The combination of "either . . . or" in the first sentence and the negative proposition after the "since" suggest that one should look for a disjunctive syllogism.

C: The conclusion is, "We must execute murderers." In the context the "obviously" helps to *cue* this conclusion.

O, R:

The general argument is the disjunctive syllogism:

1. Either we execute murderers or imprison them.
2. Do *not* imprison them.
3. *Therefore* we must execute murderers.

E: Premiss 2 is supported by a set of arguments. The first argument is a valid categorical syllogism:

4. No criminals are reformed by being sent to prison.
5. All murderers are criminals (implicit premiss).
6. *Therefore* no murderers are reformed by being sent to prison.

The last sentence of the original provides the proposition:

7. If murderers are not reformed in prison, then we waste taxpayers' money by sending them to prison.

Using propositions 7 and 6, we can, by affirming the antecedent (*modus ponens*), validly deduce the conclusion:

8. We waste taxpayers' money by sending murderers to prison.

Also note that premiss 4 is supported by the parenthetical comment about recidivism.

Evaluating the argument, we find:

F: There are no fallacies or invalid forms.

A: Premiss 1 does not offer exhaustive choices, so an alternative could be introduced to challenge premiss 1.

T: Premiss 7 might be challenged, perhaps on the grounds that reform is not the only purpose that may be served by sending dangerous people to prison. For example, prisons keep dangerous antisocial people off the streets.

E: One should search for evidence that prisoners are reformed; not *all* prisoners commit second offences.

II. There is no argument here; this example really presents a story, not an argument. However, one might feel that Mary's decision and subsequent action implicitly contain an explanation and that we could therefore supply a rule and have the following argument *modus ponens*:

1. If Mary has had enough of a party, then she leaves.
2. Mary had enough of the party.
3. *Therefore* she left.

However, we have no reason to believe that premiss 1 is true. Mary may often, for social reasons, stay at a party after she has had enough of it. So it is *illegitimate* to supply premiss 1.

III. S: The "therefore" in the middle of the second paragraph cues a conclusion. The next sentence, "It is, rather, an ideology," makes it clear that (a) Hoover is suggesting philosophy and ideology as *alternatives* and (b) the part after "It is, rather" is also a conclusion. This suggests that we have two arguments here, linked together.

C: Hoover's point clearly is to prove that communism is an ideology rather than a philosophy. So this *main* conclusion is "Communism is an ideology."

O, R:

Since the search revealed alternatives, we can expect a disjunctive syllogism. It is:

1. *Either* communism is a philosophy *or* communism is an ideology (implicit).
2. Communism is *not* a philosophy.
3. *Therefore* communism is an ideology.

E: Most of this quotation is taken up with proving premiss 2. One *could* cast this into the form of a *reductio*, for that certainly is suggested by the *tone* of Hoover's writing. However, it is most likely best presented as a pair of syllogisms:

4. All philosophies are systems (of thought) seeking ultimate truth.
5. All systems seeking ultimate truth are systems that must question premisses, conclusions, and judgments.
6. *Therefore* all philosophies are systems that must question premisses, conclusions, and judgments.

Taking this conclusion, now as a premiss, we have:

7. All philosophies are systems that must question premisses, conclusions, and judgments.
8. No communism is a system that questions premisses, conclusions, and judgments.
9. *Therefore*, no communism is a philosophy.

This gives us the second premiss of the main argument.

F: These arguments are valid. Venn diagram tests would show this for the last two. There are no fallacies.

A, T, E:

Since the arguments are valid, criticism would have to center on the truth of the premisses. Is premiss 1 an exhaustive alternative? Premiss 8 appears to be false. This alone brings the whole argument down. Once 8 is assumed to be false, the conclusion, 9, is no longer guaranteed. And since 9 is the same as 2, the main argument is no longer sound.

IV. S: The writer breaks up the piece very clearly. The first sentence states an opinion, or point of view. The argument for the opposite opinion is introduced in the second sentence by "One of the company took the other side . . ." In this, "therefore" cues the conclusion. Finally Johnson's reply is introduced with "He turned to the gentleman."

C: The only *real* argument is the second part. The conclusion is: Some medications put in warm bath waters are medicines that have good effects on the body.

O, R:

The order involves classifications and so is syllogistic. It is:

1. Some medicines that have good effects on the body are medicines that enter the body by the pores.
2. All medications put in warm bath waters are medications that enter the body by the pores. (Implicit premiss.)
3. *Therefore*, some medications put in warm bath waters are medicines that have good effects on the body.

E: No further evidence is given for these premisses.

F: A Venn diagram test shows this argument to be *invalid*:

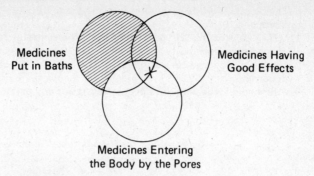

Medicines
Put in Baths

Medicines Having
Good Effects

Medicines Entering
the Body by the Pores

INVALID

(Note: Altering premiss 2 to " Some . . ." will *also* produce an invalid argument.)

A: One possible alternate is that some medications cannot enter the body via the pores when put in bath waters.

T: There is no reason to accept premiss 2 as true, given the possible alternative.

E: Perhaps a medical authority would indicate some counterexamples— medicines that act contrary to premiss 2. Or perhaps authoritative sources would show premiss 1 to be false.

The last part of the quotation gives Dr. Johnson's reply. Unfortunately, Johnson does not address the argument but uses a fallacious argument *ad hominem.* Johnson merely becomes abusive; he carries the audience, so we are told, because they react favorably to the humor of the abusive *ad hominem* remark. Hence Johnson's reply rates *very* low marks—in fact, no marks at all (except as a witticism).

V. *S:* "Because of this" signals a conclusion. There are some rhetorical passages that can be ignored, such as "people from every walk of life, business executives and union members . . ."

C: All people will vote for our party.

O, R:

1. Our party's record is a good record.
2. All people are people who always vote for a party with a good record (implicit).
3. *Therefore* all people will vote for our party.

E: The first three sentences constitute an *inductive* argument supporting premiss 1.

F: The argument as expressed above contains too many terms to provide a proper syllogism and too many terms to allow us to test it by Venn diagram. Therefore, if it is put in this form, the argument goes astray. The only conclusion that one can draw from it in this form is that: "All people who vote for our party will be people who are voting for a party with a good record."

The Venn diagram test would be difficult and confused because, as the argument is expressed, we seem to be asked to include "voters" in the class of "good political records," which is odd to say the least.

The argument can be made more respectable if we reconstruct it in this way:

1. All people voting for our party are people voting for a party with a good record.
2. All people (who vote) are people who vote for a party with a good record.
3. All people (who vote) are people voting for our party.

Venn Diagram Test for Reconstructed Argument

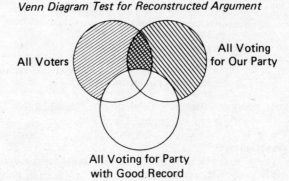

All Voters

All Voting for Our Party

All Voting for Party with Good Record

INVALID

You can see the problem in the original argument. Even if the speaker is right about his party having a good record and right about people voting in terms of record, he cannot conclude that *everyone* will vote for his party. Some people may vote for *another* party on the grounds that it, too, has a good record.

Of course, the speaker intends to *exhort* and persuade people to vote for his party. He is trying to be persuasive by showing that voting for his party is a rational conclusion, based on facts.

A: One possibility is that some people vote for other reasons. For example, they vote because the candidate is a friend or relative or because a friend or relative belongs to the particular party.

T: Premiss 2 is very likely false.

E: The alternative considered would generate counterexamples.

VI. S: This example involves mostly emotional claims. The only argument appears to be in the first two sentences.

C: Man is not made in a monkey's image.

O, R:

1. If man is made in God's image, then he is not made in a monkey's image.
2. Man is made in God's image.
3. *Therefore*, man is not made in a monkey's image.

E: Premiss 2 is supported by the claim the Bible says this.

F: The argument as it stands is a *valid* instance of *modus ponens*. The second paragraph of the original is largely emotional rant. It involves an instance of the fallacy of arguing *ad hominem*, which occurs in the attack on the college professors who are accused of being "deceivin'" and "hell-bound." A version of the fallacy of appealing to the masses is present, in that the speaker appeals to the feelings and sentiments of *all* those present by referring to "our children" going to hell. The emotive term "damnable" is purposely used to attach negative connotations to the doctrine of evolution.

A: One alternative would be that man is made in *neither* image, but perhaps just by a long biological, evolutionary process.

T: Premiss 1 will be false if it is possible *not* to be made in God's image and yet not to be made in a monkey's image either.

E: One could argue that citing the Bible in support of premiss 2 is not adequate, since the Bible contains some false claims (since it has contradictory statements in it).

Before we leave this example, it is worth noting that one might construe the initial argument in a less formal way than as an instance of *modus ponens*. One could consider it to be making its point by arguing that an absurdity, in the form of a contradiction, results from maintaining that "man is made in the image of God" *and* that "man is made in the image of a monkey." It must be one or the other, not both. Hence, the speaker rightly employs the principle that *both* of a pair of contrary or contradictory propositions cannot be true. Since the first sentence claims that the proposition supported by the Bible is true, and *known* to be true, it is *absurd* to believe the evolutionary version ("... how *can* he be made in the image of a monkey?").

An opponent might well attack this last point by arguing that the fact that both propositions in the first paragraph cannot be true only shows that one of them is false. And the false claim *may* be that man was made in God's image. (Remember that the first sentence uses the Bible as an authoritative source; some people would argue that it cannot be accepted as literally true in all respects.) Also, since the propositions are only contraries, it may be that *both* of them are false.

VII. *S:* The *search* reveals "because," which is a cue word for a premiss; the "and" cues an additional premiss.

C: The *conclusion* is, "No civilized people have public censors."

O, R:
The given argument has three statements in it. Putting the premisses (*reasons* for the conclusion) first and then the conclusion, we get the logical *order*:
1. All civilized people are people wanting freedom of expression.
2. No public censors are people who want freedom of expression.
3. *Therefore,* no civilized people are people who have public censors.

E: There is *no* further *evidence* or support for the premisses.

F: The argument is *not valid.* It appears to be a syllogism, but it has too many terms. The only conclusion following from the stated premisses is "No public censors are civilized persons" or "No civilized persons are public censors."

A: Premiss 1 is not necessarily true. An alternate is that all civilized people want freedom of expression *except* in cases where free expression might cause harm—say, by inciting riots or misleading children.

T: This argument gives us no *reasons* for believing that the premisses are true. And since there are plausible alternatives, such as the one mentioned under *A*, the premisses are suspect.

E: We do not need more evidence or a counterexample here, since the argument both is *invalid* and has at least one premiss that is probably false. But the alternative suggested above could easily be made into a counterexample. We could cite a nation that allows only limited freedom of expression—as most do—by, say, censoring films or imposing restrictions on the press in time of war.

Chapter 11. How to Construct and Present an Argument

I. S: First one must distinguish active from passive euthanasia. Active euthanasia would, for example, be administering a drug to someone in order to cause death. Passive euthanasia would be allowing a person to die naturally—for example, by not taking very special steps or using special equipment to prolong life. The case of Karen Anne Quinlan presumably was of the latter sort, in that her family wanted certain life-support machinery to be disconnected so that she would die naturally if life was not possible for her without these machines.

This topic will involve a split in opinions similar to that over abortion. On the one side, there is the belief that someone—in this case, the sick person—should have a choice. On the other side, there is the belief that everything should be done to preserve life under all circumstances. Supporters of the former position might talk of the dignity of death and having the right to choose not to burden one's relatives. Supporters of the latter position would worry about people dying who do not have to or dying for the wrong reasons; and about who should make the decision if the ill person is physically unable to do so.

C: A reasonable conclusion is that *passive* euthanasia should be allowed in cases in which the ill person is capable of freely and knowingly making the choice.

O, R:

One reason might be that one should be able to experience one's death with the same dignity and freedom of choice that one has in the rest of life. Since this involves classifications, a syllogism might be in order:

1. All aspects of life are to be experienced in the way that each person wishes.
2. The process of dying is an aspect of everyone's life.
3. *Therefore*, the process of dying is to be experienced as each person wishes.

E: One could support premiss 1 by an analogy showing how one has freedom, in most areas of living, to choose one's life style and to do things that suit one's personal sense of style and dignity. This should be extended to the process of dying.

II.   S: On the one side are the beliefs that animals have no rights, are here
          for human use, and must be used in laboratory studies and tests if
          we are to defeat human diseases such as cancer.
              On the other side are the belief that animals *do* have rights and the
          opinion that test animals suffer pain and live under poor conditions.
          Also, such tests make *people* insensitive.
      C: Animals ought *not* to be used in laboratory tests.
      O, R:
          Three separate arguments can be made, each supporting the con-
          clusion, based on the reasons turned up in the search.
ARGUMENT 1
          1. All living creatures have the right to life.
          2. No laboratory animal is given a right to life.
          3. *Therefore* no living creature should be a laboratory animal.
ARGUMENT 2
          1. No animal should have to live in poor or painful conditions.
          2. All laboratory animals live in poor or painful conditions.
          3. *Therefore* no animals should be laboratory animals.
ARGUMENT 3
          1. If the activity of testing animals makes people insensitive, then
             that activity should be banned.
          2. Testing animals does make people insensitive.
          3. *Therefore* the activity (of testing animals) should be banned.
      E: Premiss 2 in each of the first two arguments can be supported by
          arguing that test animals are not living freely or naturally and so do
          not have their proper natural rights and are in comparatively poor
          conditions. Premiss 1 of argument 3 can be justified from the more
          general position that *anything* making people insensitive is bad and
          ought to be stopped.

III. S: On the one side we have the belief that certain minorities have been
          badly treated in the past and so preferential hiring of members of
          such groups helps to make up for this.
              On the other side we have the position that all discrimination is bad
          and that to hire preferentially is to discriminate. Two wrongs don't
          make a right.
      C: There should be *no* preferential hiring of minority groups.
      O, R:
          1. All discrimination is bad.
          2. Preferential hiring is discrimination.
          3. *Therefore* preferential hiring is bad.
          The conclusion, 3, with a general claim that we ought not to do bad
          things, will produce the desired conclusion.
      E: As further support one might provide an analogy to demonstrate
          another parallel case in which two wrongs do *not* make a right. For
          example, one could suggest that we might just as well let people
          steal things if they happen to be poor or at some disadvantage and
          in this way "make it up" to them. This would provide an *analogous*
          case and would also be a *reductio* of the opponent's position because
          of its patent absurdity.

IV.   S: On the one hand we have the belief that heroin is harmful and
          destructive.

On the other hand, the belief is that people who really want or need heroin will get it anyway, so it is better to have it available legally.

C: People should be allowed to buy heroin legally.

O, R:

1. Either people will get heroin legally or they will get it illegally.
2. They should *not* get it illegally.
3. *Therefore* they should get it legally.

This is a *valid* disjunctive syllogism.

E: For premiss 1 you can argue that one cannot effectively *police* drug use. People will get drugs somehow.

For premiss 2 you can argue that it is dangerous for heroin to be illegal, because this makes it expensive to obtain—which, in turn, causes crime as people rob and steal to get the money to buy the heroin. It would be better for it to be available under government control; then the price, quality, and distribution could be controlled.

V. S: On the one hand we have the need for more energy and the fact that nuclear energy is available, in the long run, in great quantities.

On the other hand, there is the opinion that although we need energy, the nuclear route is too dangerous.

C: Abolish nuclear power plants.

O, R:

1. Any dangerous method of producing energy should be abolished.
2. Nuclear power plants are a dangerous method of producing energy.
3. *Therefore* nuclear power plants should be abolished.

This is a *valid* syllogism.

E: While there is some possible debate about what is or is not "dangerous," premiss 1 seems almost self-evident. Premiss 2 can be supported by citing examples of people being poisoned by radon gas from nuclear wastes. Several cases of such poisoning have occurred in North America when buildings were constructed on sites that consisted of land-fill into which nuclear wastes had been dumped.

Glossary

Ad hominem   *see* Fallacy.

Affirming the antecedent   a valid argument form. One premiss is a conditional ("if . . . then") proposition; the second premiss asserts (affirms) the antecedent to be true; and the conclusion asserts the consequent of the original conditional. Schematically represented, the form is:

1. If A, then C.
2. A.
3. *Therefore* C.

Ambiguity   the use of a word that has two or more meanings in a way that does not make clear which meaning is intended in the particular context.

Analogy   an inductive argument inferring that if two individual persons or things—or classes of persons or things—share a number of relevant properties, then a further property displayed by one of them will also (probably) be possessed by the other (even though we cannot *observe* that the other item has that further property).

Analytic proposition   a proposition, or statement, whose truth depends not on experienced facts, but on the *meaning of the terms* of the proposition.

Antecedent   the phrase following the "if" in a conditional, or hypothetical ("if . . . then"), proposition.

Appeal to authority   *see* Fallacy.

Appeal to ignorance   *see* Fallacy.

Appeal to the masses   *see* Fallacy.

Appeal to pity   *see* Fallacy.

Appeal to threats or intimidation   *see* Fallacy.

Arguing in a circle   *see* Fallacy.

Argument   (1) in logic, a set of propositions consisting of premises and a conclusion. (2) The act of presenting a conclusion you wish to establish and backing it up with reasons that logically lead to the conclusion.

Aristotelian logic   the system of logic developed by Aristotle, a Greek philosopher of the fourth century B.C. Its main elements are (1) categorical propositions, which express relationships between classes of things (for example, the inclusion of one class within another); and (2) syllogisms—deductive arguments that have two premises and a conclusion, all of which are categorical propositions.

Begging the question   *see* Fallacy of arguing in a circle.

Biconditional   a statement marked by "if and only if," intended to indicate a mutual conditional relationship between two simple propositions—for example, "Harry is the brother of June *if and only if* June is the sister of Harry." In this example the biconditional combines the two conditionals, "*If* Harry is the brother of June, *then* June is the sister of Harry" and "*If* June is the sister of Harry, *then* Harry is the brother of June."

Categorical proposition   a simple proposition having two terms—for example, "All *horses* are *mammals*" and "Some *pigs* are *pretty*"—and a quantifier—"all" or "some." The terms introduce classes, and the quantifier indicates the partial or total inclusion of one class within the other. Categorical propositions can be either affirmative or negative, and this characteristic is called the *quality* of the proposition.

Categorical syllogism   a deductive argument consisting of exactly two premises and a conclusion, all of which are categorical propositions.

Circularity   *see* Fallacy of arguing in a circle.

Compound proposition   a proposition composed of two or more simple propositions joined by logical connectives such as "and," "or," "if . . . then." For example, "John is late leaving work or his car has broken down again" is a compound proposition in which "or" connects the simple propositions "John is late leaving work" and "His car has broken down again."

Conclusion   the proposition an argument is attempting to prove.

Conditional   a statement using "if . . . then."

Conjunct   a component of a conjunction—that is, one of two or more simple propositions joined together by "and" to form a compound proposition called a conjunction.

Conjunction   a compound proposition using "and" to connect two or more simple propositions.

Connotation   *see* Intension and Meaning.

Consequent   the phrase following the "then" in a conditional, or hypothetical ("if . . . then"), proposition.

Consistency   *see* Logical inconsistency.

Contradictories   a pair of propositions that cannot *both* be true at the same time but are such that *one* of the pair *must* be true. (*Example:* "It is snowing now" and "It is not snowing now" are contradictories.) You can always form the contradictory of any statement simply by prefacing it with "It is not the case that."

Contraries   propositions that cannot both be true, but which are such that neither *must* be true. (*Example:* "This mug is black" and "This mug is white" are contraries.)

Counterfactual a conditional proposition in which the antecedent is false because it is contrary to fact. For example, "If I were eight feet tall, then I would hit my head on that doorframe." Even though it is false that the speaker is eight feet tall, nevertheless, if she were, she would hit her head on the doorframe.

Deductive argument an argument in which the conclusion is drawn out of the premisses. The premisses *of necessity* entail the conclusion.

Definition the explanation of a word by means of a synonym for it. A proposition that is a definition is true by virtue of the meanings of the words, or terms, involved. For example, "Bachelors are unmarried males" is both a definition and a necessarily true proposition. Unlike factual claims, definitions do not provide new information.

There are several types of definition.

(*a*) *Classificatory definition:* explanation of a term by citing subclasses of the things referred to by that term. For example, a classificatory definition of "mammal" would tell us that dogs are mammals, elephants are mammals, whales are mammals, and so on.

(*b*) *Ostensive definition:* explanation of a term by pointing out (designating) an instance. For example, if you point to a red book and say "This is red," you are defining "red" ostensively.

(*c*) *Persuasive definition:* use of the emotive meaning of a term to excite a favorable response to something. For example, "Democracy is freedom to be self-governed" uses the favorable word "freedom" to evoke a positive attitude toward democracy.

(*d*) *Real definition:* reference to the properties of things intended by a term, as opposed to a stipulative definition.

(*e*) *Stipulative definition:* the way a particular person or specific group intends to use a term. For example, in *Through the Looking-glass* Humpty Dumpty defines "glory" stipulatively as "a nice knock-down argument"; when Alice objects that this is not what "glory" means, Humpty Dumpty tells her that a word used by him means "just what I choose it to mean."

Denotation *see* Extension.

Denying the Antecedent *see* Fallacy.

Denying the Consequent a valid argument form having two premisses and a conclusion. The first premiss states a hypothetical (conditional) proposition; the second premiss denies (negates) the consequent of that hypothetical, allowing us to deduce the denial (negation) of the antecedent in the conclusion. Schematically represented, the argument form is:

1. If A, then C.
2. *Not* C.
3. *Therefore* not A.

Dilemma an argument form offering a choice between alternatives in the initial premiss; from each alternative an undesirable or unacceptable consequence is deduced. Schematically, the argument form is:

1. Either M or N.
2. If M, then O.

3. If N, then P.

4. *Therefore* either O or P.

Disjunct   a component of a disjunction—that is, one of two or more simple propositions joined by "or" to form a compound proposition called a disjunction.

Disjunction   a compound proposition using "or" to connect two or more simple propositions.

Disjunctive syllogism   a valid argument form consisting of two premisses and a conclusion. The first premiss states a pair of alternatives—that is, the first premiss is a disjunction. The second premiss denies (negates) one of these alternatives, allowing us to infer the other alternative in the conclusion. Schematically, such an argument form is:

1. Either A_1 or A_2.

2. *Not* A_1.

3. *Therefore* A_2.

Eliminating the alternative   *see* Disjunctive syllogism.

Emotive sentences   a sentence used to express the speaker's or writer's approval or disapproval—to express feelings, likes, dislikes, and attitudes.

Empirical proposition   a proposition whose truth is determined by experience—that is, by observation or experiment. In Chapter 2 these are called "factual propositions."

Enthymeme   an argument with a missing (implicit) premiss or conclusion. The term is most frequently used to refer to a syllogism.

Equivocation   *see* Fallacy.

Extension   the class of things referred to by a general, or class, term. Another word for extension is "denotation."

Factual proposition   *see* Empirical proposition.

Fallacy   a purported inference that mistakenly implies that the premisses lead to a given conclusion. The notion of a fallacy always carries with it the idea of a wrong-headed, or misguided, argument or an irrelevant or inappropriate appeal in citing evidence.

Some of the main fallacies are:

(a) *Fallacy of affirming the consequent:* the invalid argument form,

1. If A, then C.

2. C.

3. *Therefore* A.

(b) *Fallacy of ambiguity:* a general label for arguments containing ambiguous terms that cause shifts of meaning within the argument.

(c) *Fallacy of (illegitimate) appeal to authority:* the fallacious inference that a conclusion is acceptable on the grounds that some person or group of persons endorses that conclusion, even though the person or group in question does not have any special competence to decide the issue.

(d) *Fallacy of appeal to intimidation:* see Fallacy of appeal to threats.

(e) *Fallacy of appeal to the masses, or appeal to the people:* the attempt to gain acceptance of a conclusion by illegitimately appealing to and playing upon popular feelings and biases.

(f) *Fallacy of appeal to pity* (also called *argumentum ad misericordi- am*): the attempt to gain acceptance of a conclusion by illegiti- mately appealing to and playing upon the sympathetic feelings of a person or group toward something in the conclusion.

(g) *Fallacy of appeal to threats* (also called *argumentum ad baculum*): the attempt to gain acceptance for a conclusion by warning that failure to accept the conclusion will have undesirable or harmful consequences for the listener or reader.

(h) *Fallacy of arguing against the person* (*ad hominen*): an attack against the person advancing an argument rather than against the argument itself.

(i) *Fallacy of arguing in a circle:* an argument that assumes the truth of the conclusion it is trying to prove and uses this assumption as one of the premises of the argument.

(j) *Fallacy of begging the question: see* Fallacy of arguing in a circle.

(k) *Fallacy of confusing cause and effect:* when considering two events, mistaking the cause for the effect or vice versa.

(l) *Fallacy of inventing a cause:* the illegitimate assumption that two events are causally related merely because one event happens *after* the other does. In philosophy the common name for this is *post hoc ergo propter hoc,* and it is sometimes referred to merely as the *post hoc* fallacy.

(m) *Fallacy of denying the antecedent:* the invalid argument form
1. If A, then C.
2. Not A.
3. *Therefore* not C.

(n) *Fallacy of equivocation:* the use of a key term that has more than one cognitive (nonemotive) meaning.

(o) *Fallacy of hasty generalization:* the error of formulating a gen- eralization too quickly in circumstances in which the evidence is either insufficient or too specialized or extraordinary to warrant drawing a general conclusion.

(p) *Fallacy of relevance:* a general label for arguments that advance irrelevant considerations or evidence in support of a conclusion.

Generalization an inference that something which is true of certain members of a given class of things or persons is also true of other mem- bers of that class. Many people believe that a great number of the laws of nature are generalizations. For example, a Briton who sees several loudly dressed American tourists in London and who then infers that all Americans dress loudly is *generalizing.* Generalizations based on experience are inductive conclusions, or inductive inferences.

Hypothesis a belief, proposition, or theory for which there is enough evidence to give it tentative support—or for which there is enough sup- port to suggest that it is possible—but for which there is not yet enough evidence to hold it as certain.

Hypothetical syllogism a valid deductive argument form consisting of two premises and a conclusion, all three of which are hypothetical (conditional) statements. Schematically, the argument form is:

1. If A, then B.
2. If B, then C.
3. *Therefore* if A, then C.

Implicit premiss   a premiss that is hidden—either not stated or purposely suppressed—but which is *necessary* in order to produce the conclusion of the argument in question.

Inconsistency   *see* Logical inconsistency.

Induction   as applied to argument, an argument in which the conclusion goes beyond what is given in the premisses. The premisses provide support for the conclusion, but the truth of the premisses does not entail the conclusion. The classical sense of induction is generalization from particular examples or instances.

Inference   the process of affirming one proposition on the basis of another proposition or other propositions assumed to be true.

Intension   the collection of properties commonly shared by all things making up the extension of a general, or class, term. Another word for intension is "connotation."

Invalid   not permitting an inferential move from premisses to conclusion. An invalid argument can have true premisses and a false conclusion, which a *valid* deductive argument can *never* have.

Law of nature   a statement claiming a universal relationship between or among two or more classes of things, or two or more events.

Logical inconsistency   holding two viewpoints that are contradictory. Thus we can have various types of logical inconsistency: (1) A proposition is logically inconsistent if it is self-contradictory. For example, "Tom has blue eyes but Tom does *not* have blue eyes" is self-contradictory so long as "Tom" refers to the same person at the same time. (2) Premisses of an argument would be logically inconsistent if when taken together (in conjunction), they were self-contradictory. (3) An argument would be logically inconsistent if one or more of the premisses taken together with (taken in conjunction with) the conclusion produces a self-contradiction.

Meaning   several different senses of "meaning" can be distinguished:
   (a) *Extensional, or denotative, meaning:* the group of things referred to by a general term and to which the term appropriately applies.
   (b) *Intensional, or connotative, meaning:* the collection of shared properties possessed by the things belonging to the extension of a general term.
   (c) *Cognitive meaning:* sentence content that can be said to be either true or false. This is contrasted with certain emotive utterances, which are said to be noncognitive. For example, the emotive exclamations "Help!" or "Fire!" may convey information, but they are not *in themselves* pieces of linguistic expression that can be said to be true or false. A term sometimes is said to have cognitive meaning if that term can be used properly in a cognitive sentence.
   (d) *Emotive meaning:* the feeling or attitude of approval or disapproval expressed by the use of a given word.

(e) *Evocative meaning:* the feelings brought forth, or evoked, in the hearer or reader of a word or sentence.

(f) *Explicit meaning:* the accepted, normal interpretation of a word, as given, say, in a dictionary.

(g) *Expressive meaning:* a synonym for "emotive meaning."

Modus ponens   *see* Affirming the antecedent.

Modus tollens   *see* Denying the consequent.

Necessary condition   an event that *must* occur in order for another event to take place. Thus A is a necessary condition of B if B cannot occur without A's happening first; and if A does not occur, we can count on B's not occurring.

Ostensive definition   *see* Definition.

Petitio principii   *see* Fallacy of arguing in a circle.

Predicate term   the term represented by P in a categorical proposition schematically represented as "S is P." It indicates either a class to which the things referred to by the subject term, S, belong or a property of the things designated by S. The subject term introduces the subject the proposition is about, and the predicate term indicates something that can be said of (charged against) the subject term.

Premiss   in an argument, one of the statements that present evidence or reasons for the conclusion of that argument.

Proposition   the meaning expressed by a spoken or written sentence. For example, "Bill loves Jane" and "Jane is loved by Bill" are two different sentences that both express the same proposition—namely, that there is a certain relationship of love between Bill and Jane. In other words, both sentences express the proposition that Bill loves Jane. A sentence in Arabic or one in Hebrew could express that same proposition just as well.

Quality   a technical term used to classify categorical propositions as either *affirmative* or *negative*.

Quantifier   "all" or "some" as they appear in categorical propositions. *See* Quantity.

Quantity   a technical term used to classify categorical propositions in terms of whether they refer to "all" or "some" of a class. Literally to ask about the *quantity* is to ask "how much" is intended in the stated inclusion of one class within another by the proposition in question.

Reductio ad absurdum   reducing a position to absurdity by showing that an absurd consequence (a self-contradiction or a false statement) can be logically deduced from that initial position or theory.

Self-contradiction   a proposition that is false and that can be seen to be false by considering the logical nature of the proposition alone, without needing to decide the issue of the truth of any parts of the proposition. For example, "Today is Tuesday and today is *not* Tuesday" is a self-contradiction. The logical form shows that a proposition is self-contradictory even if you do not know whether the conjuncts are true or even if you do not know what they mean (as in "It is Grillitch today and it is *not* Grillitch today"). Basically, a thing cannot both *have* and *not have* a property at the same time; an event cannot both *be happening* and *not be happening* at one time. To say that such a thing is the case is to utter a self-contradictory statement.

Simple proposition   a proposition that does not involve logical connectives such as "or," "and," and "if . . . then." An example is "Jones has big feet." All categorical propositions are simple propositions. *See* Compound proposition.

Sorities   a chain of syllogisms in which the conclusion of the first syllogism is used as one of the premisses of the second. It may continue with the conclusion of the second syllogism being used as a premiss for yet another syllogism, the conclusion of the third as a premiss for a fourth, and so on.

Sound   a term applied to an argument that (1) is valid and (2) has true premisses. An argument is sound if and only if it meets these conditions.

Statistical argument   an inductive argument, the conclusion of which is a statistical proposition.

Statistical proposition   a statement that there is a certain percentage of probability that, for example, a class of objects has a specific property.

Subject term   *see* Predicate term.

Sufficient condition   an event that will bring about some other event. Thus A is a sufficient condition of B's occurring if the presence or occurrence of A is adequate to bring about B.

Syllogism   a valid deductive argument form having exactly two premisses and a conclusion. Usually, this term is used to indicate the categorical syllogism (*see* Categorical syllogism), although some other forms— such as the disjunctive syllogism and the hypothetical syllogism—are called this as well.

Tautology   a categorical proposition in which the subject term and the predicate term have the same meaning. *Example:* "Bachelors are unmarried males."

Term   a part of a sentence having cognitive (nonemotive) meaning. *See* Predicate term.

Traditional formal logic   *see* Aristotelian logic.

Vagueness   as applied to a term, the lack of precise limits to the class of objects or events to which it refers. A sentence will be vague if it contains a vague term.

Valid   the term applied to a deductive argument that has a logical form such that if the premisses are true, then the conclusion must be true. In other words, a valid deductive argument *cannot* have true premisses and a false conclusion. In a valid deductive argument the truth of the premisses entails the truth of the conclusion.

Bibliography

Chapter 1. Introduction

Baker, Samm Sinclair. *Your Key to Creative Thinking*. New York: Harper and Row, 1962. An interesting approach, with teasers to improve one's creative thinking ability.

Passmore, John. *Reading and Remembering*, 5th ed. London: Cambridge University Press, 1963.

————. *Talking Things Over*, 3rd ed. London: Cambridge University Press, 1963.

Both Passmore books are very brief introductory handbooks providing practical help and hints.

Chapter 2. The Trouble with Words

Barry, Vincent E. *Practical Logic*. New York: Holt, Rinehart and Winston, 1976. Chapter 1 has an introductory discussion of how language influences the way we see things.

Beardsley, Monroe C. *Thinking Straight: Principles of Reasoning for Readers and Writers*, 3rd ed. Englewood Cliffs, N.J.: Prentice-Hall, 1966. Chapters 4 and 5 deal with language.

Blumberg, Albert E. *Logic: A First Course*. New York: Alfred A. Knopf, 1976. Part 1 of this clearly written logic text deals with the relationship between language and argument. It focuses on the nature of human language, some uses and misuses of language, meaning, and definition.

Copi, Irving M. *Introduction to Logic*, 5th ed. New York: Macmillan, 1978. Part 1 of this standard introductory logic text deals with language. It contains sections on the various uses of language, informal fallacies, and definitions.

Engel, S. Morris. *With Good Reason: An Introduction to Informal Fallacies*. New York: St. Martin's Press, 1976. Part 1 of this easily read book contains a good discussion of words and language and illustrates the role they play in informal fallacies.

Hospers, John. *An Introduction to Philosophical Analysis*, 2nd ed. Englewood Cliffs, N.J.: Prentice-Hall, 1967. Chapter 1 covers the topics of word meaning, definition, vagueness, and sentence meaning.

Kahane, Howard. *Logic and Contemporary Rhetoric: The Use of Reason in Everyday Life*, 2nd ed. Belmont, Cal.: Wadsworth Publishing Co., 1976. Chapters 5, 6, and 7 are easy to grasp and contain many up-to-date, lively examples.

Ruby, Lionel. *The Art of Making Sense: A Guide to Logical Thinking*. Philadelphia: Lippincott, 1954. Chapters 2, 3, 4, and 5 are an interesting, easy-to-understand discussion of the role of language in logic. Somewhat dated.

Chapter 3.   Don't Let Them Fool You: Some Common Fallacies

Engel, S. Morris. *With Good Reason: An Introduction to Informal Fallacies*. New York: St. Martin's Press, 1976. Chapters 3, 4, and 5 of this easily understood text cover the major fallacies of ambiguity, presumption, and relevance. Exercises are provided.

Fearnside, W. Ward and Holther, William B. *Fallacy: The Counterfeit of Argument*. Englewood Cliffs, N.J.: Prentice-Hall, 1959. An extended discussion of the main types of fallacies.

Gardner, Martin. *Fads and Fallacies in the Name of Science*. New York: Dover Publications, 1957. A study of fallacious reasoning as it appears in pseudoscientific writing.

Hamblin, C. L. *Fallacies*. London: Methuen, 1970. An advanced book on the topic, which discusses historical treatments and disputes some of the standard interpretations of fallacies.

Michalos, Alex C. *Improving Your Reasoning*. Englewood Cliffs, N.J.: Prentice-Hall, 1970. An interesting and nontechnical catalogue of nearly one hundred types of fallacious arguments and deceptive tactics. Numerous examples and exercises.

Chapters 4 and 5.   How to Classify and How to Draw a Conclusion; Tools for Testing Arguments: Venn Diagrams

Black, Max. *Critical Thinking: An Introduction to Logic and Scientific Method*, 2nd ed. Englewood Cliffs, N.J.: Prentice-Hall, 1952. The syllogism is discussed in considerable detail in Chapter 8 of this text. Venn diagrams are also used. Some symbolic notation.

Copi, Irving M. *Introduction to Logic*, 5th ed. New York: Macmillan, 1978. In Chapter 4, Copi introduces the square of opposition, which would be of interest to anyone wishing a more complete picture of the traditional logic.

For readers wishing more advanced material on deductive logic, we suggest the following texts. Each of these will also introduce symbolic notation in its treatment.

Barker, Stephen F. *The Elements of Logic*, 2nd ed. New York: McGraw-Hill, 1974.

Blumberg, Albert E. *Logic: A First Course*. New York: Alfred A. Knopf, 1976.

Gustason, William and Ulrich, Dolph E. *Elementary Symbolic Logic*. New York: Holt, Rinehart and Winston, 1973.

Pollock, John L. *Introduction to Symbolic Logic*. New York: Holt, Rinehart and Winston, 1969.

Quine, Willard Van Orman. *Methods of Logic*, 3rd ed. New York: Holt, Rinehart and Winston, 1972.

Tapscott, Bangs L. *Elementary Applied Symbolic Logic*. Englewood Cliffs, N.J.: Prentice-Hall, 1976.

Chapter 6.   Finding Explanations and Making Predictions

Cohen, Morris Raphael, and Nagel, Ernest. *An Introduction to Logic and Scientific Method*. New York: Harcourt Brace, 1934. The second half of this text provides one of the best treatments of applied logic and scientific method available. The discussion is detailed, yet written in a manner that is easy to grasp.

Gardner, Martin. *Fads and Fallacies in the Name of Science*. New York: Dover Publications, 1957. A study of fallacious reasoning in pseudo-scientific writing.

Hanson, Norwood Russell. *Observation and Explanation: A Guide to Philosophy of Science*. New York: Harper and Row, 1971. This book covers the topics of scientific observation and explanation (plus related material) in quick fashion. It is especially suited to the student with a science background—all examples are drawn from that area.

Hempel, Carl G. *Philosophy of Natural Science*. Englewood Cliffs, N.J.: Prentice-Hall, 1966. This book offers an advanced treatment of the topics covered in this chapter. It contains technical language and symbolic notation, and will be challenging for those wishing to do further study in this area.

Mill, John Stuart. *A System of Logic*, in Ernest Nagel, ed. *John Stuart Mill's Philosophy of Scientific Methods*. New York: Macmillan, 1974. This classic work on scientific reasoning and inductive methods is worthwhile reading for anyone seriously interested in the topics covered in this chapter and the next. Although the book is a century old, Mill has more that is valuable to say on explanation, hypothesis, and prediction than most of his followers.

Olson, Robert G. *Meaning and Argument: Elements of Logic*. New York: Harcourt Brace, 1969. Chapters 14 and 15 of this introductory logic text cover the topics of confirmation and explanation. Lengthy exercises are also provided.

Quine, Willard Van Orman and Ullian, J. S. *The Web of Belief*, 2nd ed. New York: Random House, 1978. A valuable little book. It covers the topics of belief and change of belief, observation, evidence, testimony, hypothesis, induction, confirmation, explanation, and others. Exercises provided. No symbolism used.

Chapter 7.   Experience Proves the Rule: Inductive Reasoning

Black, Max. *Critical Thinking: An Introduction to Logic and Scientific Method*, 2nd ed. Englewood Cliffs, N.J.: Prentice-Hall, 1952. Part 3 (pp. 250–400) of this text provides a sustained discussion of the topics of induction and scientific method. Relevant to both this chapter and the previous one. Contains some symbolic notation. Includes exercises.

———. "Induction," in Paul Edwards, ed. *The Encyclopedia of Philosophy*, Vol. 4. New York: The Free Press, 1967. Provides some historical perspective plus a discussion of the problem of induction.

Blumberg, Albert E. *Logic: A First Course*. New York: Alfred A. Knopf, 1976. Chapters 13 and 14 of this text are devoted to the topic of non-deductive logic and its application in science and social-policy making. Some symbolic notation.

Copi, Irving M. *Introduction to Logic*, 5th ed. New York: Macmillan, 1978. Part 3 of this text gives an in-depth, yet introductory discussion of inductive logic. It is valuable supplementary reading for the material covered in this chapter and the preceding one. Numerous exercises provided.

Mill, John Stuart. *A System of Logic*, in Ernest Nagel, ed. *John Stuart Mill's Philosophy of Scientific Methods*. New York: Macmillan, 1974. Still one of the best treatments available of induction in the classical sense.

Salmon, Wesley C. *The Foundations of Scientific Inference*. Pittsburgh: University of Pittsburgh Press, 1967. An in-depth treatment of the philosophic problems of induction and probability. This book is considerably more advanced than those already mentioned.

Skyrms, Brian. *Choice and Chance: An Introduction to Inductive Logic*. Belmont, Cal.: Dickenson Publishing Co., 1966. Designed primarily for a first course in inductive logic, this book provides a detailed study of the problem of induction, the Goodman paradox, the probability calculus, and related topics.

Chapter 8.   Some Perplexing Arguments: Dilemmas and Reductios

Black, Max. *Critical Thinking: An Introduction to Logic and Scientific Method*, 2nd ed. Englewood Cliffs, N.J.: Prentice-Hall, 1952. In Chapter 6 of this work, the author discusses arguments involving alternatives. Some exercises are provided. Symbolic notation is used.

Cohen, Morris Raphael and Nagel, Ernest. *An Introduction to Logic and Scientific Method*. New York: Harcourt Brace, 1934. At the end of Chapter 5 the authors offer a good discussion of the dilemma, including the various ways of attempting to handle the dilemma when it is aimed at you.

Chapter 9.   Connecting Your Thoughts: Alternatives and Causes

Black, Max. *Critical Thinking: An Introduction to Logic and Scientific Method*, 2nd ed. Englewood Cliffs, N.J.: Prentice-Hall, 1952. Chapters 4

and 5 cover the material dealt with in this chapter. Black makes considerable use of symbolic notation and truth tables in illustrating his
points.

Capaldi, Nicholas. *The Art of Deception*. New York: D. W. Brown, 1971.
Chapter 5, "Cause and Effect Reasoning," contains a clear discussion of
several fallacies of causal reasoning, as well as some discussion of Hume
and Mill on the topic of causal reasoning.

Dray, William. *Philosophy of History*. Englewood Cliffs, N.J.: Prentice-
Hall, 1964. Chapter 4, "Causal Judgement in History," is a good example
of how causal arguments come to be applied to specific areas of inquiry.
In this chapter, the author goes into considerable detail discussing some
of the problems of uncovering causes in history.

Hart, Herbert Lionel Adolphus and Honoré, A. M. *Causation in the Law*.
Oxford: Clarendon Press, 1959. This work represents an application of
the kinds of causal arguments considered in this chapter to the question
of legal responsibility. Of special interest to students with a background
or interest in ethics or legal philosophy.

*Readers wishing further material on the argument forms discussed in
this chapter should consult the list of texts on symbolic logic given in the
preceding list for Chapters 4 and 5.*

Chapter 10.   How to Find and Evaluate an Argument

Barry, Vincent E. *Practical Logic*. New York: Holt, Rinehart and Winston,
1976. Chapter 7 of this text contains a clear discussion of how to go
about reconstructing an argument that someone else has given. The
chapter is dressed up with lively examples, and some exercises are
included.

Pospesel, Howard. *Propositional Logic*. Englewood Cliffs, N.J.: Prentice-
Hall, 1974. Chapter 14 of this contemporary text deals with identifying
"natural arguments" and then formalizing them for evaluation. Complete
with lively exercises and cartoons. Some symbolic notation.

Scriven, Michael. *Reasoning*. New York: McGraw-Hill, 1976. Most of this
text deals with analyzing arguments. Provides exercises.

Chapters 11 and 12.   How to Construct an Argument; How to Write a Paper
or a Speech

Crews, Frederick. *The Random House Handbook*, 2nd ed. New York:
Random House, 1977. A handbook that gives equal attention to the
rhetorical and technical elements of writing.

Hodges, John C. *Harbrace College Handbook*, 4th ed. New York: Harcourt
Brace, 1956. A useful manual covering all aspects of composition.

Irmscher, William F. *The Holt Guide to English: A Contemporary Handbook
of Rhetoric, Language and Literature*. New York: Holt, Rinehart and
Winston, 1972. Chapter 6 summarizes logical arguments well. Excellent
source of information on all facets of writing.

Johnson, Thomas Meidell. *Guide to Student Papers*. Minneapolis: Burgess
    Publishing Co., 1968. Covers well some principles of writing essays and
    term papers.
Moore, Robert Hamilton. *Handbook of Effective Writing*, 2nd ed. New
    York: Holt, Rinehart and Winston, 1971. Helpful on the mechanics of
    writing.

Index

About the Authors

David J. Crossley is Professor of Philosophy at the University of Saskatchewan. He received his B.A. and M.A. from the University of Toronto and his Ph.D. from the University of London (England).

Peter A. Wilson is Associate Professor in the Extension Division at the University of Saskatchewan. He received his B.A. and M.A. from the University of Windsor and his B.Ed. and M.Ed. from the University of Toronto. He did doctoral studies at the University of Chicago.